SUPREME

AUTHORITY

SUPREME AUTHORITY

UNDERSTANDING POWER IN THE CATHOLIC CHURCH

Mary Faulkner

ALPHA

A Pearson Education Company

International Standard Book Number: 0-02-864427-1
Library of Congress Catalog Card Number: 2002115288

04   03   02   8   7   6   5   4   3   2   1

Interpretation of the printing code: The rightmost number of the first series of numbers is the year of the book's printing; the rightmost number of the second series of numbers is the number of the book's printing. For example, a printing code of 02-1 shows that the first printing occurred in 2002.

Printed in the United States of America

Note: This publication contains the opinions and ideas of its author. It is intended to provide helpful and informative material on the subject matter covered. It is sold with the understanding that the author and publisher are not engaged in rendering professional services in the book. If the reader requires personal assistance or advice, a competent professional should be consulted.

The author and publisher specifically disclaim any responsibility for any liability, loss, or risk, personal or otherwise, which is incurred as a consequence, directly or indirectly, of the use and application of any of the contents of this book.

Trademarks: All terms mentioned in this book that are known to be or are suspected of being trademarks or service marks have been appropriately capitalized. Alpha Books and Pearson Education, Inc., cannot attest to the accuracy of this information. Use of a term in this book should not be regarded as affecting the validity of any trademark or service mark.

For marketing and publicity, please call: 317-581-3722

The publisher offers discounts on this book when ordered in quantity for bulk purchases and special sales.

For sales within the United States, please contact: Corporate and Government Sales, 1-800-382-3419 or corpsales@pearsontechgroup.com

Outside the United States, please contact: International Sales, 317-581-3793 or international@pearsontechgroup.com

Publisher: Marie Butler-Knight
Product Manager: Phil Kitchel
Managing Editor: Jennifer Chisholm
Senior Acquisitions Editor: Randy Ladenheim-Gil
Development Editor: Lynn Northrup
Production Editor: Katherin Bidwell
Copy Editor: Rhonda Tinch-Mize
Cover/Book Designer: Trina Wurst
Creative Director: Robin Lasek
Indexer: Brad Herriman
Layout/Proofreading: Angela Calvert, John Etchison

I dedicate this book to my parents, Betty and Athel, who approached religion and spirituality from opposite sides. My mother was a Catholic who loved the Church. For her, religion consisted of Mass, rosary beads, rituals, church bells ringing through the neighborhood, light filtering through stained glass, and hats and gloves—even in the heat of summer.

Mother didn't question religion—or the Church—and would probably not approve of my doing so. My father had no church affiliation. He loved the wilderness and found whatever connection to the heavenly realm he needed in the forest. Going with him into the boundary waters of northern Minnesota and Canada packed the wallop of high Mass at the Vatican. As I look back, his deep spiritual connection to nature is apparent to me, but he would never have used any of that kind of language, nor would I.

Time spent with him in the dark mysterious north woods while timber wolves howled in the distance and the northern lights flashed across the July sky—combined with the smell of pine needles and campfire smoke—transmitted a profound sense of nature's integrity. From my mother I inherited the love of symbols and ritual from the rich sacramental life of the pre-Vatican II Church, where we crowned Mary Queen of the Angels, Queen of the May, and where pets, crops, and family automobiles were blessed with no apparent higher ordering. These different ways of meeting God—my mother's Catholicism and my father's love of nature—took root in me. So, in their honor, I begin.

Contents

Prologue

This book is about power and authority in the Catholic Church. I approach the topic out of curiosity and a desire to understand the dynamics inside one of the largest and oldest institutions in Western culture. The urge to do so was augmented by the recent sad scandals of clerical pedophilia and Episcopal cover-up that landed the Church in the news for the wrong reasons and resurrected old questions about power.

I come to this essay as both an insider and outsider. As an insider: I was raised Catholic, attended 12 years of parochial school, did my graduate work in religious education, and studied religion and read theology from many perspectives. I come as an outsider because I am a layperson, female, and not employed by the Church in any way.

Christianity has put a big thumbprint on Western culture. Catholicism, its oldest and largest expression, has enormous influence today as a world power. Understanding Catholic power helps *us* understand *us*—as a country and as a people.

Presently, the three major religions of the Western world—Judaism, Christianity, and Islam—are embroiled in a religious argument that goes back to the beginning of our shared history. Many cultural factors are involved, but the conflict is rooted in clashing values. Interestingly, we all drink from the same well—drawing water from the same sacred literature.

Whether we think of it as growth or change, we've been in some mode of adaptation since the Creator brought the firmament out of chaos and planted us in the garden. We began our journey as a people wearing fig leaves and walking barefoot through the valley by the Tigris and Euphrates rivers. Today, we walk on the moon, visit outer space, and our thoughts can be transmitted around the world in four seconds. We're talking rapid fluctuation—and the danger of whiplash!

The catchword today is *process*. We've always been in one, but right now it seems that everything is up for grabs. We haven't quite figured out how to participate in government, business, community, church, or family—yet the ante has now been raised to a global scale.

Meanwhile, rather than making a bold play for the reign of God, the Catholic leadership seems to be settling for small potatoes—locked in a power struggle between institution and people.

Furthermore, recent events have shined the spotlight on a dark corner of the Catholic world. Sex abuse scandals have shaken both institution and members, bringing immediacy to any reordering that might be in the air.

The book begins with a look at the institutional Church in theory: how it is organized and how Church offices function. Then, after all the fine theory, it remains to be seen how Catholicism works in reality. Beginning with a brief history of the buildup of Catholic power, we'll check with several theologians whose work lends rhyme and reason to this mysterious enterprise. And we'll explore that ongoing challenge for theologians and everyone else—the great anomaly, Catholic sexuality.

But behind the lurid headlines and awkward scandals, a new spirit stirs. We will go behind the scenes, meeting some modern prophets and exploring emerging visions of a future Church.

A sign of spiritual maturity is when dichotomy resolves into paradox. As the institutional Church and the regular folks in the pew begin to merge into the people of God, an age-old power scuffle could be resolved. I believe the wake-up call has been sounded, summoning us all to a spiritual conversation. I hope that this book helps in some small way to feed that conversation.

Throughout history, the institutional Church has wasted much of its moral capital on the personal sex lives of the people—choosing to stay afloat on the spiritual waters at the expense of achieving depth. The people are ready to go deeper, and a question arises as to whether Church leaders will take us or follow us.

Toward the end of the book, Sophia—the Old Testament wisdom figure—graces the stage, bringing a new kind of power that is shared throughout the entire web of life. Her re-emergence is particularly poignant as we search for images that feed our need to put relationship back into religion: relationship between creature and creator, between male and female, between parent and child, between leaders and the faithful. From Wisdom 8:1–4:

> She deploys her strength from one end of the earth to the other,
>
> Ordering all things for good …
>
> Her closeness to God lends luster to her noble birth,
>
> Since the Lord of all has loved her.
>
> Yes, she is an initiate in the mysteries of God's knowledge.
>
> She makes choice of the works God is to do.

Sophia is God's softer side—the side that attends to creation. In the vulnerability that we all feel as the world threatens to come undone, she brings strength, taking notice and making a list of what God needs to do to bail out this troubled creation. Sophia is God's wisdom.

How This Book Is Written

This book is written in essay style, exploring topics from different perspectives. During the study of Catholic power, a second theme emerges—the dualism that has haunted Western culture from the get-go. The book explores these pervasive and related topics. For example, the current business of sexual abuse is a by-product of that dualism, while at the same time all bound up in issues of power. For all too long, there has been too much secrecy—too much cover-up. Recent events are drawing attention to all our cultural icons—and the Church is no exception. It's time to take a look at the inner workings of this huge institution. Although born in anguish and even anger, there might be the beginning of a healthy and transforming conversation here in the tired, yet ever-resilient Church.

Most of the books mentioned in this book can be found in Appendix A, along with some additional recommended reading. Appendix B contains a timeline of important events in the Catholic Church.

Acknowledgments

Special thanks goes to Michael Farrell for his editorial support and personal wisdom. Appreciation is due to my agent Linda Roghaar for securing the project, and the ongoing support she brings me. Thanks to all the folks at Alpha Books—particularly Randy Ladenheim-Gil, Lynn Northrup, Kathy Bidwell, and Rhonda Tinch-Mize. I am grateful for the encouragement of my good friends Martha Leigh and Daniel, who kept me on board even when I threw in the towel. Refusing to let go of the vision, they threw it back. Appreciation to the scholars and visionaries whose works I drew on—as well as teachers I've had through the years. And thanks for the garden's wisdom. Today, as I look out the window, I see it going to seed—getting ready to sleep through the winter; I am going to do likewise.

Chapter 1

Saints and Sinners

When headlines scream about Catholic priests and pedophilia, about cardinals and cover-ups, the world scratches its head in dismay. Amid the many sensational news stories to grace the new millennium, these pairings are perhaps most incongruous and alien to our expectations. "There is nothing new under the sun," Solomon said long ago. Yet surprises continue to ambush us, and certain sordid secrets long swept under the carpet are coming home to roost. One is clerical pedophilia.

At first there were only murmurings about this enigmatic scourge of child abuse, back in the 1980s, amid denials and obfuscations by the U.S. hierarchy. The moment, it turned out, was not ripe for outrage. But the United States and much of the world was ready to be angry in 2002 when the once small story became a sensation.

What On Earth Is Going On?

The reaction was incredulity, anger, and confusion. And, some Catholics said, ill-concealed glee on the part of would-be Catholic bashers. This was red meat for controversy not only on the part of Catholics, but also of the whole world. Old taboos were crumbling before our eyes. Cherished ideals were going up in smoke. Contemporary culture, already under siege, looked around in bewilderment. The media and the world strained to find a context that might make sense of all the scandal. The faithful and not only Catholics searched frantically for solid moral ground.

When the subject has such a long, deep history as the Catholic Church does, the search for perspective often takes people back all the way to their roots.

The world developed in a certain way, this search for perspective tells us—searchers under stress cling to old, solid truths we seldom stop to think about. Earth could have evolved in other forms (we can all think of improvements) but the slow, seemingly random process made us, for better or worse, who and what we are. The arena, then, is imperfect. In certain contexts, we call it sinful.

The Global Challenge

One of our biggest challenges was learning how to live together in our imperfect home away from home. To this end we formed groups, such as families, tribes, and eventually nations. We became multidimensional, developing interests as well as needs so that we formed other groupings such as soccer clubs and religions.

We and our preoccupations ebbed and flowed, and our associations with each other changed accordingly. Empires came and went—interspersed with bouts of chaos, which reminded us that we needed order and purpose if we were to endure. We started out at a very local level, probably chewing the fat under a shady tree. Once we were mobile enough, we formed bigger configurations, with more ambitious agendas. Eventually, we became not only national but transnational.

Martyrs, Missionaries, Saints, and Scholars

Long before our corporations went global, our churches did. A universal need was found to gnaw at us—a hunger for transcendence, and a yearning for some higher aspiration always out of reach. Although human history has many glories, our religious institutions are high on the list. Our various bodies of religious belief made their impression on our human nature. We continued to screw up on a regular basis; but overall, religion made us better.

For 2,000 years, Christianity has been among the most populous and influential of those religious systems. Today, Catholicism, with more than a billion souls, is almost everywhere; is very powerful, even by human standards; and is looked up to in most cultures and contexts.

Some bad apples were bound to be in so large a basket. Still, the Church has an exalted history of martyrs, missionaries, saints, and

2

scholars. It would be impossible to imagine what Earth would be like without the Church. Not as good a place, most people would agree.

Into this impressive picture creeps pedophilia—sexual relations with children. As if that wasn't bad enough, the transgressions were made by celibate clergy. A deluge of scandals came in its wake, such as lies, cowardice, self-interest, arrogance, cover-up, and their various pernicious offspring.

No wonder the world was shocked.

The Church in the United States and elsewhere has grown used to making headlines. It has usually used the spotlight to good advantage. But in 2002, it was making news for all the wrong reasons.

Playing the Accountability Card

The broad outline of what is called the priest pedophilia scandal is well known. The details differ with each telling. The scandal is unfinished business, so the details will continue to grow and transmogrify, and few dare to predict how the story will end.

Dismay and anger focused not only on the acts loosely labeled pedophilia, but also equally on the subsequent Episcopal decisions that added to the suffering of those who should be most protected: the children. Questions come tumbling. People want to know what has gone wrong—how could such a thing happen? In pressing the Church for answers, people are doing something that has seldom been done in the Catholic Church: They are holding their leaders accountable.

Even in the tranquil past, pedophilia was never a total secret. Stories went around of bishops lining up formidable lawyers at big boardroom tables to confront any victim who risked complaining about being molested. This usually had the desired effect: spiritual and temporal intimidation. If money changed hands, it was conditional on the victim's silence.

All that has changed. Experts in various related fields have for some time been educating the U.S. bishops regarding the effects of sexual abuse and the long healing process necessary for victims and families to mend. It is to the bishops' credit that they have taken the problem in hand and begun to face the situation squarely. Critics say that this change of heart happened only because the hierarchy could not keep the lid on the scandal any longer and feared losing all credibility vis-à-vis their flock. Despite their best efforts, however, it will be a long time before the individuals and communities they shepherd will trust them as wholeheartedly as they did in the past.

Iceberg or Tip?

Is pedophilia the tip of the iceberg or the iceberg itself?

Although the twin scandals of child abuse and the ensuing cover-up have been getting the world's attention, many have felt that neither the pope nor his curial officials were similarly preoccupied with the crisis. It is well known that the Church, accustomed to dealing in centuries rather than 24-hour news cycles, reacts with understatement to nearly everything. Still, there was a marked contrast between the Vatican's stiff upper lip and the U.S. hierarchy's headlong rush to zero tolerance and other quick remedies.

The iceberg, then, might be much deeper down.

Behind the Headlines

Behind the headlines, many suggest, there is a crisis of authority.

"The Christian church seems to have one great thing on its mind in each epoch," theologian and author Martin Marty wrote some years ago. At one time, it was the Trinity. Then it was Christology and later other preoccupations. "In our time, it is authority," Marty concluded.

This bone of contention began to make itself obvious late in the nineteenth century when Pope Pius IX called the First Vatican Council for the primary purpose of having papal infallibility declared a dogma of faith. Although papal infallibility had long been a vague theological concept tossed around by theologians, not to mention popes, it had never in the past loomed so large in the arsenal of papal power. That might be because the pope seldom needed to call on infallibility to make his point. (I'll discuss infallibility in Chapter 3.)

It was only when papal authority was threatened that popes began to grasp for it in earnest. This is a human reaction.

Ever since the Church, especially expressed by the papacy, became a world power many centuries before, the pope had a variety of ways to express and enforce his will. By 1870, however, the Holy Roman Empire of yore had dwindled to a few acres by the Tiber, and the armies of the past had been reduced to the Swiss Guard of the colorful uniforms.

In order to matter on Earth, the Church needed a different kind of clout, namely spiritual authority, of which the most cogent expression was infallibility.

A basic definition of authority is the exercise of power (the dictionary renders it as "the power to influence or command thought, opinion, or behavior"). Power, in turn, is a wide-ranging concept. We most frequently think of it in terms of physical force, but most people admire moral power more: the ability to persuade. This is the power the Church exercised most effectively, even in the days when the pope had armies at his command.

The Deeper Problem

Most professionals agree that the most common element in all kinds of sexual abuse is power inequity. This is true whether the abuse is found in the public school, scouting groups, families, or the Catholic Church. When one person has more power than the other, by its very presence, that power becomes the means of coercion—thus improperly influencing, or controlling, the behavior of the other.

Power inequities might be based on a wide variety of factors, depending on what the society values. Age, size, education, wealth, and position in an organization are some ways we establish the pecking order. (The term "pecking order" itself hints at how we regard power in the culture: The bigger, more aggressive chickens peck at weaker ones.)

Power, needless to say, is not in itself abusive. Power is as integral to the way the world is made as air or gravity: Part of the way things are; sometimes vague as a lover's power to enchant the beloved, or obvious as a hurricane's power to blow one's house down. Like so many things in creation, therefore, power is spongy, ambiguous, and at the mercy of circumstances. In the right circumstances, power performs great good. In the wrong hands, it is a killer and a despoiler of life—an abuser.

Because power has so often been badly used throughout history, many people tend automatically to be suspicious or even fearful of it. In this entire discussion, it is of the utmost importance to remember that power in itself is neutral. It is as good as the way we use it.

Accordingly, certain ways of organizing power are more likely to become abusive than other arrangements. When power is directed to responsibility and service to others, and includes accountability of the leaders to the people, it has a good chance of being a positive influence in people's lives. When it is viewed as privilege and wielded as control over others, it is abusive. Power over others means, almost by definition, power over all who are not in positions of power in the system. This in turn means power over those who are not *like* those holding power.

Rights are a close relative of power. Rights are an excellent outcome of our evolution as a human society—no one wants to argue against life, liberty, or the pursuit of happiness or the multitude of more ordinary human rights that allow people to live together without constant tension. But just as power is sometimes perceived as power "over," rights can become rights over others. When some come to believe that they have innate rights over others, the first ingredient in the abuse formula has been met.

Hierarchy: The Power Tower

Hierarchy describes a system of organizing groups of people whereby members are arranged in ascending ranks—each having power over those below and answering to those above. Although the word is most often applied to church personnel, and especially to that of the Catholic Church, hierarchies are everywhere. Hierarchy is an effective way of getting things done, especially from the perspective of those at the top. Whether it is applied strictly or loosely, it is a sufficiently common paradigm for everyday human interaction that it must be treated with respect until a better system comes along.

This, on the other hand, is the real world, where practice does not always fully live up to theory. To take a trivial example, an understanding exists in most systems that not only does the boss make the decisions, but the boss also gets the best parking space. One boss I know pushes this unofficial privilege way beyond the limit of good sense. In a seven-story office building with only two elevators, this boss has designated one elevator for his personal use, leaving only one for several hundred other employees. (It could be argued that an elevator is not what this selfish fellow needs most.)

Power Over: More Than a Parking Place

In our democratic societies, though, the parking place does not tell the whole story. At the local grocery store, the haughty boss cannot tell the underling from the workplace what to put in her or his basket, and grocery store parking spots are fair game. Workers give permission to the boss to exercise a certain amount of control over them for so many hours a week in return for a salary. Beyond the scope of the organization in which both opt to participate, the boss has no innate power over the worker. This has not always been the case. For much of recorded history, hierarchical power systems have assumed a wide range of innate rights on the part of some people over others.

In the hierarchical model, whether secular or ecclesial, power is centralized in the leader. This is especially effective when decisions must be make quickly. Furthermore, centralized power creates a focus for the members—a rallying point and a unifying identity. A community might find that being under the guidance of a talented leader is the best way of getting things done.

In practice, however, hierarchies can become problems in several ways. When leadership is imposed and exploited to exert power *over* people's lives, and when this is backed by the use or threat of force, it becomes problematic. When a hierarchical structure assumes power over others' lives, it decides what the others need and what they have to do to get what they need. Such a procedure is based on the assumption summed up by the cliché that "we know what is best for you." In such scenarios, the so-called ordinary people frequently don't enter into the decision-making either by identifying their needs or by designing the way decisions are carried out. This "power-over" model works on the assumption of a finite supply of power and assumes that only those in charge have it, so it is doled out to those below only when the ones on top deem it appropriate.

An insidious aspect of this and most other expressions of power is that the threat of coercion is usually enough to achieve compliance. Thus, to all external appearances, the system within which the power operates seems humane and polite and often even cheerful when, in fact, an unexpressed reservoir of opposition and resentment might be buried deep down. This might be true in groups as different as the army and the Church. On the inevitable other hand, a corrupt system that relies on coercion will sooner or later be overtaken by the resentment within and will eventually reap the whirlwind.

Scrambling for Power

When, by contrast, hierarchy is seen as a way of serving the needs of the people involved, it has the opposite set of assumptions. One key assumption is that even those who are not bosses know best what they need. Mutual decisions are made, and everyone looks at designing ways in which the decisions can be put into action. In this model, a high level of communication exists between the people and the leaders. Communication involves a system of feedback in which adjustments can be made and accountability can be measured. In a healthy system, no one has any innate power over anyone else. Theoretically at least, everyone now has an equal opportunity to serve in a leadership capacity. Rather than scrambling for seemingly finite power, this system concedes that power can be creative and expansive and that each person has an innate capacity for such power.

It is a dearly held belief that all persons are created equal. This is nonsense, of course, unless properly understood—all of us are not of equal height, and no two sets of fingerprints are the same. This existential inequality (one might be richer, but the other runs faster) pervades all aspects of our interactions. That is why some give orders and others take orders, why some give advice or take it, run the store or sweep the floor. Hierarchy is a given. Its modality in daily life might be benign or despotic, enlightened or foolish, collaborative or dictatorial, as you've just seen.

Hierarchy, like power, is not necessarily a bad thing. Nor a good one, either, unless the humans involved are up to snuff. Whether it's good or bad lies in how it is used.

From Ad Hoc to Hierarchy

Like most of the rest of the world, the Catholic Church uses a hierarchical governing structure. Many of the similarities end right there, however. The organization of Catholicism is one of a kind.

The pope is the visible head of the Church. The pope and all Catholics are agreed that papal authority comes from God. In this regard, though, the Church is by no means unique. Since the dawn of history, worldly rulers have frequently claimed their authority has come from above. This includes some of the most rotten regimes in history. God, meanwhile, remains distant and seldom comes down directly to say whose side he or she is on.

Christianity is one instance in which God allegedly came down and did just that. The incarnation of Jesus Christ is well documented—the four Gospels, Acts of the Apostles and more—yet his historical persona remains elusive. Despite all this discussion about power, one of the things Jesus most clearly did not flaunt was power. Rather, he seemed intent on becoming the very personification of powerlessness and vulnerability— as the world usually understands these terms.

A Blind Leap

It is an ironic and striking commentary on our human nature that the Church claiming to represent this Jesus Christ on Earth didn't go down that road toward peace on Earth. It did at first, and heroically at times; some would say that it has been historically at its grandest when its worldly authority seemed most pathetic. But eventually, given the opportunity, Church leaders grasped the more mundane model and have been running with it to this day.

Yet the Church is different, Catholics say, from every other organization. It is founded by the Son of God, for starters. The hierarchy is built around the memory of Jesus and the 12 apostles, but its authority, as Vatican II points out, derives from the Holy Spirit, who "guides the Church in the way of all truth and, uniting it in fellowship and ministry, bestows upon it different hierarchic and charismatic gifts."

When Jesus returned, as tradition reports, to heaven, the small band of followers were at a loss, by turn fearful and elated, making up the new Church as they went along. When different questions arose, they debated them, sometimes quite ardently. Their decisions were ad hoc—there was no precedent and no tradition to follow. There certainly was no talk of infallibility, nor even of a pope.

Peter stood out, it seems, because of things Jesus had said to him; and also, perhaps, because in his rough-hewn way, he was a natural leader. Titles such as bishops and cardinals were far from their minds at first, though some gradually were give lesser names, such as deacon, which, perhaps significantly, carried with it the connotation of service rather than lordship over anyone.

Ordinary circumstances—as distinct from celestial promptings or thunderbolts—had much to do with what happened and how the Church got on its feet. Peter took a trip to Rome. Between one thing and another, he decided to stay, though circumstances might have made the decision for him. Things got worse before they got better. Peter found himself on a cross like his leader, only upside down. It made sense that whoever followed Peter as Rome leader would be the main man—in time, called the pope. There were hard times in the catacombs and elsewhere, yet the group defied all odds and kept expanding.

It was only natural to get ever more organized, as humans do; and for some to be leaders and others, therefore, followers; for some to be popes and others the faithful. They had this amazing story that made so little sense on the surface one had to make a blind leap of faith to buy it.

In a group like that, authority obviously wasn't business as usual.

The Other Side of the Coin

Even a group that claims divine pedigree, however, cannot help rubbing shoulders with the world. This can benefit the group—even when the world is imperfect, as it is. Religious bodies never had a monopoly on

10

the good, the true, and the beautiful. A great many good people and structures are in what we call the secular world. These have rubbed off on the various churches. The Catholic Church has received untold benefit from interacting with the world. During certain epochs when the Church withdrew into itself—usually for the purpose of keeping itself pure from the big, bad world—it usually festered and suffered and eventually (in the famous phrase of Pope John XXIII) had to throw open its windows to let the world's light in.

The other side of this coin shows the Church tarnished by the world.

Even when Jesus walked among them, the first Christians couldn't help being human, which historically covered nearly every fault and foible from petty to greedy. There was at first, and there were frequently later, surges of great enthusiasm, fervor, and heroism, but these cannot be sustained constantly in this particular world. So imperfections and more serious problems showed up from the start. They have haunted the Church ever since.

When, however, the Church looked at itself in the great big mirror in the sky, perhaps it did not always see what others saw; did not always see its own most serious sins. The Church has long been famous for its rather odd fascination with sex—making it a major issue. It is ironic that a Church whose leaders tried so hard to distance themselves from the opposite sex should nevertheless remain so obsessed by the subject.

Meanwhile, though, as Church leaders and theorists ranted about sex, other aberrations were often allowed to go unnoticed and unreformed. Perhaps the most telling example has been its exercise of power: what some would call its abuse of power.

Over the centuries, the Church acquired extraordinary spiritual, psychological, and temporal power. Perhaps it used that power about as well as a human institution could be expected to do. But it also sinned, its critics say, both by what it did not do with that power (sins of omission) and by what it did do (sins of commission).

So here, after 2,000 years, sex and power combine to haunt this formidable and mostly idealistic institution. For all its otherworldly demeanor, these are strikingly human demons for a Church to have to deal with. In the great lockbox of sins that the Church has fashioned through the years, one could risk creating a hierarchy: from cerebral peccadilloes such as pride and envy to sex and power at the lower end of the sin spectrum. In the early centuries, if history is a reliable guide (which it isn't always, especially when a body as influential as the Church is eager to put its spin on it), the obsessions were more exalted; Church leaders getting genuinely angry about theological issues, for example, and killing heretics for what they considered to be their wrong beliefs—which took considerable spiritual chutzpah.

Today, though, the issues are sex and power. The thesis of this book is that power is the more urgent problem and a major contributing factor to the pedophilia crisis.

How It Does and Doesn't Work
The Catholic Church, as I've indicated, uses a unique hierarchical structure (the God factor), but it is otherwise similar to most systems in the secular culture in its manner of being in the world.

Because this model is pervasive, it can seem like it's the normal way of relating. We have learned to accommodate—to fit into the system like getting used to an old shoe. The following are some ways a hierarchical system works in relationship to the nonranking members. (Al-though an enlightened hierarchy might behave differently, these typical examples indicate the generally innate structural tendency of hierarchy when taken to its logical conclusion.)

1. **Identification of what is working or not working is done by the leaders.** People's experiences are not used to help define reality, which is assessed only from the perspective of those on top. For example, a worker might experience being tired, but the authority figure is permitted to name and define the tiredness. Rather than tired, the leader can name the reality laziness, or being uninterested or uncooperative. The leader's interpretation is decisive.

2. **What the people need is determined by the leaders.** This principle is akin to the previous one. The authority figure decides what is the real problem. After it has been determined that the subordinate is not tired, but lazy, this person might then need to be taught

a lesson.

3. **Leaders are the only ones who know how to get things done.**
   Regardless of what information the worker might have because of
   his or her close relationship with the situation, educational background, experience, or just plain intelligence, the leader knows
   best. Companies do this all the time. Workers know better and
   more efficient ways of getting things done, but the authority figure
   needs to maintain authority and shuns losing face.

4. **Communication is one-way only: from leaders to subordinates.**
   All communication originates at the top and is passed down
   through the ranks. The higher-ranking figure seldom, if ever, has
   direct communication with members more than one level below.
   This maintains the illusion that the leader knows everything.

5. **Accountability is one-way: up from people to leaders.** Each
   level of worker is responsible to the level above, regardless of the
   circumstances. Because the separation between highest and lowest
   can be quite great and communication is limited, there is a lot of
   room for impossible situations to develop—and they do.

6. **Opportunity for leadership is reserved for certain types of people, often based on race, gender, or religious affiliation.** The
   hierarchical system has an undeclared, therefore secret, procedure.
   Membership depends on some genetic factor or belief system that
   is shared among the leaders and defines who is in or out.

Obviously, for a whole variety of reasons, hierarchy works better in
some instances than others. One would expect it to work to the optimum
in a sophisticated, educated, highly motivated body like the Catholic
Church, and occasionally it does. Many religious and secular institutions are nevertheless incorporating principles of shared authority and
mutual responsibility. This communal system, as it is sometimes called,
depends on the capacity and goodwill of the personnel, but then the
same is true of full-blown hierarchy or any other system. The dynamics
are the opposite of what you have seen in the previous list:

1. Identification of what is working well and what is a problem is
   done mutually, between the people and the leaders.

2. Needs are determined mutually, by the people with the leaders.

3. Design of how needs can be better met is by mutual agreement.

4. Communication is two-way between people and leaders.

5. Mutual accountability exists between people and leaders.

6. Leadership is open. Qualifications for leadership are determined by members.

Hierarchy Marries Patriarchy

Patriarchy literally means rule by fathers. It has traditionally been understood in a broader way to mean male rule, with leadership passing typically through sons or brothers. In a traditional patriarchal system, the father in the clan or family had supreme authority. Wives and children were legally dependent on the patriarch. In keeping with this family relationship, inheritance passed from father to son.

Although this traditional understanding of patriarchy is no longer a strict model in contemporary society—cracks are emerging in the glass ceiling—its legacy of male domination in society in general and in most religious institutions remains very strong.

The Rule of the Day

The Judeo-Christian origin of patriarchy generally traces back to the Old Testament patriarchs such as Abraham and Isaac and extends to Moses. Patriarchal time designates a period of approximately 400 years, from the first half of the second millennium B.C.E. to the conquest, in the thirteenth century B.C.E., of Canaan (Palestine) that followed the exodus from Egypt during the reign of Ramses II.

The seminomadic thirteenth century Hebrews evolved into statehood of sorts around the middle of the eleventh century B.C.E. The society increasingly excluded women from public and religious activities and introduced a stricter regulation of female sexuality.

During this same period, the Eastern Mediterranean area was undergoing similar dramatic changes. The social and religious institutions were likewise strongly patriarchal—marked by the diminished status and role of women.

Athens did not allow women to be citizens or own property. A Roman wife who committed adultery could be put to death, although her husband had complete sexual freedom. A Roman father was the undisputed ruler, acting as priest, judge, legislator, and, sometimes, executioner in his own household. He performed his duties as he saw fit—without any particular concern for the rights of his wife and children.

Christianity inherited the patriarchal system from all these sources. This happened for secular and historical rather than religious reasons. Although the Hebrew Bible gave the patriarchal legacy to the Judeo-Christian world, it did so because patriarchy was the rule of the day, not because it was the God-given way.

Against this backdrop of patriarchy, the radical nature of the teachings of Jesus can best be understood. He established a revolutionary or transforming community. His message, insofar as one can read it between the lines of the New Testament (which was written by men who still had strong patriarchal leanings), was startlingly ahead of its time in terms of the parity and uniqueness attributed to women.

Following Christ's death, Christianity continued to make inroads into the patriarchal system. The early Church became a haven in which women and children were treated as valuable and important beings in their own right. This radical liberation agenda was rewarded by increased membership as poor and downtrodden women flocked to it. But the revolutionary changes inherent in the early Christian movement gave way soon enough to the cultural influences of the time, and the Catholic Church gradually organized itself according to hierarchical and patriarchal patterns.

Taking Dominion: Defining Reality

The principles of hierarchy and patriarchy combine to create an all-male ruling structure. This ruling authority is believed to be God-given—therefore not open to question. Thus, in the Catholic Church, the highest-ranking male—the pope—has unique access to God that isn't available to everyone. He stands between the people and God. Through him, all must pass to reach God. He is, therefore (with due allowance made for those who know no better), their means to salvation. However, his rank and privilege do not belong to him personally, but come to him through his position in the organization: the Church. The Church, then, becomes the means to salvation through which all must pass. Because this deals with something as important as salvation, a primary preoccupation of those in charge is to preach and maintain this self-serving status quo. Such a church is not likely to shed its power lightly.

In this model, the authority figure's accountability is to God, and the accountability of the members is to the authority figure.

The hierarchical system forms the basis for how we understand our relationship with creation. Its roots are in the creation story of the Old Testament, where God gives man dominion over the earth. This particular relationship with creation has never been popular with certain of Adam and Eve's descendents, nor with other non-Western religions, nor with indigenous people all over the world.

An innate oppression inherent in a hierarchical/patriarchal system is that the leaders define reality and that leadership is restricted to those most like those already in power. Thus, during the past two millennia, the all-male leadership of the largely European Catholic Church exercised inordinate influence over the developing Western world. From this position of power, the hierarchy for all practical purposes defined reality and set the standards for all other cultures, including the culture of women and children.

This Huge, Powerful Church

The Catholic Church has grown from a humble movement within Judaism to represent one fifth of the world's people. Today, there are over 1 billion Catholics worldwide. Although there are 61 million Catholics in the United States, approximately 24 percent of the population, the numbers are even greater in Latin American countries. Central America, for example, is 85.5 percent Catholic, and South America is a little more than 87 percent Catholic. In the United States, the Catholic population is higher in certain cities than in others. Boston, for example, has 2 million Catholics, a little more than half the total population. Los Angeles has 3 million Catholics, or 30 percent of its population. Chicago and New York each have about 2.5 million Catholics—41 and 45 percent of their respective populations.

Considering, therefore, how many lives are touched by Catholicism, it is only natural, amid this pedophilia brouhaha, for inquiring minds to want to know what's going on.

Besides sex abuse, there is something more basic here, and ultimately personal to practically everyone. For more than 1,500 years, Christianity and Catholicism were one and the same thing. Before that, all Christian roots go back to Judaism.

It is impossible to measure how much U.S. culture is influenced by its European heritage. Those to whom we frequently refer as the nation's founders were a group of largely Protestant men, not far removed from their European homeland. For a long time, when people spoke of an American, they had a picture in mind of a person of European ancestry. That began to change only late in the twentieth century when the black civil rights movement and other quite recent developments brought attention to long-ignored cultural realities. Yet, regardless of our current multicultural awareness, U.S. culture has been constructed largely according to European customs and culture. Both patriarchy and hierarchy, therefore, are built into the way our culture, including our democracy, works.

So the culture in which we live, do business, and work out our various individual and communal destinies is steeped in the Judeo-Christian ethos. To understand ourselves as a culture, we must understand our origins. And our very origins are in play here—these are not merely juicy or dirty stories about eccentrics attached to an outmoded institution belonging to the hoary past. To a considerable degree, this is here and now and all of us.

In Conclusion

The Catholic Church is a study in paradox. Power and scandal have accompanied it throughout history and are once again rocking the boat. At the same time, it has been the primary spiritual expression for a large number of people over a big portion of time. It is good to remember that the Church is the story of *people*, so it is filled with human imperfection. One cannot look at the Catholic Church without looking at Western culture, and the reverse of this is likewise true. It was shaped by the cultures in which it was formed, and it left its imprint as well. The process continues today. The history that many Americans share through the 1,500 years of common experience can be helpful in learning more about ourselves as both a religious and political community.

Chapter 2

Inside the Catholic Church

The pedophilia debacle is, obviously, not the first crisis in the history of the Catholic Church. The crisis that split the universal Christian Church between East and West in 1054 was greater, as was the crisis that climaxed with Martin Luther's revolt in 1517 and the Reformation that followed. In these and other instances, issues about abuses in Church life became magnified into power struggles whose outcomes could scarcely have been foreseen. Because the current crisis has not completely played itself out, we are left to speculate about its final seriousness and to hope for a benign outcome.

Humming the Canticle of Change

The devastating impact of some previous scandals culminated in the loss of millions of Church members, who frequently went on to form competing denominations with different belief systems and power structures. In a church whose founder prayed so ardently that all might be one, this repeated urge to disunity has been a recurring scandal.

One reason for hope that the current crisis will not result in similar loss of members is the paradoxical fact that millions of Catholics are more casual about their Catholicism than their forebears once were. Not so long ago, the faith was so rigid, and so rigidly enforced, that an all-or-nothing adherence to the Church's dictates was the only acceptable posture.

Trumping Papal Power

A new attitude was fostered throughout the 1960s by the questioning that surrounded and followed the Second Vatican Council. (You'll find more about Vatican II in Chapter 5.) The faithful who had been brain-washed, many said, to pay, pray, and obey, awoke to the possibility that all doctrines and dictates were not of equal significance for salvation. This view suggested that Catholicism need not be all or nothing.

A crucial stage in this evolution toward what its critics call "cafeteria Catholicism" was a decree by Pope Paul VI, soon after the Vatican Council, to the effect that artificial birth control would not be allowed after all. Because millions of Catholics, led to believe that the old ban was history (a special worldwide commission had been set up to examine the matter, and the scuttlebutt said it would look favorably on artificial birth control, which it did, but the pope then rejected its report), were already practicing birth control, they now had a formidable dilemma.

A century or even a generation earlier, the options would be clear: Get off the pill or get out of the Church. At the Vatican Council, however, a crucial new element had been introduced into the old equation—the inviolability of individual conscience. This, the council flatly stated, trumped even papal power. (It was presumed, of course, that this would be an "informed" conscience, and what exactly constitutes an informed conscience has also been the subject of hot debate in the meantime.)

Hanging Tough

So the Catholics, or at least most of them, stayed in the Church. From this and other experiences grew the new realization of an old truth—that the Church was not for perfect people but for sinners. People still part company with the contemporary Catholic Church, but not for the old reasons—not because they were expelled (with the rarest exceptions) or because they did not feel worthy. Sadly, a prime reason people "fall away" nowadays, to judge by the anecdotal evidence, is a vague feeling in many quarters that the Church has become irrelevant. The fear of eternal damnation that for centuries kept Christians in line no longer exerts the same absolute hold on believers. The new, more pragmatic approach needs to see a payoff, often even a temporal one, that the blind faith of the past did not presume to expect.

So now, as the headlines yell out about clerical pedophilia, related improprieties, and cover-ups on the part of the leadership, Catholics have serious decisions to make, including the decision to do nothing and think nothing—the drift toward irrelevance.

And most Catholics, it seems, are hanging tough. Even the pedophilia victims and their families, instead of throwing up their hands in disgust or despair, are speaking out, organizing, criticizing, and refusing to let the leadership call the shots as they had done for centuries. The significant factor is that these and other dissatisfied Catholics are choosing to seek reform from within the Church rather than walking away from it.

The Church is so big and so opaque, it takes time and distance to see how it's doing. Whether the outcome of all this recent trauma will be an erosion of papal power or a whole new configuration within the Church remains to be seen. What has happened, in short, is that the sex abuse crisis has drawn many Catholics into deep reflection on issues of faith and what it means to be a Catholic.

Big Church, Little Church

When Catholics talk about "the Church," they frequently sweep aside fancy ecclesiastical lingo and talk instead about "big church" and "little church." They do this to distinguish broadly between the clergy and the laity. The clergy are the ordained members of the Church—deacons, priests, and bishops. (They will be discussed in detail in Chapter 4.) All the rest of the people are laity.

A few years ago, I co-authored a book called *The Complete Idiot's Guide to Understanding Catholicism* (see Appendix A), which told the story of "little" church—what being an "ordinary" Catholic is like. The book looks at beliefs, practices, traditions, organization, and history as the people's story, as distinct from the story of the Church leaders. In writing that book and later in presenting the material in workshops and seminars, it became increasingly apparent that two distinct experiences of the Church are expressed in the terms big church and little church. This book looks at some of the differences between big church and little church, but with a particular focus on the elements of big church.

In this down-home model, a key factor is ordination, which in the Catholic Church is a sacrament. Because the distinction between priest and (other) people is vital to the thesis of this book, it seems worthwhile to pause and put sacrament in perspective.

Brother Sun and Sister Moon

Catholics like to say that theirs is a sacramental church, and behind that lies a sacramental consciousness. By this, they mean that God and God's grace enter the world in all sorts of worldly ways. This is a gloriously upbeat view. It sees all aspects of creation as good because God made creation full of good things; all of which can be inroads to later glory. St. Francis epitomized this optimistic aspect, seeing salvation in Brother Sun, Sister Moon, a rabbit, or a bird. Well-known author Fr. Andrew Greeley has likewise sung the praises of sex and other mundane pursuits such as music, dance, and a good time. English author Hilaire Belloc is frequently quoted in this context: "Wherever the Catholic sun doth shine, there is music, laughter, and good red wine. At least, I've always heard it so; *Benedicamus Domino*." Not to excess, of course—this is still the Catholic Church. And the purpose is not just to have a ball, but to meet God in God's creation.

The ramifications are widespread. Sacramental consciousness should show itself in such contemporary terms as ecology, community, and engagement with all aspects of the world rather than retreating from God's lavish gift of creation.

Even for many traditional Catholics accustomed to dire warnings about sin and damnation, this positive picture comes as a surprise. Indeed, the Church's teaching has frequently flagged in its enthusiasm for the world. Yet the sacramental aspect is a profound distinguishing feature between Catholicism and other Christian denominations. Most Protestants subscribe to the principle that God is so above and beyond us that ordinary earthly intermediaries are unworthy of his splendor and inadequate means of touching divinity. Only Jesus Christ, by his incarnation, death, and resurrection, is an adequate intermediary, the prevailing Protestant view insists. This more severe, puritanical Protestant approach is individual and aloof—between me and God—compared with the communal, all-embracing

Catholic attitude summed up by novelist James Joyce's rollicking definition of the Catholic Church: "Here comes everybody."

Seven Sacraments

This sacramental interface between humanity and divinity has been concentrated in the life of the Church into seven specific channels, or sacraments. These are not haphazard; directly or indirectly, tradition claims, they were established by Christ as visible signs and integral instruments for working out spiritual salvation within the Catholic Church. They cater to the predominant needs of the human soul at crucial moments on its journey through life.

Every Catholic of a certain age learned early to rattle off the seven sacraments:

- Baptism
- Confirmation
- Eucharist
- Penance
- The sacrament of the sick (which lacks the drama of its old name, Extreme Unction)
- Holy orders
- Matrimony

Holy orders is the sacrament through which ordination is conferred on priests in the Church. (Deacons and bishops are also ordained to their ecclesial offices, as you'll see later.) The fact that a sacrament marks this passage from the lay state to the priestly state underlines its crucial role in the overall salvation scheme.

Although little church and big church are tidy handles for making some basic distinctions between Church personnel, they scarcely represent what Jesus was presumed to have in mind when he got his popular movement off the ground. The adjectives big and little, however, do betray a feeling all too prevalent in the Church: that the unfortunate, uneven distinction between "us" and "them" is not a figment of people's imagination.

The Institution/People Dichotomy

The long debate before, during, and after the Vatican Council about who or what is the Church finally highlighted a distinction long eclipsed, yet crucial to any discussion of ecclesiastical authority: that between the Church as institution and the Church as people of God.

Older Catholics grew up with the notion—and many cannot shake it to this day—that the Church is the pope and his subordinate hierarchy, the buildings and bureaus, from the Vatican to the local Rosary and Altar Society.

It is insidiously easy to fall into such a trap. Usually the institutional aspect of the Church makes the news and forces itself on the public consciousness. When the pope travels, he's featured in the evening news. When a scandal breaks, the Catholic on the street is seldom asked her opinion; rather, some bishop, theologian, or other institutional person is asked. Equally often, for many Catholics, and even more so for people who are not Catholic, mention of church means the building rather than those in it. Whether secular or sacred, it is an understandable inclination for those who run institutions (often vaguely called bureaucrats) to emphasize the institutional rather than the individual. It makes the bureaucrat seem more important, for one thing, and confers more power on the bureau.

The wave of new thinking that culminated in the Vatican Council turned this misconception on its head. The Church is the People of God, the new-old paradigm says. The idea, of course, was as old as Church history. It all started as a group of people of like mind—no churches, no rites; not even titles to name themselves.

Of course, there had to be an institution when the early Christians realized that they were here on Earth for the long haul. It was natural that the members then focused on the institution. It was bad for everyone, though, when the institution became "the Church." Popes and saints made this happen, often with good intentions. Efforts to restore the balance between people and institution have never quite succeeded—not even now. The best efforts of the progressive leaders and theologians to instill this key concept in the so-called ordinary faithful have been thwarted by what is called the restorationist efforts of Pope John Paul II and a curia all too willing to turn back the calendar.

This has enormous impact on the daily life of the Church— especially in times of crisis such as this pedophilia scandal creates.

Meeting in God's Creation

It's about power—not military or muscular, but moral. And indeed, the way the U.S. pedophilia story has played out in mid-2002 hints that the pope and the institution have not been able to take back totally the power they once possessed. If they had, the scandal would have been swept under the carpet as many so often had before; victims, other Catholics, and even bishops and other bureaucrats would not have been allowed to display such dirty laundry so publicly.

The people of God are not the same thing as the little church. The people of God, as understood by Vatican II, include the laity, the pope, and everyone in between. But with the different terminology comes a difference of perspective. The new emphasis is on people (or, as they used to be called, souls). With perspective comes a more profound change of attitude and outlook. With attitude and outlook comes the way power will be exercised.

Among the many ways of dividing up the Church (and as we shall see, there is a multitude of ways), perhaps the most resounding current division is between conservatives and liberals (or, as they would usually prefer to be called, progressives). In the contentious post–Vatican II tussle for the soul of the Church, the conservatives tend to emphasize loyalty to the pope, which in turn leads to a predilection for the institution. The progressives, which include priests, bishops (but not many), and possibly a (very) occasional cardinal, go beyond lip service (which everyone gives) in fostering the people of God as the ideal expression of Christ's Church.

The Complexity of Catholic Power

The organization of the Catholic Church is so complicated, and the interlocking networks of its power so convoluted, that they can only be attributed to the human element of what Catholics call the body of

Christ rather than to the divine element, which is said to be utterly simple.

This stupendous complexity did not happen overnight. From the first few bewildered disciples, who had a profound fortifying experience on the first Pentecost, grew a number of small local communities. They were Jews, like Jesus. There were no buildings. They met in neighborhood houses. They borrowed their liturgies from the synagogue and elsewhere. They had no dogmas—no canon law. They made no distinction between clergy and laity. In an early letter, Peter talks about a royal priesthood, but he applies it to everybody—Church history came full circle when the universal priesthood of the laity was reaffirmed at Vatican II.

The early emphasis was not on what each one believed, on doctrinal orthodoxy (so much a preoccupation of the pontificate of John Paul II), but rather on praise and thanksgiving. The new Christians were amazed at having discovered the new secret of life, and the overarching attitude was gratitude—which literally means Eucharist—which is now a synonym for the Mass and still the heart of Catholic worship today.

Humans can't spend long together, however, without needing to get organized. The apostle Paul became a key architect of the growing Church. Paul was sold on the idea that the Spirit of God would shape the destiny of the growing community. The Spirit was accorded a big role in deciding local leadership. (They were called presbyters at first, a word that was later translated as priest but in Paul's day was merely Greek for older guys, or elders.) These Spirit-guided, early leaders, then, were not so much managers or CEOs, but rather charismatic gurus. The early Church was looking up rather than around.

This carelessness about administration needs to be understood in context. The early Christians believed the end of the world would happen any day, so there was no incentive to build basilicas (which they knew from the Romans) or form committees. But as time passed and no end appeared, they began to think in terms of the long haul.

More important than buildings, for the long term, was the story. Tell the same story to 10 people, and they will all feed it back differently. After the apostles died, to whom could Christians turn for the authentic message? There was a rush to write it all down. Already, there were gaps and contradictions in the story. Some of these might well have been deliberate. The authors of the historically quite imperfect New Testament were products of their culture. It was natural to want to leave out aspects of the account with which, perhaps, they were not comfortable. Jesus might be the Messiah, but he sure did and said some odd things. He didn't keep women in their place, for one thing. So if women were at the Last Supper, as many suspect, there was a temptation to leave that out of the account, and the evangelists gave in to the temptation. Today, this little omission has huge repercussions in the debate over women's ordination.

Not everything was written down, then. But in addition to the Scriptures, there was an oral tradition. This, too, was finally written down, or what was remembered of it—a loose legacy that, along with Scripture, eventually became what some called the deposit of faith.

This deposit might all be divine, but it wasn't all clear. Who meant what by this or that? Huge controversies, and eventually occasional wars, were waged about seemingly harmless words or concepts. Heresies sprouted. Later conflict would be about power, as theologian and author Martin Marty noted, but back in those more formative centuries, it was primarily about what to believe.

From the earliest days, anyone could see an arbiter was needed. After Jesus left, Peter was the obvious candidate. But after Peter, then what? The idea of "apostolic succession" became very important—an unbroken line stretching back to the apostles. Even in the late first century, Pope Clement laid this down as a bottom line for authority. And 2,000 years later, every bishop in the world must have this connection going back to the apostles to be recognized by the universal Church. Catholic power is complex, all right.

After two millennia of evolution, the deployment and exercise of that complex Church power is outlined in canon law—the Church's essential rule book—and elaborated in a more reader-friendly fashion in the *Catechism of the Catholic Church.*

All the members together are described as "the Christian faithful," but also as the people of God. They become members by the sacrament of baptism. These Christian faithful are basically divided into two groups—

the hierarchy and the laity. (A third category is called "consecrated life" by the catechism, though these are more popularly if less accurately known as religious orders; you will meet them later.)

To generalize, the hierarchy means the bishops, including the bishop of Rome who is always pope. The laity is nearly everyone else. We will return to them in later chapters.

Some Are More Equal Than Others

Cynics might be forgiven for reading into some of the *Catechism* descriptions (it was compiled under the aegis of the Vatican) a beguiling condescension more appropriate to an earlier, less sophisticated age. There exists among all the faithful "a true equality," the *Catechism* tells us. This is only an equality of "dignity," however, and does not mean, for example, that anyone who wants to can be pope. Rather, we exercise our equality "in accord with each one's condition and function." This is about as helpful as saying the president of the United States and his fellow citizen sleeping under a bridge in the inner city are equal.

The catechism tries further to polish this silver lining to charm the laity: "The very differences which the Lord has willed to put between the members of his body serve its unity and mission."

This is cold comfort to women especially. There lurks here, like the elephant in the parlor, a radical prior separation even within the lay membership. That separation is between male and female. Of course, natural differences exist between males and females, but there is no problem unless power goes with the difference. And a power goes with being born a Catholic boy baby that isn't extended to Catholic girl babies. From birth, a male Catholic will have the option to become a priest and the potential to progress through the ranks as his vocational call directs, all the way to the top—he can become pope. Female Catholics don't have this option. When difference brings privilege, as is the case with ordination, there is a problem.

Few would claim that the Church is wantonly inflicting this seeming injustice on half (at least) of its membership. A mountain of tradition piled amid the dust of 20 centuries of arguments, encyclicals, councils, synods, theologians, popes, and the formidable assertion that "we always did it this way" add up to an anomaly that—in this age of burgeoning equality in nearly all levels of society and nearly all cultures—is difficult for many observers to swallow.

For men who opt not to become priests—or, according to Catholic theology, are not called by God to be priests—a comparable discrepancy remains between laity and hierarchy. The catechism's own words are so telling that one cannot resist using them: "To the apostles and their successors [the hierarchy], Christ has entrusted the office of teaching, sanctifying, and governing in his name and by his power." This might seem like the lion's share of the work of salvation, but not to worry. "The laity are made to share in the priestly, prophetical, and kingly office of Christ." This sounds great, but is a fistful of smoke that as a job description lacks heft; and one must not forget that the "priestly" office described here is the more diffuse gift shared by everyone and in no way entitles the man, any more than the woman, to perform the most exalted aspects of priestly ministry.

Hierarchy as a Case of Mistaken Identity

This laity-hierarchy dichotomy scarcely begins to describe the complex arrangements and structures that have grown up through the centuries to facilitate the governance and sanctification of the people of God.

Some say, perhaps a bit tongue in cheek, that this hierarchical ordering was authenticated and consolidated in the sixth century through a case of mistaken identity. A relatively obscure Syrian theologian was writing under the assumed name of Dionysius the Areopagite, a name he borrowed from a convert of the apostle Paul. Dionysius got the idea of a hierarchical ordering system for the Church by observing what he saw to be a "divinely ordered structure of the entire universe." In this worldview, everything in creation was seen to belong to a hierarchical order of being; for example, three orders of angelic beings. Dionysius believed this divine order was intended to be reflected in the hierarchy of three ordained orders within the clergy—bishops, priests, and deacons. Putting logic to the test, or believing that good things always come in threes, he believed that, divine order was further mirrored in three orders of lay hierarchy: religious orders, laity, and catechumens (those studying to become Catholic).

In the Dionysian world, "higher" orders were seen to have power over "lower" orders. This theory firmly established the laity at the bottom of the ladder: passive recipients of grace bestowed by the clergy. Thanks to his *nom de plume*, Church historians mistakenly thought Dionysius actually *was* the contemporary of St. Paul; in which case, he would be directly involved in the formation of the early Church and consequently an authority of some stature.

As Catholics often say when they're confused, God works in mysterious ways.

The hierarchical formula was gradually woven into Church identity among both the clerics and the laity. When the Council of Trent (1545–1563) was called to make much needed Church reforms necessitated by abuses in hierarchical power, council members wrestled with the idea of a divinely ordered hierarchy and with issues of a separation between clergy and laity, but decided not to make any serious changes in this critical area.

Changes that would reflect a more communal relationship among the people of God would not be effectively addressed for another 500 years—at the Second Vatican Council. Many of those Vatican II recommendations have not yet been enforced as official Catholic policy. Rather, there has been an entrenchment of the old order based on the traditional hierarchical power structure. (Dionysius the Areopagite could be said, incidentally, to have gotten his finger into even the great American pie because most of the institutions in Western society are organized roughly according to the same divine order he conceived a millennium and a half ago.)

Who's Who in the Catholic Church

The hierarchical structure of the Catholic Church is a top-to-bottom power flow. Here's a thumbnail sketch of how the offices are ordered. The main division is between the nonordained and the ordained. The pope is at the top, and is the final decision-maker. I'll describe how each of these offices function a bit later in this chapter and in Chapter 3. I'll also take a look at some expressions and modifications of ecclesial authority. (Those that do not get a separate chapter later, as the pope and others do, will be outlined here.) These reflect how the Church works in practice.

Here's a quick look at the structure:

Pope (Supreme Authority). The pope, who is the bishop of Rome, is at the top of the hierarchical chain of command. Power: absolute.

Roman Curia. The Roman Curia are the pope's closest advisors. Power: highly influential, unofficial.

Cardinal (College of Cardinals). The College of Cardinals is not a university, but it describes the collegial relationship of the men (cardinals) who work together assisting the pope in governing the Church. Power: collegial/advisory.

Archbishop. An archbishop is a bishop with a greater administrative position than a bishop. Power: collegial/advisory.

Bishop (Hierarchy). A bishop is the head of a diocese. Power: collegial/advisory.

Priest. Priests have no official decision-making capacity beyond the administration of the church or parish where they serve, and those decisions must be in agreement with the bishop. Ordination to the priesthood is necessary before moving up to decision-making level.

Deacon. Permanent deacons are ordained and serve the bishop and assist priests. Transitional deacon describes a position that will eventually lead to ordination into the priesthood.

Clergy (Ordained). Clergy are the ordained members of the Church: deacon, priest, and bishop.

Laity. Laity are the nonordained members of the Church. There is an unofficial order, generally expressed as *seminarians* (men studying to become priests); *brothers* (men in religious orders); *nuns* (women in religious orders); *lay professionals* (lay professionals fill a variety of positions in Church life, including the study of theology, teaching, Directors of Religious Education, pastoral ministry, music, chaplains, and spiritual direction); and finally, the *regular folks* (the one billion practicing Catholics who fill the churches, receive the sacraments, and assist the priest in carrying out the Christian mission in parishes all over the world).

Administrative Offices

In addition to the individual offices, there are administrative offices and ways that Catholics organize themselves and are part of the function of the Church, although not directly involved in decision-making. The Church is in a transition time following Vatican II, when the power was more evenly distributed—theoretically. The shift is in process and moving fairly fast according to the Catholic clock.

The *Roman Curia* is the central administration of the Church. It is composed of departments similar to most secular governments, though some of the portfolios are different. (Few governments have a bureau for liturgy.) These are usually directed by cardinals or archbishops but also staffed by priests (many of them monsignors, a largely honorary title), nuns, and laity. Everyone serves at the pleasure of the pope.

In terms of the exercise of power, there has often been a tension between the curia and the local Church: not only the individual parish priest, but also bishops and national conferences of bishops and other groupings whose members privately feel that they know more about conditions and spiritual needs in their own neck of the woods than does an Italian (most frequently) bureaucrat with a briefcase. But there is no denying the fact that some members of the curia, who have the ear of the pontiff, have huge influence over the direction of the Church.

The Vatican does not confine its influence to Church politics. It also has a worldwide network of embassies or nunciatures to interact with secular authorities around the world.

The *College of Cardinals* is a body of Church dignitaries chosen by the pope for a variety of purposes but most importantly to elect the next pope. Cardinals do not fit neatly in the hierarchical chain of command. Indeed, they are regarded by many as uncomfortable relics of a medieval past when princes dressed in finery and were better served by whom they knew than what they did. A unique feature was that they did not have to be ordained, though nowadays loopholes have been filled. With the circulation of the 1917 Code of Canon Law, only priests or bishops can become cardinals, and in 1962 John XXIII determined that all cardinals then and henceforth would be ordained as bishops.

In modern times, there are usually approximately 150 members in the College of Cardinals. These are distributed around the world, but a preponderance of them are at the Vatican.

The *diocese* is a geographic district containing many parishes, which is under the direction of the bishop. The diocesan Church is called a cathedral. An archdiocese, led by an archbishop, describes a larger or more prestigious geographical center, usually in a major city.

The *presbyteral council,* a relic of the early Church, was recently reinstated in the spirit of building cooperation between bishops and priests and helping move the Church toward collegiality at a local level. The presbyteral council relates to the diocese as parish councils relate to the local Church. The bishop usually determines how they are used. However, there are some matters about which the bishop must consult with the council, such as building a new church, merging or dividing parishes, and decisions about a pastor's salary.

The presbyteral council is composed of priests in the diocese who serve as advisors to the bishop. Members of the council can nominate members, but membership comes by invitation of the bishop usually in consultation with other bishops. The bishop presides over the council and sets the agenda, though members may submit items for the agenda. How much power is shared through this council depends on the leadership style of the bishop.

The People's Church

The People of God is not so much a monolith as an amalgamation of local communities—parochial, diocesan, national, and other less tidy manifestations. *Collegiality* means that all these churches and their leaders share with the pope (and his curia) a common privilege and responsibility in the governance and pastoral mission of the Church.

The problem is that the pope is not known as the *supreme* pontiff for nothing. Over many centuries, he has gathered unto himself an enormous amount of unquestioned authority—to say that his sway does not equal that of a king or dictator might be literally true but is also coy evasion. Hence, a tension continues between the role played by the pope vis-à-vis the local pastor, the local bishop, the Episcopal conference, and international synods (set up at Vatican II as instruments of collegiality, but degraded by the Vatican into glorified Episcopal workshops without clout).

The two popes who reigned most of the years since Vatican II, Paul VI and John Paul II, have paid lip service to collegiality but in practice exercised a robust form of papal primacy.

Most Catholic life happens at the local *parish*—a geographical area with a church, and sometimes a school, as its center. Occasionally (not often), a parish is defined by sociological factors such as nationality or language.

Parishes are administrated by a pastor. Usually the pastor is a priest. Currently, because of the large numbers of Catholic parishes and the dwindling number of priests to serve them, nonordained people are being trained to function as pastors. Each parish is responsible to the bishop in whose diocese the church is located. However, the bishop is required to consult with the presbyteral council when making important decisions about parishes in his diocese.

The parish is now the closest approximation we have to the original Church of Christ's first followers; that is, a small group in a local area, making most of its own decisions (there was no one yet in Rome to write to) and solving its own problems. It was very personal and based on charity—"Behold how they love one another," strangers allegedly said. As Catholics fight for the future of the Church, a key factor is perspective: Are Catholics to be seen primarily as one huge monolithic institution or as a local community that has its own life and expression?

In the average healthy parish, an immense amount of energy is generated and a wide variety of ministries, services, and activities are organized and administered. *Parish councils* are often the engines behind this pulsating parish life. They are a Vatican II development designed, among other things, to create more participation by lay members who are invited to share in the administrative business or in local ministries. Councils are under the direction of the parish priest. How much decision-making authority the parish council has might depend more on the leadership style of the pastor and his willingness to empower the members than on anything written in canon law.

Here, as throughout the universal Church, tensions can arise between the pastor and the people. Properly handled, even the tensions can be creative and the collaboration help the local Church—in a way, it *is* the local Church. Badly handled, the parish can soon display in miniature the travails of the universal Church. Complaints about parish councils come from both sides of the table. Sometimes, the parish members don't feel that they have any real say in the decisions and are simply taking on more work with no sense of power. Sometimes, the pastor complains that the parish council is just a lot of extra work and that people don't volunteer and take an active interest in participation. Parish councils represent a process new to Catholics who are used to turning all responsibility over to the priest.

In Conclusion

The Catholic Church continues to struggle with the division between clergy and laity that creates a sense of separation. The hierarchal and patriarchal nature of its organization imposes elitism that is not in keeping with the mission or the model on which it was founded—the early Christian communities. This disconnection between the leaders and the people means that the experiences of the people at the bottom of the structure is often very different from the leaders at the top. A collegial form is emerging and is in its earliest stage of development—existing more theoretically than realistically for the time being. It is probably moving along about as fast as it can given the nature of this organization, and both the people and the leaders have to make adjustments that secure a smooth transition. If you're looking for quick changes, you're in the wrong pew!

Chapter 3

Papal Power:
Theory and Practice

There's nothing quite like it in any other religion. The pope has come to visit some far country, which was once a mere outpost of Christendom, maybe even mission territory. Now, a plane flies in self-importantly—most likely the national airline of the host country, or a plane repainted in papal colors for the occasion. Every nun who could get the day off from her ministry is there, as are phalanxes of priests and crowds of the faithful, all agog. Not only are the local bishops there, the red trim of their outfits betraying still a hint of worldly ostentation, but civil notables are also there, perhaps a president or prime minister—all paying homage to one man.

Then follows the ride in the popemobile. In the days when popes seldom left home, they were carried around on ceremonial occasions on an elevated throne called the *sedia gestatoria*, a relic of the regal splendor with which the papacy was once surrounded. Today's popemobile, with its bulletproof glass, is more practical than pompous—a safety measure, among other things, in an age in which someone would not hesitate to shoot a pope.

Next day, in the local football stadium, a million Catholics or more are gathered, often amid considerable hardship, for the papal Mass—people straining to catch even a glimpse of the white dot in the distance that is the pope. They believe he's the Vicar of Christ on Earth. No other religion makes any comparable claim. It makes sense, then, to be excited and even in awe of the pope.

What Is a Pope?

Although he's perhaps the best-known person on Earth, there is no simple way to say what a pope is. The response depends in part on whether one turns to the Gospels or to canon law or to history for an answer.

For starters, he is the bishop of Rome and head of the Catholic Church—although that's not where everyone would start. In Latin, the word for pope means *father*, or more precisely, *papa*. He has many other descriptive titles such as the Vicar (substitute) of Christ, Vicar of Peter, Successor to the Apostles, Supreme Pontiff of the Universal Church, Patriarch of the West, Sovereign of the Vatican City State, and Servant of the Servants of God.

Within certain limitations, therefore, the pope is the final authority on everything that goes on in the Catholic Church. Whether it was the intention of the founder, most popes also wielded power outside the Church's boundaries. The result has often been disastrous, especially when popes were recognized more as temporal than spiritual leaders. Yet, in a quiet way, the Church has also been an influence for good in the larger society. For example, Pope John XXIII exerted salutary papal influence during the Cuban missile crises of the 1960s and helped effect a positive outcome. Although spiritual by definition, Catholicism is engaged with the world and therefore is not immune to its controversies and conflicts.

In his book *Conclave*, John Allen explains the pope's formidable clout: "One way of putting the point: The pope can push a button in Rome and see something happen in Singapore in ways the archbishop of Canterbury or the Dalai Lama cannot."

And renowned Vaticanologist Peter Hebblethwaite wrote: "The papacy is not a static institution, frozen once for all in its present form. And popes are not just a mass-produced series of figures in white who appear on distant balconies and mouth interchangeable platitudes. It matters very much who is pope. Each pope makes his own distinctive contribution."

Late in the pontificate of Pope John Paul II, the paradox that is the papacy becomes even more pronounced. When the door of the big plane opened, the man who struggled to descend the ramp was old and bent, willing himself to take one painful step after another just as many said he was willing himself to stay alive because it was his destiny to guide the Church—first into a new millennium and then into some unspecified new Christian era. Years earlier, in 1981, he was shot and seriously wounded. For years, he has been suffering from Parkinson's disease and other ailments. His voice is as weak as his body is frail, and he sometimes falls asleep in the midst of all the pomp.

Contrasts are everywhere. The esteemed pontiff seen from the distance is a sick old man when seen up close. The glamour of being the intermediary between Earth and heaven grows pale under the burdens of office. Head bent as the crowds applaud, the pope sits on a lot of secrets—some of them sad ones.

As the pedophilia storm rages and accusations fly about which bishops knew or covered up this or that horror story, it is natural to ask what secrets the pope himself has been sitting on. He has not been a remote presence, but a hands-on, activist overseer. It need not be that he knew names or details, but it is not consistent with the image of him cultivated over 20 years to say that he was out to lunch while rumors, accusations, and even lawsuits were hinting to the world that a scandal was waiting to break. It need not be, either, that he is guilty of any wrongdoing or sin. But it would be delusional to divorce the pope from the real life in which he is said to be so immersed.

Even if he knew that there were a serious pedophilia crisis, this assuredly was not the only problem confronting John Paul. Probably more than anyone else on Earth, a pope sits at the crossroads of the world's aches and pains. Yet some problems more than others seem to leave religious leaders with a dilemma: those that might give scandal to the faithful or the wider world.

This bugaboo of scandal needs to be confronted, advocates of reform have long grumbled. Church leadership, from the pope to the local pastor, has constantly and often conveniently used scandal as a reason for covering up unpleasant aspects of Church life that needed to be aired. "The faithful would be scandalized if they heard about it" was a constant refrain the Church used before sweeping various ills under the carpet.

This, of course, was often an insult to the faithful, who were judged to be so immature that they could not handle reality, warts and all.

Awesome though papal power may be, it is as limited as the pope's human nature. That's why there is a constant need for reform. Leaders, no matter whom or what they lead, seldom respond enthusiastically to demands for reform. For one thing, such a demand implies that they have not been doing their jobs; if they were, the club, corporation, or church would be a more perfect organization. This is especially true in the case of Christianity, which is believed to be a perfect society by its members, at least potentially if not actually (a handy distinction that its philosophers have long relished), and which for 2,000 years has proclaimed ideal life with commendable persistence.

What a pope is, then, is important.

The Past Is Prologue

On one famous occasion, Jesus was said to say: "Thou art Peter, and upon this rock I will build my church, and the gates of hell shall not prevail against it. And I shall give to thee the keys of the kingdom of heaven. Whatever you bind on Earth shall be bound in heaven, and whatever you loose on Earth shall be loosed in heaven" (Matthew 16:18).

Few quotations preserved by history are as powerful as this one. Modern biblical scholarship has concluded—something totally unacceptable to literalists or fundamentalists—that every word attributed to Jesus in the New Testament was not necessarily said by him. Rather, in this view, the gospel stories had an oral history before they were written down; there were no tape recorders; human memory is fallible; human nature is often inclined to remember things to the advantage of the speaker or writer, or to the advantage of others one admires—such as the head of one's community; such as Peter, the fisherman turned apostle.

On the other hand, there's no good reason to believe Jesus didn't say this or some equivalent. But perhaps it didn't matter: The new group that was soon to lay the foundation for Christianity believed that the Spirit was guiding it in any case. Some wild leaps of faith were taken in the early Church, as they are to this day. They are at the heart of religion.

Jesus' words confirmed the belief that Peter was special. Indeed, Peter went on to lead a tumultuous and significant life. Because spreading the good news was central to Christ's message, Peter, like many of the others, soon took to the road and eventually found himself in Rome. He obviously made an impact there as well. He was crucified by the authorities—upside down, they say. Just think of it.

Fishers of Souls

Because he was bishop of Rome, we have grown accustomed to calling Peter the first pope. But here again, we might be on thin ice. In his book *Lives of the Popes*, theologian Richard McBrien writes that there is no evidence of Peter being involved in establishing the Church community in Rome or serving as its first bishop. One reason for saying so is that Rome, up to the middle of the second century, did not have a single bishop and neither did other early Christian communities. "The Roman community seems instead to have had a corporate or collegial form of pastoral leadership," writes McBrien. "Those counted among the earliest popes, therefore, may very well have been simply the individuals who presided over the local council of elders or presbyter-bishops." They might simply have been the most prominent or respected local Christians.

It was only with Pope St. Pius I (approx. 142–155), according to this version, that Rome had one sole bishop and thus an obvious candidate for pope.

Not that it mattered much at the time (it's one of those cases that has come to matter much more with hindsight), because early popes had little clout outside their own neighborhood anyway. Rather, local Christian communities took care of their own spiritual and temporal affairs and settled their own differences. Rome was far away and was, furthermore, a hostile place—headquarters of the occupying power that had killed their Savior.

It was only in the fifth century, with the pontificate of Leo the Great, that Peter was identified with the title of bishop of Rome. It might be loose history, but it became important ecclesiology. Symbolism was central. If the Church were just another superpower, it could draw a line in the sand and whack whoever crossed it. But if the appeal were to the spirit, hearts and minds responded more willingly to symbols.

"That They All May Be One ..."

The Church's identification with Rome is one of its most effective creations. The Messiah, especially on the crucial last evening before he was captured, made an impassioned appeal for unity among his followers. "That they all may be one, as you, Father, in me, and I in you," he prayed (John 17:21). That unity was dramatically sundered on a number of occasions, such as Luther's Reformation. These tragic schisms aside, the unity that the Catholic Church has maintained for so long, considering its turbulent history and all the urges to disagree, has been among its most impressive achievements.

The papacy has played a central role in maintaining this unity. In the course of twenty centuries, popes have so incontrovertibly established papal primacy and have so finessed their own papal identity as practically synonymous with the identity of the Church that breaking away has become nearly unthinkable for anyone who cherishes Christianity.

Catholics might argue whether this is a good or a bad thing. Certainly, unity has been good for the Church. Yet, if it's wielded as a psychological weapon, it can become an oppressor. Bishops, as already indicated, don't even exist without the apostolic succession that connects them to the apostles. The papacy, of course, is the arbiter of such apostolic succession. This is just one of the many ways in which popes have exploited unity to consolidate power.

A glance at Church history shows how enormously the papacy has grown from almost nothing. The break between the Eastern Church and Western Catholicism in 1054 seems to have been a catalyst. Indeed, one is tempted to wonder if the great spiritual energy of the Eastern Church—one thinks of great centers such as Constantinople, Ephesus, and Nicea, which hosted some of the Church's great ecumenical councils—might not have been a salutary influence to keep the early Church in balance.

McBrien points to the pontificate of Gregory VII as pivotal. Before that, popes were more mediators than rulers. They were not called anything so imposing (or, some might say, self-important) as Vicar of Christ. They did not appoint bishops (that was done back home). They did not have a Roman Curia worth mentioning. They did not impose clerical celibacy. (In addition to Peter, several of the other early popes seem to have been married.) They did not write encyclicals—that is, when the tough questions were asked, they did not presume to be the sole, universal teacher for the entire Church.

In the second millennium, in short, the popes took over.

Amidst Aberrations and Crises

One could say that the pope has been accumulating power, or one could take the bite out of it by saying that he has been assuming responsibility. If a pope were to take to heart the responsibility entrusted to him, it might well keep him awake at night.

Despite aberrations such as the pedophilia crisis, the Church seems very successful today. (Admittedly by worldly standards: No reliable spiritual measure has yet been devised.) The pope is a superstar. The numbers are up. There is little serious dissent or challenge from within. Yet anxiety lurks below the surface. Beyond the comfortable paycheck and the contemporary icon of ubiquitous fun, people of all creeds or none are searching for meaning in life, for transcendence, for wonder, and for *something*. Huge numbers of those searchers walk past the church door as they also walk past the mosque or synagogue door. Catholicism and other religions are constantly challenged to be relevant. This vague requirement is a Holy Grail often sacrificed to orthodoxy, fear, smugness, and the status quo. The easier procedure is not to rock the boat.

Jesus said that he would always be with the Church, but he never said how big or small that Church might be. A self-satisfied or out-of-touch papacy could find itself in charge of a flock diminished in numbers or, worse, in faith—that all-or-nothing attitude and energy that makes a church transcendent and not merely a club.

It's Not Easy Being Pope

In this context, leadership is crucial. Always and everywhere, leaders who let hubris go to their heads eventually reaped the whirlwind. For a while, beginning with the reign of Pope Pius IX in the late nineteenth century, there existed what some called the cult of the reigning pope. One bishop went so far as to call Pius an incarnation of Jesus Christ.

One can't always blame a pope for what certain sycophants who surround him do or say. It's no secret that there is no place like the Vatican for attracting careerists for whom expediency and advancement are more important than God's truth. And that's not only at the Vatican: Lower prelates everywhere fall over themselves to pay homage to the Vicar of Christ. In this atmosphere of obeisance, few bishops or priests are likely to look the pope in the eye (if they should get that close) and tell him that he should drop some of the fancy titles, that he should spread the responsibility around because most Catholics are wiser than he thinks, or even that women should be ordained.

Whether in papal or other circles, this is sometimes called speaking the truth to power. It is not frequently found in the corridors of power. It's hard to blame people—no one wants to lose one's job—unless one stops to think how much more might be at stake.

But the alternative sure is easier. A glance at the *Catechism of the Catholic Church* (to take a recent example) will quickly reveal the homage the writers lavish on His Holiness. Some will see this as overweening and others as giving the great man his due. In the course of centuries, in any case, the praise and the titles pile higher. The resulting figure (*figura* is a great Italian word full of nuance) can be at least intimidating, at worst a caricature.

It seems highly unlikely that anyone this past century has said "Now, wait a minute, Pope ..." or its equivalent to the person in white at the head of the table. In a glasshouse environment such as this, it's hard to muster the backbone to be real or to thrash things out, as Jesus and the disciples seem to have done. But maybe, in our day, in our post-feudal, sort-of-democratic culture, this would be a great thing for the Church. If the pope wants to be humble, he has the power to do it.

The personality of each pope plays a part. It matters what kind of person the Church gets, as Hebblethwaite indicated. Yet popes seem to have been sufficiently of a kind that for centuries the Church has been moving steadfastly in the direction of a more powerful papacy.

The controlling pope who insists that papa knows best, as many recent popes have done, might be well advised to take the Church's own advice and trust the Holy Spirit. This would presumably lead in turn to greater trust in the far-flung Church to whose members the Holy Spirit is also attentive.

As he puts out the lights at the end of a weary day, one wonders whether the pope occasionally realizes that this formidable worldly institution over which he holds sway is a far cry from what Jesus seemed to have in mind when he walked the dusty roads of the Middle East, talking to plain folks and making them feel better in soul and body.

Papal Packaging: All Shapes and Sizes

In response to the suggestion that all popes are alike, one has only to point to the interesting diversity of the most recent popes:

- **Pius XII** (1939–1958) was an austere, ascetic aristocrat—an aloof diplomat who spent his entire priestly life well removed from the pastoral arena where priests usually meet souls. It was his fate to sit on the (metaphorical) throne of Peter during the most difficult years of the century, during World War II. Since his death, accusations have arisen about his role vis-à-vis Hitler's "final solution" of the Jewish question. During his papacy, he ruled with such towering authority that Catholics wondered at his death (as some probably do at every pope's death) how even the Holy Spirit could find an adequate replacement.

- **John XXIII** (1958–1963) was in almost every respect different from Pius. The bureaucrat was replaced by a jovial, pastoral type—a leader who enjoyed people and trusted them and believed God would see to it that things worked out fine in the end. One of 13 children from a peasant family, John was 77 when he was chosen as a compromise candidate: He would keep the seat warm

45

until a pope for the long haul was elected next time, the electing cardinals figured. John surprised them and everyone else by calling the Second Vatican Council, which changed the course of Church history.

- **Paul VI** (1963–1978) inherited the whirlwind unleashed by John's council. His was a steady, measured papacy, which cautiously steered the questioning, often rebellious but reinvigorated Church that was the legacy of the council. Paul was called the "pilgrim pope" by some because he made several trips overseas—an innovation at the time.

- **John Paul I** (August 26–September 28, 1978) was born into a poor family, was a man of simple tastes and quiet achievement, and called "the smiling pope" after his untimely death. There were rumors, and then books, to the effect that his death might have been foul play on the grounds that reactionary elements in the Vatican feared that he would take the Church in new and unpredictable directions.

Old-Fashioned Charisma and Star Quality

The current pope, **John Paul II** (1978–), is in turn different from those who came before him. He is the first non-Italian pope in 500 years and the first Slav pope. Prior to his election, he served as archbishop of Krakow, the capital of Poland. An overachiever since his youth, he was a brilliant student, he became proficient in a wide variety of languages (which as pope he showed off to great effect on his trips around the world), and he became a philosopher—while dabbling in poetry, drama, and a variety of robust sports such as mountain climbing.

One of his early edicts as pope was against priests and nuns participating in politics. Then he himself went on to become one of the most politically active popes of modern times. He had lived under the Nazi regime and then under the Communist regime, and these had far-reaching effects on his psyche and pontificate. One example is his suspicion of liberation theology—a revolutionary new model that worked especially effectively in poor cultures. John Paul II resisted it mainly because it was couched in Marxist terminology. Early in his papacy, he is given credit for helping in bringing down Communism in Poland and eventually nearly everywhere else.

John Paul II has seen his mission as bringing the Church of the East and the Church of the West into better relationship with one another. Another objective has been to put an end to what some conservatives describe as post-Vatican II drift away from strong papal leadership and toward a general updating of church practices that many traditionalists regard as core to Catholic identity.

This "restorationism" is in direct opposition to the recommendations of Vatican II and a source of great concern to progressive members of the Church. The pope has slowed the progress of reform, which was the central aim of the council, through the appointment of an ultra-conservative Roman Curia and by reasserting papal authority to appoint bishops, and then by filling vacant seats all over the world with conservative candidates.

A particular focus of Vatican II was improving Catholics' relationship with other Christian denominations. John Paul II felt that this spirit of ecumenism eroded Catholic identity. He has corrected this by placing emphasis on certain Catholic teachings that other Christian groups find most puzzling or most difficult to accept—such as infallibility and teachings about the Virgin Mary. He has reaffirmed Catholic teaching on birth control, emphasized obligatory priestly celibacy, and recommended to nuns that they return to wearing their habits. Critics say he goes out of his way to refer to homosexuality as a "disorder," while ignoring statistics that show what, under the circumstances, can only be an embarrassing increase of gay men in the seminary and priesthood—now estimated at anything from 25 to 80 percent.

Regardless of his unquestionably conservative views, he is enormously popular with young Catholics. With his charismatic and charming style, he is described as having star quality. He has survived an attempted assassination, surgery for a noncancerous stomach tumor, and a couple of falls that resulted in broken bones. It is surely no exaggeration to say that his passing will mark the end of an era.

Supreme Law: The Papacy in Practice

Catholic beliefs derive mainly from two sources: Scripture and tradition. Scripture is "closed"; that is, since the death of the last apostle, no new revelation will be added, so nothing in the New Testament can be changed. Tradition is less fixed. It describes customs or beliefs handed down from generation to generation, eventually forming a set of precedents that define a culture—in this case, the Catholic culture. The role of Catholic tradition has long been a tricky theological area. It was one of the most hotly debated topics at Vatican II, which in turn means power was somehow at stake.

The supreme authority of the Church rests in the collective body of bishops in union with the head of that body, the pope. Although the pope is the head of the bishops, most Church scholars insist that he is supposed to make decisions in a collegial way. Exactly how this happens greatly depends on the personality of the pope and the politics of his inner circle, who have considerable influence. The pendulum that swings back and forth—between those on the right advocating papal supremacy and those on the left who feel it's all about collegiality— is currently swinging to the far right.

Shaking Up Tradition

The matter had been festering since the Reformation. Luther and his followers chose to rely on Scripture alone as the basis of their belief. There's a lot more to Catholicism than you'll find in Scripture, the Council of Trent then responded. There are all the teachings of popes and councils—all the hubbub of lived Christian life. There is an ongoing process of getting to know more about the faith, century after century, not only by studying it, but also by living it. Trent, being strongly on the pope's side, insisted that the magisterium (which was always under the pope's wing) was the arbiter of what was tradition. Tradition was even the interpreter of Scripture. (And whoever can interpret, name, or put spin on reality is the one with the power.)

Time passed. Tradition calcified and became static. Such stagnation means that original thinking has been locked away in favor of the status quo. At Vatican II, the conservative curia wanted to keep it that way, but the new theologians (such as Yves Congar, in particular) and progressive theologians won the day and concluded that the Church, through its theology, philosophy, art, liturgy, the lives of its saints and even its sinners, the education in its schools, and whatever is involved in the daily living of faith (and not excluding Scripture, of course) all form a dynamic medley that is Catholicism in real life.

Some of these traditions remain as tradition and can be reinterpreted or changed over time. Other traditions in time take on the status of official teaching. This means that they are officially added to doctrines that have been accepted as teachings of Jesus Christ and the apostles, even without written evidence.

Although the pope is the supreme authority regarding doctrine, his authority is limited by *precedent*. That is, papal decisions about Catholic beliefs must conform to beliefs already established and to the code of canon law, the official compendium of Catholic rules to live by. When a belief has been around for a long time, it might not technically be a doctrine of faith, but it can still be a matter of faith. This is currently the status both of celibacy and women's ordination.

These issues have been around for a long time, but have not *officially* reached the status of doctrine. However, members of the pope's curia, who are generally in favor both of more papal authority and more doctrine, are talking like these practices have already achieved doctrinal status. The pope appears to be treating the women's ordination issue, especially, as doctrine because he has forbidden further discussion on the subject. Progressives point out that celibacy and women's ordination have never been pronounced on by the bishops, and therefore are not infallible.

Lodged, Law, or Papal Letter?

Once something enters the realm of Catholic tradition, there is a tendency for it to become permanently lodged there. The Church does not like to make mistakes—in fact, it believes it *can't* make major mistakes because of the infallibility aura hanging over it. So Church leaders find themselves in an occasional bind. By insisting that an unspecified amount of its ordinary teaching is somehow infallible (something not at all envisaged in the Vatican I pronouncement on papal infallibility), it finds that it can't change or modify, without considerable embarrassment, certain teachings that are now clearly seen to have been inadequately expressed or downright wrong in the past. This was the case when the pope ruled against removing the ban on birth control, fearing that adopting a new posture would imply that a mistake had been made and therefore that other mistakes might follow. Critics say this inflexibility is the cause of the Church's slow response to many current crises.

The interpretation of canon law is highly complex. A unique, overarching instruction guides the process. It says that in the final analysis, the salvation of souls is the supreme concern of the law of the Church, and the law is to be applied to the spiritual benefit of the people—never to their detriment. The principles of justice, equity, economy, and pastoral discretion must also be applied to the interpretation of canon law. This provides a bit of grace or wiggle room whereby dispensation or relaxation of a Church law can be granted when the spiritual good of the people requires it.

New developments in the culture bring new theological questions making interpretation and application of canon law necessarily an ongoing evolution. Recent discoveries in the emerging field of genetic engineering, for example, pose new problems and will call for new canonical solutions. Interpretations will determine the Catholic position, and a new Catholic teaching will eventually follow. The hierarchy turn to Catholic theologians to assist in applying Catholic policy to new situations. The development of theology, likewise, is a careful process, and the Church is painstakingly slow in accepting new thinking. Two thousand years of accumulated precedent is naturally conducive to a cumbersome process.

A new papal teaching usually takes the form of an encyclical. Encyclical means *circle* because the letter will now be "circulated" throughout the Church by bishops who will pass it along to parishes to be read at Mass. Through them, the pope patrols the boundaries of Catholic faith. He challenges or corrects what he considers to be errors. These letters indicate his priorities, and through them he frequently shapes his administration. Encyclicals determine where Catholic energy will be focused and what will or will not be tolerated, so they are highly influential in

Catholic practice even if most Catholics never read them. Catholics are expected to honor the teachings of papal encyclicals, although they don't constitute official Catholic doctrine—at least not yet.

Congregation for the Doctrine of the Faith

Of the many congregations that form the administrative wing of the papacy, some acquire more prominence than others depending on circumstances and on the vision and objectives of the reigning pope. During the pontificate of John Paul II, by far the most influential has been the Congregation for the Doctrine of the Faith (CDF). This fact underlines the pope's clear determination to rein in the innovations and ex-periments, particularly in the area of theology, that were the Vatican II legacy. It is a given that the ruminations of creative thinkers eventually trickle down to become part of the lived life of the Church, and neither the new pope nor his new circle of advisers were keen on further trials and errors.

Riding Herd on the Faith and the Faithful

This office was first established in 1542 by Pope Paul III, and was called the Sacred Congregation of the Universal Inquisition. Its mission was to protect the Church against heresy and heretics. (You can read more about the Inquisition in Chapter 8.) Its powers were virtually unlimited. Over time, the office has been redesigned many times. Because of the fearsome reputation of the Inquisition, the name was long ago changed to the Holy Office. Then, two days before the closing of Vatican II, Pope Paul VI changed the name again, to the Congregation for the Doctrine of the Faith.

Its job is to safeguard the "purity" of Catholic doctrine, protect the faith and morals of the people, and develop scholarship designed to deepen understanding of the faith in all matters. It is where understandings of the Church's relationship to new scientific developments and cultural changes are worked out.

Although reformed by Vatican II for the positive purpose of encouraging sound theology, the CDF has come to be regarded as a watchdog organization. It oversees publications that relate to any matters of

Catholic belief, including publications by any other agencies in the Roman Curia. Membership in this office is by papal appointment. It has the power to investigate any and all writings that seem contrary to or dangerous to the faith. It issues warnings when appropriate, and can call theologians and authors on the carpet to explain.

A Prerogative of Change

If the CDF has acquired notoriety during this pontificate, it owes it all to its current head, Cardinal Joseph Ratzinger. Born in 1927 in Bavaria and ordained to the priesthood in 1951, he was appointed to his present position in 1981 by Pope John Paul II. Ratzinger is the most controversial and thus best-known member of the Curia—both because of the power of the office he holds and his increasingly more regressive views, which have alienated many Catholics.

In his book *Cardinal Ratzinger: The Vatican's Enforcer of the Faith,* John L. Allen identifies the crux of the struggle in the Church today as a clash between pre-Vatican II thinking and post-Vatican II thinking, asking, "Who has better claim to the legacy of Vatican II: reformers who seek a servant church more tolerant of diversity, or restorationists who want the church to accept its traditional guarantee of unity in strong papal control?"

Concern over Ratzinger, voiced by Allen and others, traces back to their desire to see the vision of Vatican II brought to reality. They have noted a 180-degree reversal in Ratzinger's thinking—from his progressive position at the time of the council, to almost the opposite position during the John Paul II papacy. Here are a few areas in which the cardinal has changed his position:

- **Collegiality.** Once a proponent of the collegial relationship between the pope and the bishops, Ratzinger has shifted to a decidedly pro-papal power preference. In doing so, he has withdrawn his support of bishops' conferences, for example.
- **Loyalty oaths.** Ratzinger, who once supported the reforms to the Congregation for the Doctrine of Faith recommended by Vatican II, has switched his position. A key indicator and sore spot is his

demands that theologians sign loyalty oaths in order to teach in Catholic institutions. Many theologians feel that this is a clear abuse of the office in an attempt to gain more control over them. (Read more about this in Chapter 6.)

- **The development of tradition.** Ratzinger has made a shift from his Vatican II understanding that revelation is subject to the growth, progress, and knowledge of the faith and is subject to change accordingly to retreating to the belief that the understanding of revelation cannot change.

Cardinal Ratzinger's strong sense of papal authority has often pitted him against local congregations on numerous issues. Thus, he has recommended that many of the changes in liturgy enacted by Vatican II be reversed, such as turning the altar back around so that the priest again has his back to the congregation, such as returning to the Latin mass, and such as restricting people's participation as Eucharistic ministers. His policy regarding Catholics' relationship with other Christians and with other faith communities outside of Christianity is nondiplomatic to the point of being openly critical of John Paul's decision to bring representatives of the world's faith traditions together in prayer.

Infallibility: Never Having to Say You're Sorry

In any discussion of the Catholic Church, the issue of infallibility invariably comes up. It is defined as a gift of the Holy Spirit that protects the pope against human error when he discerns matters of faith and morals for his people. Infallibility does not assert that the pope is morally better than anyone else, that he can accurately predict the weather, or that he can't make a wrong turn in traffic. The pope teaches with infallibility only in particular circumstances related to revelation.

Since infallibility became a doctrine of faith, it has only been invoked twice. Both times were in regard to beliefs about Mary—that she was conceived without original sin, and that she was taken up into heaven body and soul at the end of her time on Earth. Once a belief has been declared an infallible article of faith, it becomes part of the Catholic religion, debate ends, and it cannot be changed.

From the Chair of Peter

The doctrine of infallibility became an infallible teaching of the Catholic Church at the first Vatican Council in 1870, which makes it a relatively recent development given Catholicism's long history. The council described the infallible teaching authority of the pope in the following words:

> *When the Roman Pontiff speaks ex cathedra, [from his chair] that is, when ... as the pastor and teacher of all Christians in virtue of his highest apostolic authority he defines a doctrine of faith and morals that must be held by the Universal church, he is empowered, through the divine assistance promised him in blessed Peter, with that infallibility with which the divine Redeemer willed to endow his church.*

According to Church scholars, there are criteria that surround the definition of infallibility:

- The pope isn't himself personally infallible, but is drawing on an infallibility bestowed by the Holy Spirit that resides in the whole Church. The pope only speaks infallibly when he is in his official capacity—not as a personal theologian.

- The pope's infallibility does not exclude the possibility that others can also use this power along with the pope, namely the bishops.

- A "doctrine of faith or morals that must be held by the Universal church" is directly connected to divine revelation. What that really means continues to be the source of much theological debate.

- Once issued, the pope's decisions cannot be reformed and are not dependent on the consent of the governed.

Building Tradition

The development of beliefs about the Virgin Mary offer a good example of how the concepts of infallibility and dogma build on one another. Through various declarations, beginning in 325 and continuing until

1950, Mary went from being a young Jewish girl to become the Mother of God, became sinless (meaning born without original sin), and she was taken up into heaven body and soul where she "reigns with her son." Here, in outline, is how it happened.

- **The Council of Nicea (325).** Two infallible declarations regarding Mary were inadvertently set in motion in 325 at the Council of Nicea, when it was declared that the *son was of the same divine substance as the father*.

- **The Council of Constantinople (381).** This council ratified the teaching of the previous council regarding the divinity of Jesus *and* his fully human nature.

- **The Council of Ephesus (431).** This council declared that in Christ there is one divine person—fully God and fully human. This declaration made Mary the Mother of God as well as Jesus, and she was given status as *Theotokos,* Mother of God.

- **The Council of Trent (1545–1547, 1551–1552, 1562–1563).** This council declared that original sin left us subject to death and decay, weakened the will, and left an ever-abiding inclination to evil.

- **The first Vatican Council (1869–1870).** This council declared Mary's Immaculate Conception, meaning that she was conceived without the effects of original sin on her soul. (Not that she conceived Jesus without sinning, as is often the mistaken understanding of this doctrine.) This doctrine became necessary to assure that her body was a suitable vehicle in which Jesus would reside for nine months—sinless and minus the inclination to evil; neither of which would be appropriate in this case.

- **The papal declaration of faith by Pope Pius XII (1950).** In 1950, Pope Pius XII declared Mary's assumption body and soul into heaven. This belief evolves out of the previous one stating that she is free of the effects of original sin—specifically, death and decay of her body in the tomb.

In Conclusion

The pope is an important symbol of the Church's unity. In the global world we are now living in, a strong papacy can bridge cultural gaps and create a sense of common identity, shared vision, and purpose. This is true only if the strength of the office is not achieved at the expense of its connection to the pulse of the people. Catholics are fond of saying that the Church is not a democracy. However, neither is it a dictatorship. Catholics are perhaps more polarized between conservative and progressive ideologies than ever before. In the 1960s, many disenchanted Catholics left the Church. Today, Catholics who find themselves in disagreement with their leaders are more apt to remain in the Church as dissenters. It will be interesting to see how this dynamic gets played out.

Chapter 4

Holy Orders: Mystery, Power, and Service

In a new century and millennium, when hope and promise should be beckoning, Catholics see instead a landscape of pain and disillusion. Although clerical pedophilia has been thrust front and center, it is by no means the whole story. There were enough sins to go around, whether within or outside the Church—from greed to hypocrisy to despair to your own particular peccadillo.

This is not a particularly upbeat time for the human race. It is also a surprisingly somber time for the Catholic Church. The steadfast members are getting old. The young are often not steadfast members any longer. The body of Christ is sorely split into conservatives and progressives. The euphoria that followed Vatican II has dissipated. Despite John Paul II's great popularity, there is a sourness at the heart of the institution. Compared with other ills, pedophilia is a godsend for the media—not too abstract, and something they can dig their teeth into.

The Priesthood in Profile

All the bad things that need to be said about priest pedophiles have already been said and, especially, written. What might readily be overlooked is that a very small number of priests are pedophiles or involved in cover-ups.

Spare a thought, then, for priests who are not pedophiles. They're sinners, too—even the pope goes to confession. Some might be selfish, lazy, smug, careerist, or alcoholics. They have been taken down unceremoniously from the pedestals on which the faithful had so long elevated them. But they are more than fallen idols.

A priesthood—by whatever name—has been an integral part of the divine-human relationship since we emerged from prehistory. Often awestruck by their particular divinity, people usually felt unworthy or afraid, so they chose an intermediary to represent them before God. More often it was a man, but sometimes it was a woman, as indeed, at times, it was the goddess to whom they paid homage.

The intermediaries have had various names, depending on the culture—shamans, medicine men (or perhaps medicine persons), witch doctors, druids, priests. Although perks were often attached to their roles, their lives were not always easy. They were expected to be better than others. And it fell to some of them to offer sacrifice, sometimes human sacrifice. Although they got to lead the celebration of life's joys on good days, the knock always came to their door first when there was trouble, illness, or death.

It was inevitable that Christianity, which adopted and adapted so much from so many cultures, would have a priesthood. Despite the bad ones (one must, alas, cover one's tush with caveats), priests have been a triumph of the Catholic Church. Some climbed the career ladder and became exalted and famous. Many were heroic in a variety of ways—martyrs, missionaries, scapegoats, or workers of unaccountable miracles—though it must be added that comparable heroes and miracle workers could be plucked from the ranks of the nonordained.

Perhaps most worthy of mention at this time are the so-called ordinary and unnoticed priests. Those priests get up each morning to strive for an intangible goal (as distinct from the usual motivations provided to others by money, family, advancement); go it alone as good priests ultimately do (if celibacy were not a sacrifice, there would be no brouhaha about it); put service and compassion ahead of other considerations—that vague, tantalizing, ruthless call to charity; settle for the humdrum (while presumably not deaf to the great cosmic gong that reverberates for us all); simply persevere day after day—during tough times like these, Catholics hope fiercely that such priests exist, or else it's all a con game.

Yes, since Vatican II, more than before it is the age of the laity, who possess their own estimable priesthood. And yes, even those who sincerely oppose women's ordination ought to regret that women could not yet be part of such a glorious dispensation. It is not the good priest's fault that the world is not perfect.

Uncomfortable with his Roman collar in this climate of suspicion, afraid to put his hand on a child's head lest he cause alarm, getting old and waiting in vain for new vocations to replace him, the priest's self-esteem and very identity have taken a beating. Long ago, on a glorious morning of his youth and idealism, he lay flat on his face before some altar and promised faraway God that he would be faithful unto death. He is a hero if he sees it through. Spare a thought for him.

The world's literature has never been able to ignore the priest's unique place in society. From Graham Greene's drunk in *The Power and the Glory* to George Bernanos's *The Diary of a Country Priest* to John McNamee's *The Diary of a City Priest*, the fascination lingers.

"I've thought a lot about the question of vocation," confides a character in *The Diary of a Country Priest*. "I think that long before we were born—to speak humanly—Christ met us somewhere, in Bethlehem, or perhaps Nazareth, or along the road to Galilee—anywhere. And one day among all the other days, his eyes happened to rest on you and me, and so we were called, each in his particular way, according to the time, the place, the circumstances."

Corruptio optimi pessima, an old saying goes: The corruption of the best is worst. That is why there is sadness as well as indignation about clerical pedophilia.

Sacramental Call

The word *vocation*, in the Catholic context, usually means a calling to the priesthood or religious life. It is believed that God calls a person into service. For men, this calling will be to the priesthood or other religious state such as brother or deacon; women have usually been called to be nuns, though new forms of lay religious service are beginning to replace traditional roles.

Holy orders is the sacrament of ordination into the Catholic priesthood. There are three levels of ordination: deacon, priest, and bishop. (There isn't any other order, and even the pope can't be ordained any higher than bishop of Rome.)

Holy orders has traditionally been identified as a higher calling. A character to the office says that the person accepting this role will have to live up to loftier standards. This priestly character or stamp has been said to be permanent. Hence the expression, "a priest forever," though this is nowadays taken less seriously than in the pre-Vatican II Church. In the old days, it was a big deal when a priest resigned his priesthood; but nowadays, it is almost taken in stride.

Scholars agree that Jesus called disciples to follow him and be an integral part of his work, though there is no evidence that he ever spelled this out in detail. After Jesus' death and resurrection, the twelve formed a collective leadership that guided the nascent Church. The priest as we know him was a later development.

Ignatius of Antioch, bishop and martyr, writing around 107 C.E., began to distinguish between the offices of *overseer*, a position that would later be known as bishop, and *presbyter*, the office that preceded priest and deacon.

In approximately 220 C.E., the Christian writer Tertullian used the terms "ecclesiastical order" and "priestly order," identifying these offices as apart from the laity. At this time, there were various interpretations of what would later become holy orders and ordination. Tertullian understood them to be institutional terms, denoting power over rather than ministry for the Church. Later evolution restored the more spiritual aspect, but to this day a tension remains between these two dimensions of Church office top to bottom.

The medieval period left its imprint on the character of priesthood, with particular emphasis on liturgy, especially the Eucharist. Holy orders increasingly meant the *power* of the priest to consecrate the body and blood of Christ in the sacrifice of the Mass and to administer the sacraments. The priest *alone* had the power to act in Christ's name and enact the awesome miracle of transubstantiation of bread and wine into the body and blood of Christ. His special ability set the priest above the people. Similarly, only the priest could forgive sins in Christ's name—another reason to think of him as above the community he served.

The Second Vatican Council in the early 1960s spoke specifically of the institution's struggle with clerical separatism. The priest had grown apart from the people and was seen as above them. The Council recommended instead a more communal identity that many feel more closely reflects the apostolic Christian communities.

Vatican II marked a significant development in Catholic thinking regarding holy orders in another way: It acknowledged the distinction between the ordained priesthood and lay priesthood, recognizing that they were different in character and confirming the validity of both. The Council reminded Catholics that baptism calls all the faithful to be a priestly people. It named three specific roles the people share: prophet, priest, and servant of the kingdom of God. This became the basis for lay people being allowed to administer the Eucharist and perform other functions from which they had long been excluded.

The priesthood of the faithful means that all Catholics are expected to act in a way consistent with the teachings of Jesus Christ and the Church, perform acts of charity, attend Church services, receive the sacraments, assist in parish life, and learn about their faith. In this way, Christian priesthood is rooted in Jewish understanding and tradition. The Jewish people saw the entire Jewish nation as a priesthood because of God's covenant with them. They were called to live so that their lives were a sacrificial offering to God and so that through them all nations would come to know the goodness of the God of Israel.

Another change enacted by the Council was reinstatement of the permanent diaconate. In the spirit of Vatican II, we will explore holy orders from the bottom up, beginning with deacon and progressing to bishop.

Priests: The Power to Serve

The priestly role has always been cloaked in mystery and power. As I mentioned earlier, in indigenous traditions the priest or shaman, spiritual healer of body and soul, stands between two worlds with a toehold in each. Over time, the connection between these two worlds has found its way into the subconscious—or into the imagination. The role, therefore, contains a touch of magic because the imagination of the people must be engaged to link them successfully to their God. The mystique of the priesthood is reinforced by celibacy and the nonordinary status brought about through ordination—both elements veiled in mystery.

Thanks to the cinema, this priestly magic has taken on mythic proportions. Through movies such as *The Bells of St. Mary's* and *Going My Way,* characters such as Father O'Malley, played by Bing Crosby, became part of our national culture. Spencer Tracy's portrayal of Father Flanagan, founder of Boy's Town, helped turn the dream of an Irish immigrant priest into an enduring institution of 75 years. These and other film versions of priesthood presented a strong, focused, idealized, celibate man and taught America that priests aren't like everyone else. They can, for one thing, be trusted. Celibacy contributed to this priestly aura.

Celibacy: To Be or Not to Be?

Priestly ordination nowadays requires a lifetime promise of celibacy, which means that the candidate can never marry. Priests in religious orders take a vow of chastity. If properly observed, these amount to the same thing: Although his sex he has always with him, for the priest sexual gratification is out.

Celibacy has a complex and controversial place in Catholicism. There is wide disagreement among scholars, hierarchy, and people on whether to continue to mandate celibacy or allow it as a choice. But there is no disagreement at the Vatican. Pope John Paul II has said that the rule stands and has discouraged discussion of the matter. Just as those doors were closed, however, another flew open in a controversy over sexual orientation and gay priests (see "'Lavender Rectories': Gay Priests," later in this chapter).

At least in the Western world, the Church first introduced celibacy as a higher state and as a lifetime commitment. Before Christianity, the world didn't place much value on sexual abstinence for the sake of religion or anything else. In the ancient world, soldiers sometimes abstained from sex before battle, but only until the war was over. Vestal virgins attended the temple of the Roman goddess, but it's not clear what exactly that meant, and it probably wasn't a lifetime commitment.

According to biblical scholar Jane Schaberg, celibacy was uncommon in Judaism. There were incidences in which it was practiced in first-century Egypt, particularly among some Jewish monastic groups. Jewish author Trude Weiss-Rosmarin says that celibacy was considered unnatural among the Jewish people, and therefore against God's will. It is generally believed that ancient Jewish tradition made the arrangement of a son's marriage a primary parental obligation, and that marriage was a requirement before becoming a rabbi.

The celibate state is referred to as a spiritual discipline in Hindu writing predating Christianity—where it is called *Brahmacharya*, is described as exceedingly difficult to accomplish, and was not in any case a lifetime commitment. Guidelines for its practice include not speaking to or looking at women lest the weak-minded man be filled with passion. If the celibate feels a desire for a woman, he should fast and also stand chin-high in water for three days.

The Complete Idiot's Guide to Understanding Catholicism describes how the end of the world was expected at any moment by the early Christians. At a certain time during Mass, therefore, people went outside to check if the world was ending. Bringing new life into the community under these circumstances made no sense, and celibacy became part of a personal witness and preparation for the coming reign of God.

The writings of St. Paul strongly influenced the Church's decision toward adopting celibacy (1 Corinthians 7:1–9, 27–28, 36). At that time, it was practiced as an option. Although Paul advocated the practice, he also stated that not everyone was given the grace to live it. For those who were not, he recommended marriage to avoid sin.

Keeping the Door Open a Crack

Celibacy began to be considered a lifetime commitment during the late third century, after being introduced as part of the ascetic desert life along with prayer, fasting, and meditation. Previous to that, no official rules were governing celibacy. But now Christians were beginning to take sides on the issue. Some boycotted services led by married clergy; others frowned on bishops who left their wives and families for the Church. It was proposed and rejected as a Church rule at the first Coun-cil at Nicea in 325, though already creeping into Church practice. The first step was prohibition of marriage after ordination. Later, remarriage after the death of a spouse was forbidden.

The Eastern Church allowed priests and deacons to remain in mar-riages contracted prior to ordination. This same rule still applies for them.

In the West, celibacy was not uniformly practiced for the next thousand years. Pope Benedict VIII (1012–1024) took steps to secure celibacy largely to protect Church lands from inheritance by priestly offspring. Under Pope Gregory VII (1073–1085), the practice became more uniform in its observation, but had not fully worked itself into the fabric of clerical life. Many priests still married, and many more, while officially unmarried, did not practice chastity. The Council of Trent (1545–1563) made celibacy an absolute requirement for clergy. It noted, however, that this was a Church law, not a divine law, leaving the door open for change in the future.

Vatican II took up the discussion on celibacy once again, making three points:

- Church practices (as distinct from divine law) are shaped by history, and thus subject to change.
- Modern psychology suggests reasons to question the effects of celibacy on the human development of the clergy.
- Cultural differences in many non-European countries legitimately challenge the wisdom of celibacy as an absolute requirement worldwide.

Since that time, Pope Paul VI initiated the practice, and Pope John Paul II continued it, of married ministers from other denominations (specifically from the Episcopal church) entering the Catholic Church as priests while remaining married. So now there are married Catholic priests. Many think that this is unfair to priests who were Catholic from the start.

In Africa and parts of Latin America, celibacy is culturally unacceptable, and Rome has closed its eyes to widespread breaches of the celibacy requirement. In Peru, for example, an estimated 80 percent of the clergy live with women in various arrangements including unofficial marriages. These lapses give reason to suspect that although the door to discussion is closed, it hasn't been locked.

"Lavender Rectories": Gay Priests

Fr. Andrew Greeley and others have pointed out that the U.S. bishops don't know how to deal with the "expanding numbers of gay priests, and have simply resorted to denial." In an article called "Bishops Paralyzed Over Heavily Gay Priesthood," in the *National Catholic Reporter* in 1989, Greeley describes the result as "the toleration of lavender rectories and seminaries."

"Love the sinner, hate the sin," is the official policy in the Catholic Church. There is no explicit ban on homosexuals in the priesthood, but the practice of homosexuality is considered a sin. Most Catholics seem to have no objection to the ordination of gay men, but they expect them to practice celibacy so long as their straight colleagues are obliged to practice it. People seem more likely to judge a man by his work. There is some concern, however, about a gay culture arising in the Church if greater numbers of gay candidates should discourage others from seeking the priesthood. Whether there are more gays among the clergy, or simply more of them "coming out," no one knows. Estimated numbers of gay clergy vary from 25 percent to as high as 80 percent.

Donald B. Cozzens, rector and professor of pastoral theology at Saint Mary Seminary in Cleveland, and author of *The Changing Face of the Priesthood*, believes that homosexuals are attracted to the Catholic Church for the same reasons as heterosexuals: They feel called to the ministry. However, many wonder if the all-male environment of Catholicism plays a role.

Cozzens makes the point that many gay men possess the qualities that contribute to good ministry, such as a caring and sensitive nature, a natural aptitude for ritual, and the desire to be of service. Also, for some gays, the celibate life of Catholic priests can provide freedom from the expectations of family and friends who wonder why they don't date or are not married. And there are cases in which celibacy helps provide boundaries for sexual feelings they have not yet come to grips with.

Cozzens says seminaries must adapt their training to new and differing needs. He believes that straight seminarians might be distracted by a growing gay subculture. He is likewise concerned that preparing gays for the priesthood requires a different emphasis that isn't currently being addressed. He worries that counselors, teachers, and spiritual directors lack the training and skills to assist seminarians to meet these additional challenges.

Seminary Training

Preparation for the priesthood ordinarily requires seven or eight years of study beyond high school—if it did not already begin in a high school seminary program, though these are dying out. Armed with a four-year degree, the candidate will then attend a theological seminary where he will earn either the Master of Divinity or Master of Arts degree. Theological course work usually includes Scripture, canon law, moral and pastoral theology, preaching, Church history, and liturgy. Along with these studies, seminarians engage in fieldwork where they have direct experience of ministry.

Entrance requirements to the seminary include psychological testing and extensive interviews with trained staff, psychologists, and spiritual directors. Formation is an ongoing process, assisting the seminarian toward maturity on all levels—emotional, intellectual, and spiritual. This includes education on how to remain celibate.

Critics believe not enough attention is paid to the difficulties students will face regarding celibacy, and are recommending more time be given to understanding what the commitment entails and how to live up to it. Likewise, in light of the current focus on sexual abuse, seminaries are being advised to pay closer attention to the testing and interviewing process of candidates prior to acceptance—with the expectation of weeding out those who have unresolved sexuality problems.

Priests are encouraged to continue their education after ordination. Graduate work in theology is offered at many Catholic universities around the world, particularly in Rome. Students can choose fields other than theology—psychology, sociology, education, science, medicine, and ethics, to name a few. Continuing education credits might soon be required, as they are in many other professions.

Young men are never denied entrance to the seminary for financial reasons. Diocesan priests are paid a salary, which differs from parish to parish, averaging about $13,000 per year, with additional benefits such as a car, expenses, room and board, health insurance, and a retirement plan. If a priest takes on additional services in the diocese such as teaching, he might be further compensated. Because priests (and sisters, too) who belong to religious orders take a vow of poverty, their earnings are traditionally contributed to their community.

Deacons: Mini-Power

The office of deacon originated during apostolic times and is mentioned in the New Testament. It is also described as the office of "minister." At that time, both women and men were ministers and deacons. A combination of factors contributed to the diminished role of women deacons over the next 500 years, although little is recorded of this process. By the sixth century, women's participation as deacons had ended for Western Christianity.

By the seventh century, the diaconate was being absorbed as a stepping-stone to priestly ordination. It continued to be a transitional step (usually of about one year's duration) until Vatican II called for its reinstatement as a distinct and permanent ministry. This was one of many examples of the Council reconstructing the Church as it was believed to be at the time of the apostles.

Permanent deacons are attached to a diocese and subject to most of the same conditions as priests—the most obvious exception being in the area of celibacy. They can choose whether to wear clerical or regular clothing. The Church does not pay its deacons, so they are usually employed in secular jobs to support their work in the Church.

The main qualifications for deacon are as follows:

- Unmarried men 25 years of age or older. Deacons may not marry after their ordination.
- Married men 35 years of age or older may be ordained deacons with the consent of their wives. Married deacons may not remarry if their spouse dies.
- Preparation includes a time of formation and course of study, usually for a period of three years.

- Deacons practice their ministry under the direction of the local bishop.

Deacons preach, teach, counsel, preside over retreats, and assist the priest in any other way they are needed. Liturgically, they officiate at baptisms, weddings, wakes, and funerals. They are expected to participate in pastoral service and perform charitable acts in the community. They carry out prison ministries, visit the elderly, assist the poor, and work as campus ministers. The office of deacon is not intended to take away from the participation of lay members, but to provide additional assistance to the priest. Their pastoral responsibility can be extended to include limited leadership roles in the absence of the priest.

Bishops: The Power of Magisterium

The Latin word *magisterium* both denotes the authority to teach official Church doctrine and describes those who do it—the bishops. Bishop is the final level of ordination.

Bishops have three main responsibilities—preaching, leading, and sanctifying. They interpret, explain, and preach matters of faith. Theologians have teaching authority as experts in their subjects, but only bishops share the authority Christ gave the apostles to teach in his name.

Bishops have a collegial relationship with the pope in decision-making for the whole Church (see Chapter 3). In addition to their individual role, usually at the head of a diocese, they serve as members of the college of bishops. Bishops are also pastors—indeed, that is their primary, though often overlooked, responsibility. As such, they administer the sacraments and participate in other Church rituals, including celebration of the Eucharist, usually in the cathedral, their parish church. Only bishops can ordain priests. The other sacrament they most frequently administer is confirmation, though priests can do it.

Bishops are appointed by the pope, acting on recommendations from many sources. It was not always so. Sometimes the people of a diocese elected their bishop, sometimes the canons of the cathedral chapter elected him, sometimes the emperor of the day appointed him—and in that case he was probably a close friend, brother, or son of the emperor.

Insisting on the power to appoint bishops is one of the most effective grabs for power on the part of the modern papacy. Through this, he can control practically everything.

Unmitigated papal power is an area of concern not only for progressive Catholics but for bishops as well. To oversimplify, Vatican I was the council that gave the pope what he wanted; the thrust of Vatican II was to give the bishops what they wanted, including restoring the balance of power. Out of this dynamic came the notion of collegiality between bishops and the pope. It was to include bishops' conferences and other group mechanisms. But as soon as the council ended, the pope and his curia proceeded to take back what the council had given away, and currently collegiality takes a back seat—way back—to papal authority.

A common-sense point in favor of collegiality is that it draws on a larger source of wisdom, as distinct from the few who have the pope's ear in Rome. Centralization has resulted in decision-making that is not representative of the Catholic people. Church credibility becomes challenged, as it has in several areas. Papal decisions with regard to birth control, celibacy, married priests, and women's ordination betray how new scholarship and the views of the people are currently being sacrificed to the conservative papal circle.

The Consecrated Life

At first glance, history seems crowded by popes, bishops, priests, and people strutting their hour on the Catholic stage before moving on to their reward. But something is missing from this picture. Behold in the background the religious orders, men and women, usually out of the spotlight, not strictly part of the hierarchical power structure, yet greatly influencing the Church's body and especially its soul.

It's not even accurate to call them religious orders; some are, but technically others are congregations, institutes, and such. We know them when we hear their names: Trappists, Benedictines, Carmelites, Jesuits, Dominicans, hundreds of groups. They are priests, sisters, brothers. Some orders incorporate both men and women; others go solo. They have their own arcane nomenclature—there are monks, friars, some called sisters, and some called mothers.

They have done a great many things in the course of Church history, yet they might be more important for what they are than what they do.

The official Church bundles them together as "the consecrated life" and explains: "the state of life which is constituted by the profession of the evangelical counsels." The latter are better known as the three vows of poverty, chastity, and obedience. These counsels are variously vowed: some groups make simple vows, some solemn; some vows are temporary, some for life. These gestures become a sign to the world that God matters, and his love trumps all other values. Like so much in the Church, religious orders make more sense when seen in the context of history.

Philosophers, Clowns, and Popes

Early Christians, after waiting for a while for the expected destruction of the world and the return of Christ in glory, eventually realized that they were stuck on Earth for a while. So they settled in, built churches, became organized, and, yes, became humdrum. There were, to be sure, challenges and rewards, martyrdoms, and other victories. But a Christian had to work hard not to become settled in the world.

Along came Anthony of Egypt as the third Christian century turned into the fourth. He was disappointed that the religious fervor and heroic life of the early Christians was depleted. He left society as his contemporaries knew it, moving instead into the nearby desert to pray, fast, and resurrect the heroic, ascetic life that was already evaporating from the Church. The local bishop wrote a book about Anthony. It became immensely popular. People flocked to do like Anthony was doing. Some spirit was still left in people.

This being Earth, the experiment wasn't perfect. As well as the holy, some weird people followed Anthony to the desert to escape the law, to escape slavery, and to work various cons. Many, often with the best of intentions, became extreme in their religious practices, scourging themselves mercilessly, for example, and, in the case of one Simon Stylites, literally living up a 60-foot pole for 30-odd years without coming down.

The reform needed reform. It wasn't good for people to be alone like that. (They were called anchorites, meaning they "withdrew" from the world.) Various bishops proposed instead a cenobite movement: that is, getting people back together in community. This regrouping was rationalized and organized by St. Benedict and others, and religious communities were born. Time and again, they had to be reformed on account of the human condition being always prone to go a little off the rails.

Religious communities multiplied and became one of the glories of the Church. During the Dark Ages, religious monks kept the spark of learning and civilization alive. In the intervening centuries, men and women of religious orders have been at the forefront of innovation and experiment within the Church and in the world. Not as rooted in the status quo as the secular clergy (as some call them), religious have been risk-takers. They have been in the vanguard of missionary activity and have devoted their considerable resources to educating, feeding, and otherwise helping the poor. Imbued with a more independent spirit than the bishop-led local Church (though the pope runs them all), they have been at the creative edges of society, from philosophers to clowns, and some of course have also been popes.

Compassion: Who Among Us?

It is a disquieting sign of the times that membership in religious orders is dwindling. Their way of life seems to be in transition. They seem likely to be replaced by lay volunteers or some other expression of whatever Christianity becomes in the near future—it's always a work in progress.

In the meantime, the religious orders are not going quietly. In August 2002, the annual meeting of the Conference of Major Superiors of Men took issue with the resolutions of the U.S. bishops issued in Dallas a short time previously with regard to pedophilia.

The bishops—in a belated but, some say, exaggerated reaction to the scandals—had voted for zero tolerance for molesters, while failing to take any action against their own members who covered up and otherwise helped perpetuate the child-abuse epidemic. The religious men decided, by a big majority, that sexually abusive members of their orders should be kept away from children, but should not be expelled.

This action highlighted several differences between the two groups. The diocesan priest, while under the aegis of a bishop, nevertheless lives a somewhat individual and independent life—no vows of poverty or obedience, alone or in small groups in rectories. Religious orders, by contrast, live in community.

The religious community and the pedophile made a deal, a long time ago, that they would be there for each other, sinners all: the vows binding them until death. Members of religious orders can be expelled and sometimes are, but the bond created by the three vows is special and enduring. "Just as a family does not abandon a member convicted of serious crimes, we cannot turn our backs on our brother," the religious orders' statement said.

This decision also points to the perennial Catholic belief in compassion, forgiveness, and redemption. These are not a few bleeding hearts. They represent approximately 15,000 of the total 46,000 U.S. priests.

In this light, pedophilia poses a dilemma that would test the mettle of wise Solomon. If the bishops' stern stance had been *de rigueur* in the Church of yesteryear, Fr. Larry N. Lorenzoni wrote in the Jesuit magazine *America*, we would have been left bereft of such famous penitents as David in the Old Testament, Magdalene in the New, Paul, Augustine, and even some of the apostles.

Making the case for mercy, Lorenzoni writes of "this harsh, no-exceptions-considered, shamelessly unforgiving attitude toward some elderly Catholic priests who, yes, may have sinned once thirty/forty years ago in a moment of weakness, of depression, of loneliness, but for nearly half a century have proved themselves, through an unblemished life of service, beloved and revered by parishioners and friends."

There is no perfect solution. But once again, the religious orders are living up to their calling and reputation for being a balancing influence in the heavyweight arena of the hierarchy.

Other Voices, Different Views

The Catholic hierarchy's preoccupation with authority has been described by Catholics and others as a neurosis, an addiction, a dysfunctional system, grandiosity, and more. Recent scholarship finds little justification for this overemphasis on roles, status, and other manifestations of power.

Hans Kung, a controversial Swiss Catholic theologian whose criticism of the Church resulted in his status as a Catholic theologian being revoked, was one of the leading theologians of Vatican II. His book *The Catholic Church, A Short History* reminds readers that at the end of the New Testament period, many different styles of ministry existed, and all believers participated in "apostolic succession." The entire Church was an apostolic church as described in the fourth-century Nicene Creed.

The distinction between clergy and laity came after apostolic times, about 110 C.E., when the three offices that would later become bishop, priest, and deacon were established—not during apostolic time, as the Church now maintains. About this same time, the leadership decided that the Eucharist could no longer be celebrated without a bishop, thus solidifying the hierarchical structure.

Originally, charismatic prophecy stood side by side with the more structured teaching office of bishop, and both were considered gifts of the spirit. The charismatic aspect, less predictable and therefore less easy to control, was gradually suppressed.

Jose Orlandis, Spanish Catholic historian, and former chair of history of law at the University of Saragossa, presents a different understanding of the Church's beginning in *A Short History of the Catholic Church.* He defends the traditional view that Jesus Christ established the Church and bestowed primacy on Peter when he said: "on this rock I will build my Church" (Matthew 18:18). The official birthday of the Church is on Pentecost, Orlandis claims, when the Holy Spirit empowered the disciples to go and teach all nations.

Orlandis describes life inside the Christian communities as reflecting the social structure of the Roman world—hierarchical. Thus the churches of the first century were managed by a "college" of priests in charge of liturgical life and keeping order. Bishops shared in the power to ordain that had been granted to the apostles; a power Orlandis describes as breaking the boundaries of time. This is a reference to apostolic succession, which incorporates the belief that Peter was the first bishop of Rome and that Jesus intended that this special gift of the spirit would be passed down through the ages under the auspices of the Roman Catholic Church.

Orlandis assures us that although Christian charismatics, endowed with exceptional gifts of the Holy Spirit, played an important part in the development of the early Church, they had virtually disappeared during the first century of the Christian era. They were replaced by a *divinely instituted clergy*—bishops who were assisted by priests and deacons.

Mary T. Malone, retired chair of the Graduate Department of Religious Studies at the University of Waterloo, describes in *Women and Christianity* a free association between men and women, an arrangement unheard of to that time. Because it threatened the established social order, it drew criticism. Malone portrays early Christians seeking to live in an inclusive kinship of shared discipleship. They seemed to have genuinely regarded each other as sister and brother through the new life of baptism. They entered a "new creation" in which the old social order no longer held.

Malone writes that women exercised authority in the early communities, including the positions of prophet, co-worker, apostle, and teacher. She cites Junia, a woman and a prominent apostle, whose name was changed by male scholars to the male Junias. Junia's Christian ministry existed prior to Paul's, which means that she did not depend on him for authorization, according to Malone.

As female theologians, biblical scholars, and historians re-examine biblical texts, a different story of the early Church emerges. Women's involvement sharply contradicts the idea of an all-male ministry. It places women at the very heart of their communities. Consequently, a different picture of Church emerges: a community in which friends gather to share resources and do good works. There is no mention of hierarchical structure, sharp lines of division, or privilege.

In Conclusion

The Catholic Church's sense of spiritual authority and religious leadership is based on the belief that it has an unbroken connection to apostolic times, specifically to the apostle Peter whom it believes was equivalently the first pope. Today, and throughout history, Church decisions regarding faith, ministry, leadership, and worship are modeled on the community established by Jesus Christ and his followers in the years immediately after the resurrection. Yet, there are different understandings of how the early Christian communities functioned spiritually and institutionally. People use the same sources to document very different understandings, and draw different conclusions as to who was in the circle and who was out, what that means, and what were the intentions of the founder. However, the Church created a structure and offices that have escorted it through 2,000 years of holding people together, and hopefully—if intentions matter at all—helping us bring in a common vision of God's reign.

Chapter 5

Catholic History: Staying Power

At the same time the pedophilia scandal was hitting the papers, corporate greed was coming home to roost in the secular world. Names such as Enron, WorldCom, and Halliburton shared the front pages with Boston's Cardinal Bernard Law and a steady parade of clerical sex abusers. The scandals are fundamentally similar: variations on the corruption of power. They derive from the same dark side of human nature. Sex, money, and power are good until they go bad.

These were not the shenanigans of average criminals and sinners. Higher-ups are the focus. Even in an advanced civilization such as ours, average people have surprisingly little say in the way the world turns. Millions of honest ordinary people lost their jobs and billions of dollars. An unknown number of victims suffered from clerical pedophilia. In both cases, higher-ups did it—leaders, that strange, indefinable assortment. They become leaders for a wide variety of reasons: because they inherited the privilege, were smarter, or had the money, the guile, or the luck to edge ahead of the pack. There are good leaders and bad leaders. In daily life, the led get lumped together as the people; in the Church, they get lumped as the faithful.

Like so much on Earth, these truths are so commonplace that neither leaders nor led stop to think about them. When, occasionally, the people or the faithful do stop to consider and when they don't like what they see, things sometimes happen—small or big things, from a book like this to a war.

The Sense of the Faithful

In civil society, the relationship between leaders and those being led has taken many forms: that between the chief and members of his tribe;

between emperor and peasants; between citizens and their elected representatives in a democracy, which we in the West say is the best strategy yet devised for living together.

In these and other models, complicated wrinkles developed over time, ways of thinking and being and doing that would make us happier and more creative and prosperous—or at least keep us from killing one another.

In religion, a similar evolution took place. At first, when it thundered, people thought God was angry, and they were afraid and did extraordinary things, including human sacrifice, to appease the angry God. They gradually finessed their religion, learned to pray, be thankful, and talk back to God. When things were going really badly, the Jews had a custom of putting God on trial.

Then God came along (so the story goes) in human form, in Galilee, way back then. People had a new opportunity of relating to divinity. True to form, they behaved unpredictably. Reactions were all over the place: from Mary Magdalene's to Judas's to Doubting Thomas's to Pilate's, to name only a few. In spite of being so much alike, people are amazingly different from each other. If not even two fingerprints are alike in all of history, obviously no two people ever thought exactly the same about God. Religious leaders should keep this in mind.

If the faithful are so unpredictable, it would be foolish to take them for granted.

When dealing with a concept as elusive as power that can't be bottled, wrapped, bought, sold, or won in a lottery, the energy, imagination, resourcefulness, creativity, and willpower of the so-called ordinary people—the led, the governed, or the plebs—should all be treated with caution and respect.

In secular society, this people power has led to revolutions, renaissances, and surprises of all sorts—usually when they were least expected (in religion, likewise). In religion, it used to be called *sensus fidelium*— the sense of the faithful. Another term for it is collective consciousness. The *sensus fidelium* probably had its finest hour in the early years of the Church, before authority became organized.

A powerful stand-by of organized religion—or organized society, for that matter—is "we always did it this way." Neither Jesus, Peter, nor even Mary is known to have used this phrase. The early disciples were making it up as they went, honoring God by the seat of their pants.

This lack of precedent allowed room for the *sensus fidelium* to have its say. "What do you all think?" one can imagine St. Peter asking when a conundrum arose (but not St. Paul, who always seemed to have an answer of his own). And the faithful, in the first flush of their enthusiasm (after Pentecost, for example), shared their views and brainstormed, and there were as yet no creeds, encyclicals, or bureaucrats to slow them down or rule them out.

The sense of the faithful is considered exotic, and is especially dear to the intellectually and spiritually adventuresome because it comes accompanied by the notion that it was prompted by the Holy Spirit. Although no one could readily prove this point, it lingers.

Then things gradually got organized. The charismatic side of the young Church gave way to the organized, rationalized side. Although one could lament such a down-to-earth attitude, common sense says that it's the only way for a human institution to stay in business. But if it were to stay divine as well, there had to be room for the unexpected, unscripted, maybe even irrational promptings from above and beyond.

The history of the Church has been an attempt to balance these two powers. This chapter outlines the dance they danced.

Most of the time, the institutional power has prevailed, although not often enough, institutional types say. Catholics are patient, they say; the Church is in no hurry; it deals in centuries. But the Holy Spirit is no such slowpoke, progressive types respond, the speedy Spirit is tired of dragging the reluctant Church out of the past. Sometimes the more free-wheeling right-brained side of Christianity glowed brightly; most times the more orderly, left-brained side prevailed.

Love: The Essential Message

Jesus, in a profound sense, came out of nowhere. Although some scholars say that he might have been illiterate or an unruly rebel, the prevailing persona that remains is that of teacher, healer, and then savior. He taught mostly in parables. His primary message was the reign of God—an event predicted in Hebrew scripture. The reign of God does not constitute a church, but describes a process with an emphasis on seeking peace and justice in the world. Jesus symbolizes God's real presence in our human struggle and his action on our behalf. Jesus taught that the kingdom of God was in our hearts.

He soon began drawing huge crowds from the small villages and towns of Galilee where he preached the traditions of his Jewish religion. He talked about faith in the one God, God's unique covenant with the Jews, and the proof of God's love that existed in the Torah—the written law of the Hebrews. He preached about placing love of neighbor—and even love of one's enemies—above all other parts of the law. His unorthodox views began to attract the attention of both the religious and political authorities. Three years into his ministry, he made plans to go to Jerusalem to observe Passover with his friends. This decisive event placed him precisely in the wrong place at the wrong time.

The priority Jesus placed on love over law put him on a collision course with both the religious and political leaders, who viewed the power and authority of the law as critical. He had drawn their attention by the odd way he behaved and the strange things he said. He neglected to observe the Sabbath in the traditional way. He associated with sinners, to whom he promised salvation. He scandalized and outraged the leaders of the day—referring to God as his father. When they heard about him bursting into the Temple and disrupting business by chasing away the temple merchants and driving shoppers out into the street, it was just the chance they were waiting for. A fatal conflict with the establishment ignited, and Jesus was eventually arrested. Over the next few days, he ate the Passover meal with his followers, prayed in the Garden of Gethsemane, and was betrayed by Judas, an act that resulted in his death by Crucifixion at the hands of Roman soldiers.

His followers were devastated. But on the third day after his burial, he somehow arose from the dead. During the following weeks, his friends would have many encounters with him. This event, which cannot be proven, forms the central mystery of Christianity.

To borrow a contemporary phrase, all this was counterintuitive—not what you'd expect. A movement so untypical of its time, that began so inauspiciously—even tragically—is not marching to the beat of the usual drummer. A different logic is at work—and long odds against eventual success.

A Movement Evolves into a Church

The written Church history is mostly the history of the institution. It would probably be impossible, in any case, to write a history of the sense of the faithful. Still, that sense of the faithful seeps through. It can be noticed especially at history's turning points, when the unpredictable often happened.

The Catholic Church draws its primary identity as a religious institution from the New Testament understanding of the ministry and teaching of Jesus and the early faith communities formed by Christ's apostles and disciples. Catholics believe that Christ is still present to his Church, and continues to guide and direct its spiritual activities in the world by virtue of an unbroken line of properly ordained bishops they trace from the Apostle Peter to the present pope.

However, if the apostles were to visit St. Peter's, or if contemporary Christians were to be transported magically to apostolic time, neither group of time travelers would recognize the other. It is likely that the Swiss Guards would stop Jesus and his dusty band of followers at the Vatican front door and escort them back into St. Peter's Square.

The changes in the Church are evident not only at headquarters, but everywhere. Today, more than 4,000 bishops are attending to the needs of thousands of churches located all over the world. Each year, 18 million baptisms are performed to welcome new believers into the Church. An administrative staff of more than 3,000 people works at the Vatican. Each Sunday, all around the world, bells ring calling one billion Catholics to worship. Bread and wine are changed into the body and blood of Christ and distributed to the faithful worldwide. Mass is said in more languages than were heard at Pentecost. But the beliefs expressed by the words are essentially the same.

How this enormous organization has maintained unity among such a vast and diverse membership has been described as both amazing and disturbing. Using an authority the leaders believe was given them from above, they struggled and at times waged war to maintain what they believe are the essential truths of Christianity. Church historians point to pivotal moments and focus on decisive events in the acquisition of Catholic power.

Organizational Power

As the Church spread throughout the Greco-Roman world, the rise of Gnosticism (one of the many religious sects peripheral to Judaism—you can read more about it in Chapter 8) and other theologies made it clear to Church leaders they could no longer rely on spontaneous charismatic testimony as a means of spreading the authentic gospel. They would have to organize to protect the message.

Over the next 300 years, therefore, Christianity became institutionalized. As a movement makes such a shift, there is always a trade-off. Some of the spontaneity, hope, and joy that characterize it in its early stages are sacrificed to stability, maintenance of the structure, and systematic growth.

At first, leadership was chosen by appointment by the community. Members who were recognized by their companions as having special gifts of the Spirit were chosen and ordained—first by proclamation and later by the laying on of hands. The distinction between ordained and nonordained was not solidly defined, and the entire Church was still considered as belonging to the "priesthood."

The role of bishop in the early Church followed the established Jewish model of Church elder. Congregations elected both bishops and deacons as they needed them, and the leaders governed collectively. By the end of the first century, a system called *monarchical episcopate* was in place, meaning that one bishop governed each diocese. The Greek term for *bishop* means overseer or supervisor, and the office of bishop gradually assumed leadership in worship and the administration of the sacraments.

The position of bishop eventually became the highest authority, but the character of leadership in those pristine days was service.

Setting the Record Straight

Stories that had been told and retold about the life and teaching of Jesus were selected and recorded. Which writings would be included as official records were generally agreed upon by the second century. During this time, essential beliefs were refined and defined, and forms of worship were taking shape.

As Christian communities were scattered over an increasingly larger area, communication became a challenge. Assemblies were organized where problems could be discussed and solutions found. Gradually, larger churches gained authority over smaller communities, and eventually the largest population centers, such as Rome, Alexandria, and Antioch, assumed authority over smaller metropolitan areas. Rome's position as the capital of the Empire and its financial prosperity contributed to making it the logical choice to be the center of the Christian Church. In addition, Rome was where both apostles Peter and Paul had lived and died.

Rome was prospering under the watchful eyes of its gods, as well as under the guidance of the Emperor who himself often had near-divine status. The Christians, however, were saying publicly that there was only one God. Roman authorities noticed that these ideas were catching on, and it made them edgy. The Romans usually practiced uncommon religious tolerance, but when they realized that the Christian agenda included triumph over all other religions, they felt threatened.

The Blood of Martyrs

So the persecution of Christians began. Sporadic at first, by the late second century it had intensified. The blood of martyrs is the seed of the Church, was a true observation. The Church continued to grow. With heaven on their side and the end of the world expected any day, the zealous Christians were indomitable.

The final, most intense onslaught against the Church was launched in 302 by Emperor Diocletian. Things were not going so well in Rome, and Christians became the scapegoats. Edicts were issued to destroy all Christian places of worship. It became illegal for Christians to gather. At first, Roman fury was focused on the clergy—bishops, priests, and deacons—but later any available Christian was hunted down.

Those early persecutions have been written about in gruesome detail and lofty prose. Because history was not yet scientific, there is plenty of room for interpretation. What shines through, however, is that the Church is closest to its ideal self in times of extreme trial. When the living is easy, being good is a cheap option. But when everything is on the line—not only possible death, but also torture beforehand—the option to take the Messiah at his word and to make that absurd leap of faith soon strips away all the baloney, posturing, and pettiness and puts in a new perspective the greed, lust, or hunger for power that at other times have such appeal for most humans. Christianity becomes all or nothing then. It has happened at occasional, glorious junctures throughout Christian history.

These are the occasions, all too rare, when the sense of the faithful was uniform: when those in authority and those subject to authority were on the same page, motivated by the same spirit—or Spirit— toward the same exalted end. If the bishop and the illiterate Christian pauper are going to be thrown to the same lion, a common consciousness is likely to well up from some deep spiritual place.

Christianity Gets the Green Light

That reign of Roman terror continued until 312, when Emperor Constantine came to power and made Christianity legal. The story goes that on the eve of the most significant battle of his life, the Milvian Bridge, he had a vision of Christ, who told him that in the cross he would be victorious. Constantine ordered the symbol to be displayed by his army, which was indeed victorious, and he emerged the new ruler of the Western world. Constantine did not become Christian, but showed his gratitude by making the new religion legal. Although he had mixed, namely political, motives, he promoted Christianity enthusiastically. He lavished the Church with generous gifts, built splendid basilicas, and extended favors to the clergy, such as exemption from military service. Christian principles were even built into Roman law. And conversely, bishops were more and more invested with civil authority.

Good News, Bad News

It is quite reasonable to suggest that the mingling of Roman power with Christianity both saved the new religion and did it immense damage. Constantine's Edict of Milan in 313 identified the Church with power and the status quo. Christianity moved definitively from being a movement to being an institution.

One of the most striking—and enduring—consequences of the Church's more exalted worldly status after Constantine's intervention was that its authority figures became more powerful and more lavish in lifestyle as they learned to imitate the way the world did things. Soon, bishops lived and acted like princes. It seems a law of nature that the more some increase, the more others must decrease. The more Church leadership, from priest to pope, exerted authority, the more those below them diminished in institutional significance.

The sense of the faithful was seldom heard or heeded, but it was there. And that communal consciousness dusted itself off at times and insisted on being heard. It is surely no accident that it was most frequently heard when the Church needed reform—which, like other human institutions, it regularly did.

In a perfect world, the sense of the faithful would mean every soul in the church from top to bottom, laypeople, priests, and pontiffs. But given the way the institution developed, it has largely come to stand for the Spirit speaking from the bottom up. It was most likely to make itself felt when the status quo was awry at the top.

When Pope Gregory IX established the Inquisition in the thirteenth century to bring heretics back in line, this notorious scheme soon got out of hand, torturing and killing fellow Christians who often in good conscience disagreed with authority. People in a position to tell the pope— or the secular powers, who did the torturing and executing—that the Inquisition was a crock either feared for their lives to do so or did not want to jeopardize their careers.

But the laity did occasionally speak out, in a manner of speaking. From time to time, inquisitors were murdered or at least beaten up. This is not a refined expression of the sense of the faithful. Yet, at a time when courage was scarce, individual consciences stood on their own hind legs and did what must have been really risky deeds rather than wait for those in power to find their consciences again.

It's hard to say which is worse: to oppress the faithful or ignore them altogether. When papal power was at its most expansive, popes, eager to hold on to it, devoted great energy to regulating bishops and priests. But they forgot about the laity. This happened time and again throughout history—an extraordinary fact in light of the founder's focus on individual people, especially poor and sick ones.

But sometimes the faithful took their destiny in their own hands. A funny thing happened in the Middle Ages. Whole populations began to move from the countryside into the cities. The Church, however, had all its resources, priests, and buildings—the spiritual infrastructure such as it was—deployed in the country. The people were thus left spiritually adrift in the growing and turbulent cities.

The *Sensus Fidelium* Organizes

The faithful in the cities started lay movements devoted to prayer and piety, acts of charity, or the practice of evangelical poverty. One such group was called the *Humiliati*, the humble ones, who looked after the very poor. Another was the Waldenses, who likewise catered to the poor. The latter went a step further and started hearing confessions—in those early inner cities, there was no one else to do it. This, of course, got the Waldenses in trouble with the authorities, and they are now remembered as heretics. But their gesture recalls another frequent phenomenon. When reforms were needed, and the Church often failed to do anything about the situation, the laity went outside the law, and only later did the law catch up with the new practice. The leaders of the Church led by following.

If an individual can be said to do it, perhaps the most famous manifestation of the sense of the faithful was Francis of Assisi. He gave up a life of wealth at a time when opulence was king of church and state. He attracted followers from among the poor and downtrodden as probably nobody had done since Jesus. He went against the grain. But it turned out that he, and not the Church, was in step with the spirit of the time.

Yet, even as we cheer for the *sensus fidelium*, another factor raises its head. The huge numbers of mendicants (beggars) who followed Francis were, before long, tamed and institutionalized. He had welcomed the poor and illiterate. But as the new Franciscan order became organized, the better educated took over—priests for the most part—as distinct from brothers such as Francis. The saint himself was pushed aside in old age. There was a tragic split in the membership. The factions became violent at times, and people were killed.

Despite differences in theology, the humble spirit of Francis endures through images depicting his love of even the smallest of God's creatures. He is the patron saint of animals, as well as defender of the poor.

Human nature is fragile and needs organization. But if there is no room for free spirits, life can become tragedy.

Battling with the Barbarians

Pope Leo I (440–461) surpassed the ambitions of all his predecessors by claiming the pope possessed supreme authority. He was still a deacon when elected to the papacy, but soon he was dubbed "the Great"—a title one suspects he did little to discourage. As the sun was setting on the Roman Empire, Leo aimed to ensure that it would continue to shine on the Roman Church. Drawing from the scriptural image of Peter as "the rock" upon which Jesus built his Church, Leo was the first pope to claim to be Peter's heir and therefore supreme ruler, highest teacher, and undisputed judge of the whole Church. After Leo's decree, all other bishops were relegated to supporting roles.

As the Roman Empire fell, the Church stepped into the resulting void, wearing both miter and crown—the central force in the Western world.

The monastic movement, meanwhile, played an important role in the Church's missionary expansion across Europe. As Roman rule stretched into the hinterlands, monasteries rather than towns became the cultural and religious centers. Not concerned with religious or state politics, monasticism brought a spiritual vitality to the Christian culture, developing prayer life, scholarship, and literature for the whole Church. In an unlikely way, in spite of the pomp and circumstance at the top, the sense of the faithful was creeping into the Church by the back door. Bishops were recruited from the monastic movement. They brought their ascetic heritage with them, influencing the practice of celibacy and also contributing to the Church's identity, as well as its sense of holiness and of otherworldliness.

The Holy Roman Empire

As Christianity entered the Middle Ages, its hierarchal structure was locked in place, its beliefs were codified, and it had struck an alliance with the state that permeated every aspect of religious life. Church enemies were perceived as political enemies, and vice versa. This deadly alliance all too often resulted in the persecution of nonbelievers as a political necessity. Establishing Roman rule usually meant conversion to Christianity—or death. Entire villages and towns joined the Church—not by individual choice, but because it was the custom to follow the leaders.

In *A Concise History of the Catholic Church*, Thomas Bokenkotter writes of the Church in the Middle Ages: "Out of the wreckage of the Roman Empire in the West, a new social order came into being: Christendom. It was preeminently the creation of the popes, but also owed much to the anonymous labors of the peaceful monks."

Even Christendom did not bring the reign of God. Europe would be engulfed in wars for centuries. The Church was often in the thick of it. At one point, Pope Leo III (795–816) sought the protection of Charlemagne, head of the Franks.

What began as a courtship between church and state during the time of Constantine now became a marriage. During Christmas Mass in 800 C.E., Leo crowned Charlemagne Emperor of the Romans, and together they created the Holy Roman Empire, welding church and state for the next era. Having secured the survival of the Church and the people of the Empire, the partnership looked like a good one. However, having two such leaders ensured that a struggle for power would follow.

Prosperity and Problems

The first big problem occurred in 1054 when the Church of the East broke away from Rome. Differences over power, liturgy, and language all contributed.

The Roman Church grew increasingly more authoritarian. Its pastoral image gave way to a military image. Church and state combined to launch the Crusades. In 1095, Pope Urban II called on the nobles of Europe to assist in the first of a series of holy wars to wrestle the Holy

Land away from Islamic rule. Crusaders were allowed to keep the spoils of war, and this became an opportunity to pillage, rape, and murder at will. The Fourth Crusade (1202–1204) resulted in the near destruction of Constantinople—the city with which Rome shared a close bond in the early years of Christianity.

In 1215, Pope Gregory IX called on the secular authorities to assist him with the Inquisition, which became a 300-year reign of terror. Its declared goal was to rid the world of heretics—including Jews, Muslims, and pagans (people practicing the indigenous religions of Europe). The agreement was that the Church would turn the victim over to the state, thereby washing its hands of guilt in a vast campaign of torture and death. (See Chapter 8 for more on the Inquisition.)

Martin Luther Blows the Whistle

Pope Boniface VIII (1235–1303) expanded papal power when he asserted his dominion over both religious and temporal realms. He then wrote appropriate canon laws to back his claims. The hierarchical Church with the pope as its head was set in a place in which it would remain for a thousand years until it was challenged in 1963 at Vatican II.

Yet the Church, often referred to as the ship of Peter, seldom enjoyed smooth sailing. Now it was fated to fall into the arms and under the influence of the nobility. Temptations of money, power, and authority ate away at its core. Corrupt Church practices weakened its integrity and eroded its authority vis-à-vis the people. Three particular practices would eventually bring it to its knees: selling sacred objects, selling Church offices, and selling indulgences.

Martin Luther (1483–1546), a German monk, listed 95 complaints against Church corruption. He threw in some theological tenets with which he disagreed, and nailed this list to the cathedral door in Wittenberg, or so it is said. And Protestantism was conceived.

Not long after Luther's rebellion, King Henry VIII (1491–1547) got into a power struggle with the pope over history's most famous divorce case. Henry wanted to dissolve his marriage with Catherine of Aragon, who had failed to bear him a son, and Pope Clement VII refused his request. As a result, Henry left Catholicism behind to create his own version, the Church of England, declaring himself its head.

At the same time that the religious ground was shifting, the political landscape of Europe was changing. The continent was being carved into smaller states, creating new political leaders. Tired of funneling money into Rome, these leaders sought their independence, which meant independence from the Catholic Church as well as from the Holy Roman Empire. Europe was engulfed in yet more war. When the dust settled, most of the northern countries had split off from Rome, becoming Protestant, and most of the southern lands remained Catholic.

Catholic Reformation: Too Little, Too Late

The Protestant Reformation was a wake-up call to the Catholic Church, which countered with its own reformation, instigated at the Council of Trent in 1545. Historians concede that the agenda had as much to do with holding on to Catholic identity and authority as with Church reform. Still, the hierarchy that emerged from the 18 years of the Council was focused more on the spiritual life, and stronger for their efforts.

The issues of authority discussed at Trent are as relevant today as they were then. For example, Catholic belief in two sources for revelation, scripture, and tradition was argued at Trent, and the Church upheld tradition as a true source—an area of conflict within the Church today.

The Council wrestled with Church corruption, the relationship between clergy and laity, rules for adequate seminary training, and more local control for bishops—all topics in the news today. The relationship between clergy and laity continues to be defined; experts are calling for better seminary training; and Catholic bishops recently met to discuss their responsibility in submitting Church authority to the state laws regarding delays in reporting sex abuses of minors by clergy. In so doing, the Catholic Church continues the discussion begun more than 450 years ago at Trent.

Vatican I: Securing Papal Power

In the centuries following the Catholic Counter-Reformation, the Church found itself increasingly at odds with the general culture. Protestantism continued to grow. European thinkers were embracing the power of human reasoning—an oblique way of saying that human nature was good. Unleashing a passion for freedom, they were defining the Enlightenment. Totalitarian systems were giving way to democracy as the French Revolution signaled the end of the Middle Ages, including the end of unquestioned Catholic power. The world now began to turn to science for truth. The Catholic Church looked the other way, dismissing progress, repudiating new scientific discovery, rejecting the notion that human thought evolves—even the Church's own thought.

Vatican I (1869–1870) was called by Pope Pius IX, smarting from losses of power and status, as a means to combat modern ideas such as rationalism, materialism, and atheism. He particularly wanted to halt the growth of liberalism, which he saw as a threat to religious authority. In preparation for the Council and prior to his announcement of it, the pope prepared what became known as the *Syllabus of Errors.* It then became an unspoken agenda of the Council to condemn these "errors." (See Chapter 8 for more information on the *Syllabus of Errors.*)

Many historians agree that the Council was rigged from the beginning. Members of Vatican commissions believed that just as the Church had survived the barbarians by a strong papacy, strengthening papal authority would once again protect them—this time from barbaric ideas. They surprised the Council with a prepared document—the doctrine of papal infallibility—introduced as a way of shoring up flagging papal power.

Opposing groups strongly disagreed on both historical and political grounds. By the end of the Council, it became a Church dogma, although opponents were able to make a few modifications. The *Syllabus* failed to become dogma. Having saved face, the Church turned its back on the emerging world of new ideas, especially science, and fostered a new identity as separate from the world.

Vatican II: Power to the People

Vatican II (1962–1965) made a big impact not only in the Catholic Church, but also all over the world. It is difficult to imagine how different the world of this Council was from the preceding one. Vatican I was held by candlelight, and delegates arrived by horse-drawn carriages; delegates to Vatican II arrived by jumbo jet, and the Council made the front pages of every newspaper, magazine, and the evening news on television. It was the largest Council ever held, bringing together 2,600 bishops and 480 theologians and other experts, 52 lay members—of whom 29 were men and 23 were women.

The Spirit of the Times

The Council did as it was directed to do—it captured the spirit of the times. And the times were eventful, marked by shifts in the popular culture: Students challenged universities; American flags, draft cards, and bras burned as young men questioned the war in Asia and women questioned everything, including much of the world their mothers knew. The birth control pill kicked off a sexual revolution, and the American dream of freedom was advanced as African Americans gained civil rights that had officially been granted but not yet realized. Every aspect of life was critically examined in light of a new social ethic: How well does the Church work from the perspective of the people? Vatican II gave voice to many parallel questions and concerns in the spiritual and religious world. The focus shifted from big Church and Church leaders to little Church and the people.

If the agenda could be captured in a word, it might be *collegiality*— not merely in the traditional Catholic understanding of the word as power shared among bishops, but a much broader sense of power shared equally among all people. Pope John XXIII reached across time and space to mend the Christian fabric and directed Church leaders to do the same. He challenged the way the Church had used authority as a means of separation: separating Christians from one another, separating Christianity from other religions, and separating Catholic people from their Church.

Perhaps most significantly, he reconnected the Catholic Church to the world in which it resided. He called, among other things, for the end of authoritarianism. His mission was to recreate a Church that more closely resembled its beginning with Jesus Christ.

Lifting the Lid off the Power Keg

Power that had been locked up in the papal chambers was being redistributed among the bishops where it had been originally located. Five key events from the first session indicate that the changing sense of authority called for by Pope John was taking place. They are drawn from the discussion of Vatican II in *The HarperCollins Encyclopedia of Catholicism* (see Appendix A):

- The first glimpse we get at the new agenda is John's opening speech in which he named the work of the Council, "[that] the earthly city may be brought to the resemblance of that heavenly city where truth reigns [and] charity is the law." The radical nature of the pope's focus is underlined by the fact that this was the first council in Church history called to *look at itself*, not to declare a heresy or defend itself from a hostile world—purposes that characterized all prior councils.

- Another indication that the rules had changed was the bishops' refusal to accept the very conservative Roman Curia's plan to nominate the ten council commissions—thus stacking the deck in their own favor. Rather, the bishops insisted on regional groups to choose the best qualified people for the positions. In this way, the bishops asserted their authority and took the Council out of the control of the Curia.

- A shocking turn of events occurred during the liturgy debate. Objections by the Curia went past the time limit, and the microphone was cut off. The assembly applauded. It was becoming clear that a major shift in power was happening.

- The fourth issue strikes at the heart of authority within Catholicism. Progressives attacked the traditional position that there are two sources for revelation: Scripture and tradition. Tradition is that sticky wicket that would concede the hierarchy's right to declare an article of faith based on a revelation that only they receive. The progressives asserted that Scripture as the word of God is the only proper source of revelation. Traditionalists outvoted the progressives, and the matter was about to be dropped, but the pope intervened and ordered that a new commission be formed to study the subject further.

- Finally, when a complete redrafting of the document on revelation mentioned previously was called for by Council members, it was greeted by strong applause—once again showing that the Council was not to be the voice of the Curia but the voice of the people.

The old paradigm, based on patriarchy and domination of others, has been passed down for many generations within both religious and political structures. Vatican II understands Church as the people of God, and refocuses Catholics on their interactions with God's people all over the globe. In this way, the Church more closely resembles the community led by Jesus. Rather than create a new paradigm, the Council attempts to reconnect the faithful to their origins in Christ.

Becoming User Friendly

Here are seven principles drawn from Council documents that reflect the spirit of Vatican II and the shift in power it represents:

1. The Church is a symbolic representation of Christ's presence with the people, not primarily an institutional organization. The term *Church* includes all the People of God, not just the hierarchy, clergy, and religious communities.
2. The Council added the mission of working for peace and justice in the world to the mission of preaching and sacramental life.
3. The Council changed the use of the term *Church*, which is often appropriated by Catholics to mean the Catholic Church, restoring it to include all Christians. It formally recognized that salvation exists outside the Catholic Church.
4. The Council declared that the Church is a community in process, not yet the realized kingdom of God.
5. The Council greatly reduced the sense of hierarchical separateness by stating that laypeople directly engage in the mission of the Church, not just by assisting in the mission of the hierarchy.

6. Perhaps the most radical statement of the Council was that the Church is to learn from the culture. This not only changed the Church's identity as being separate from the world, it also put the Church in the role of learning from the secular culture—an entirely new concept for the Church.

7. The document on religious liberty describes the freedom to practice one's faith without coercion. It recognized that not all "official" beliefs are equally binding and that it isn't necessary to believe everything the "big church" says in order to be a good "little" Catholic. Again, this was a completely new direction for the Church.

Good Pope John

People like to say that Pope John XXIII opened the Church windows and let in the fresh air. Vatican II created a new understanding of Church power: away from hierarchy and placing power in the community.

John's vision harkened back to the Old Testament covenant between God and his people. The Church had drifted from its original vision when it emphasized the hierarchy, the buildings, and the pomp. The new Church would emphasize the people of God.

Rather than seeing the world as unholy and a threat to the faith, Pope John felt the presence of the Holy Spirit there. He spoke about paying attention to the "signs of the times," where he saw the Spirit at work ending colonialism, emancipating working people, and bringing women into full participation in society.

Post-Vatican II Blues

Despite the high ideals and novel ideas expressed by Vatican II, many of the recommended changes were never put into practice. Rather, there has been a return to the closed system that characterized the Church for much of its history. For many, the result is a sense of betrayal. But for others, it is a relief as they strive to recover the old-style Church. Catholicism is divided.

The Sense of the Magisterium

Why is it that no one seems satisfied? At first, it seemed that the sense of the faithful might be about to make a breakthrough. The musty theological documents prepared by the Roman Curia were quickly rejected. The risk-taking Pope John seemed open to the world and to the Holy Spirit nudging believers to rethink life. The new theology that had been germinating for half a century seemed consistent with the exciting and challenging contemporary world.

The publicity was great. The Vatican II documents were bestsellers. But on closer inspection, they betrayed an ambiguity that was bound to disappoint all but the cheerleaders. On the sense of the faithful, for example, *The Dogmatic Constitution on the Church* had this to say:

> *The whole body of the faithful who have received an anointing which comes from the holy one (see 1 John 2:20 and 27) cannot be mistaken in belief. It shows this characteristic through the entire people's supernatural sense of the faith, when, "from the bishops to the last of the faithful," it manifests a universal consensus in matters of faith and morals. By this sense of the faith, aroused and sustained by the Spirit of truth, the people of God, guided by the sacred magisterium which it faithfully obeys, receives not the word of human beings, but truly the word of God (see 1 Thessalonians 2:13), "the faith once for all delivered to the saints" (Jude 3). The people unfailingly adheres to this faith, penetrates it more deeply through right judgment, and applies it more fully in daily life.*

Those who believe that the Council laid an egg see in this passage the mouse that roared. It seems to be saying that the faithful should be good little Catholics and should be sensible about the faith passed on to them (by the hierarchy, naturally). The passage could equally be described as "the sense of the magisterium."

Retrench, Revise, Reinterpret

There is no hint that the people, the laity, have a religious contribution to make by themselves; that it might be a separate source of Catholic tradition entirely distinct from the pope and his hierarchy. If there is no such separate dimension, the faithful—unless of course when the pope is up there leading them—are relegated again, despite their vaunted "royal priesthood," to their pray, pay, and obey roles.

It is probably fair to say that the vast majority of those voting at the Council—all bishops—meant to accord more clout to this deep collective consciousness that time and again has made its mark on the history of the Church. It was, after all, a very human group hammering out those Vatican documents. Positions hardened. Egos got in the way. Cultural as well as theological differences cast their shadows over pages of obscure (Latin) text. A word or a phrase often became a battleground.

Time and again, the result had to be all-too-human compromise. All they had to work with was human language. So they found a more vague phrase, a less objectionable expression, and got on with it. The Church could clarify later—the living, teaching, practicing Church. In short, the sense of the faithful would take over.

No one seemed to suspect that a new pope and his carefully chosen team would pull back, retrench, revise, and reinterpret to the extent that the spirit of Vatican II has become becalmed.

Vatican I (to generalize) gave the papacy pride of place; Vatican II put the bishops front and center; the next ecumenical council (but not, please, at the Vatican) might finally be the turn of the laity.

In Conclusion

The Church, despite trying occasionally to turn its back on the world, has been vitally involved in the culture, both influenced by it and making a mark on it. Early in history, the Church began to build a power base used throughout time to assure a Christian presence and to maintain unity among members. This authority then became the defining characteristic of the hierarchy, and at times the Church has not hesitated to use it to keep its own people in line. Vatican II initiated a new paradigm, calling the Church back to revisit its origins. A shift in power from hierarchy to the people was made, at least in theory. Shortly after the Council, however, the papal office began taking corrective measures to halt what it considered a dangerous post-Vatican II drift (away from papal authority). Since that time, power has again been centralized in the Vatican. But the people have smelled freedom. Establishing the new boundaries between members and leaders will continue. For most Catholics, there is no going back to the pre-Vatican II Church.

Chapter 6

Theology: Brain Power

There are no atheists in foxholes, the saying goes. At certain difficult times, in other words, when death is only a bullet away or some other calamity presses upon us, God suddenly becomes more important than usual. This has less to do with God than with us. God was there all along, or not. But we, who were not paying attention all along, are suddenly interested: pleading for help or sorry for sins that might land us in the wrong boat on the other side.

In a crisis—confronted by faith-shaking scandal, say, or told we have incurable cancer—we're not likely to reach for a theological tome to study "God 101." Rather, we leap to old conclusions—for example, that what so many say is true must be true, so there must be a God; that, among all the likely options, this is surely a good God who helps people, especially people in trouble; that God must be mighty, so he can do it— on and on. And amazingly, this comes to us all in an instant—in the time it takes to dodge a bullet in a foxhole.

They're all assumptions. We don't know for sure. We're trying to come to terms with our crisis and straining for a solution to save us— to cure the world. We might have given God scarcely a thought for 20 years or more, but the anecdotal evidence says that when the options get lean, God frequently leaps into the foreground and suggests, "I'm still an option."

All this takes a leap of faith. This is overwhelmingly a leap of the imagination. We don't wait to work it all out. There is no time—and probably no inclination—to apply logic.

It's not exactly theology. But somewhere in the background is theology, which after it trickled down into our lives, a little or a lot, became part of us. How we act in an unexpected crisis might depend on which aspect of neglected God remained alive in psyche or soul.

The Big Story

Theology, then, has huge power. It intersects with most lives in their extreme moments. It influences people in their biggest decisions. When one multiplies this fact by all the members of a group as big as the Catholic Church, the result is a formidable force driving or coaxing the institution in this direction or that.

One simple explanation of theology is: It's the big, basic story we tell ourselves about ourselves—where we came from, why we are here, and where we are going. Whoever gets to put the spin on that story has more power than armies. If the story is told persuasively—whether it strikes the people with fear or fills them with hope—it can move immense numbers of lives in the same direction for the same purpose and thus dramatically change life on earth.

Faith Seeking Reason

In a basic sense, everyone is a theologian, and theology is the study of their particular divinity—there is probably nobody of sound mind who has not put together a few thoughts about God.

There have been many efforts to describe or defame theology precisely. Perhaps the most widely known effort at defining it is that offered by eleventh century St. Anselm: Theology is "faith seeking understanding." The bottom line is, faith might take a leap of faith into the unknown (or, as some have said, the absurd). But in the meantime, how much of all this can we wrap our minds around? Questions arise that we try to explain; ambiguities emerge that we try to interpret; doubts creep in that we try to come to terms with.

Historically, it took theology a long time to get organized and, especially, rationalized. This should be no surprise. It is all about something above and beyond our comprehension. It is, in a sense, about hunches. We suspect that there is something bigger and better, but we can't be sure in the usual human way, so we remain tentative. As civilization evolved, we tried every approach to see through that glass darkly mentioned in the Bible; we tried astronomers, soothsayers, and then philosophers and, perhaps most commonly, storytellers getting deeper and deeper into their subject generation after generation. People are curious, and they hunger for an explanation of themselves, so they wanted to know more— most of all, they wanted to know the final outcome of the story.

Various early religions gradually developed something like a system. The Jewish tradition is the one Catholics know best. Out of the Jewish world grew Christianity. It would be impossible to sum up all the tomes that have been written about Catholic theology, so the aim here is to present an impressionistic overview.

In *The Christian Tradition: A History of the Development of Doctrine*, Jaroslav Pelikan writes that for the first 500 years most theologians were bishops; from 600 to 1500, they were mostly monks; and since 1500, they have been mostly university professors.

Extraordinary bodies of work were written by theologians who have fallen into anonymity and by others who became household names, such as St. Augustine, St. Thomas Aquinas, St. Catherine of Siena, and St. Theresa of Avila. (It boggles the mind to think what they would have written with computers.)

A Christian tradition was developing. Theology interacted with real life and was written down. In the monasteries—in the popular memory at least—all that brain power intermingled with the prayer of the monks in choir. In the new universities, despite drawbacks (the faith factor), theology vied with more worldly disciplines, and in the Middle Ages it was called the queen of sciences.

The study of theology was broken down early into narrower disciplines such as Scripture, patristics, ecclesiology, moral theology, and liturgy. For most of its history, it was viewed from the top down. That is, it started with God as a given, looked at divine intervention in the world (Scripture especially), and strove to deduce what the reality of God meant for humanity. Faith was seeking understanding, but beyond that theology had the practical purpose of leading the faithful to live better lives.

It took 20 centuries for theologians to think of a radically different way to approach the subject: from the bottom up. You shall see later in the chapter how liberation theology, instead of looking up at God, looked around at people for a starting point.

Catholic theology draws on both Scripture and tradition (the body of knowledge, over and above Scripture, that evolved from living Christianity and studying it and the resulting trial and error of Christian life). These were passed along, from generation to generation, in seeking to understand God's will for the faithful. Theology brings new understanding, and in that capacity it functions in a prophetic or visionary role. A delicate balance exists between conserving important beliefs and allowing growth of new ones. Disagreements can generate power struggles between the official Church and its most creative thinkers. When power rather than truth is the driving force behind the development of theology, there is always the danger of subverting the truth to maintain the status quo. Likewise, if change for the sake of change is the agenda, new thinking can depart from tradition to the extent that it loses its Catholic sensibility.

The People's Voice

During much of its history, the Church granted admirable freedom to its theologians to explore the faith. Their mandate was not merely to regurgitate the battened-down teachings of the magisterium, but to explore new ways of understanding life and afterlife. Had they not done this, Christianity would be a sad, stagnant pool today. Theologians jousted with the spirit of their age, reacted, and reinterpreted. They went outside the Church and learned new ways of seeing the world. Thomas Aquinas and others went to the pagans—especially Aristotle and Plato—Christianized them, and emerged with monumental new perspectives.

They admittedly also got into trouble at times. The Church occasionally lost its nerve, as if worried new truth might be found with which it could not live comfortably. Aquinas was silenced, but made a good recovery and was soon canonized and called a Doctor of the Church. Aquinas was a Dominican monk, and therefore easy to rein in. Similarly, until very recently, most theologians have been priests, so it was easy for a pope to be loose when he had only to lift the phone or sound a cymbal deep in the Vatican to get official teaching back on track. With the numbers of lay theologians on the rise, seemingly the pope feels he needs to shorten the reins.

Late in the twentieth century, though, especially since Vatican II, the laity have become seriously involved in the study and teaching of theology. Women are significantly more prominent than before. Because they cannot become priests, the Church does not exercise the same control over what they teach or write. For the moment, however, the Church does control most of the infrastructure—seminaries and such—within which Catholic theology is taught. This is an immense power affecting a great many people, so it matters. As this long pontificate winds down, theologians wonder what will follow. Many hope that it will be more propitious for theologians than the John Paul II–Ratzinger era.

Theology Doldrums

Theology's recent dog days can only be appreciated in light of the bright promise of the Second Vatican Council. The Church of the 1960s was emerging from an obscurantist period when fear of reason, fear of modernism, and fear of the world had left Catholics intellectually and spiritually stranded. The Council offered hope of a new spring and engagement with life. John XXIII reminded theologians that the Church had always made room for new insights and fresh theology. And although bishops did the voting at the Council, mostly theologians made the ammo they fired. Soon, everyone was writing theology books.

Then came Pope John Paul II, who soon applied the brakes. His first encyclical, *Redemptor Hominis*, reminded everyone that the job of theologians is "to serve the magisterium, which in the Church is entrusted to the bishops." It was easy to read the rest between the lines. A whole bureaucracy was put in place—most notably the Congregation for the Doctrine of the Faith, or CDF—to ensure that orthodoxy, the new mantra, would not be messed with.

Priest theologians, traditional bearers of the flame, were most vulnerable to the growing clampdown on innovation and experimentation.

A long process began of theologians, especially those who wrote their thoughts in books, getting called to Rome and being subjected to a heavy-handed process of interrogation and often intimidation and punishment. You will meet some of them later in the chapter.

There were no burnings at the stake. But, to rearrange an old saying, the more things remained the same, the more they changed. Although many careers were aborted, it was now possible to do an end run around the Church: to a public university, for example, where one could do theology out of reach of the Vatican. Once upon a time, such a dissident could not run far enough to escape divine wrath. But the inviolability of conscience was now brought to bear. And in the public arena, even theologians had civil rights.

For a long while, writers kept on writing and teachers kept teaching. The CDF, established primarily to encourage theology, became its ferocious watchdog. What should have been the joyful creativity of new visions, angles, and paradigms of transcendent Catholic life—all human efforts, of course—became cat and mouse games with Cardinal Ratzinger and his willing assistants and far-flung spies writing letters reminiscent of the old Soviet Union to land their neighbors in theological hot water.

The theologians grew weary, worn down by Rome. Among the clergy especially, creative theology quietly ground to a halt.

The Laity Steps In

Still, other signs of the times were emerging. The living Church made adjustments almost in spite of itself. There were no landmark institutional decisions. Rather, the effect was like a huge animal turning over in its sleep in the night. In the morning, theology was still in the doldrums, but the context was changed. The laity were taking theology into their own hands. They were going to theology schools, and then teaching in parishes or high schools or *doing* theology as ministry.

The resulting theology would take time to develop. New expressions were being tried and making their mark. It began with liberation theology in Latin America and was soon followed by Africa and Asia. It caught on in the United States, and was written from the perspective of women, African Americans, environmentalists, and other political viewpoints.

The Vatican, the pope, and collegiality still mattered, but at the CDF it looked like the nightfall of enforcement. As Martin E. Marty points out in *A Short History of American Catholicism,* "In the modern free world, the Church must make its way through persuasion, not coercion."

This point had been spectacularly demonstrated in the 1960s when the encyclical *Humanae Vitae* gave thumbs down to artificial contraception and very few Catholics saluted. Everyone saw that the sky did not then fall. Thus grew the practice of selective adherence to the Church's teachings. It used to be that all sins were the same in seriousness: An impure thought and a massacre would land one in the same hell. Catholics began to doubt that. Their doubt, in turn, created worry in Rome over the dangers of relativism.

So used to getting away with coercion, the official Church has not, up to the pontificate of Pope John Paul II (and despite his popularity), learned the art of persuasion. Yet it is a resilient Church that has survived centuries of clashes with the culture. In the twilight of the Wojtyla era, people say his successor will face great challenges, but it's likely they also said that about most of the previous popes.

Breathing Life into Tradition

Tradition is a key concept in Catholicism because at its best it is alive and influences beliefs and practices. Currently, dissension is focused on clarifying what teachings fall into the category of tradition that cannot be discussed further and what teachings and practices are open for further development.

In his book *Inventing Catholic Tradition,* Terrence W. Tilley believes that theology should offer ongoing critique to the accepted way of Church thinking. Although theologians are usually (but not necessarily) Catholic, Tilley places them outside the purview of the organization. It's their job to stand at the periphery and challenge the power structure and its theology. They must be far enough removed to gain perspective, yet close enough to be representative of the tradition.

He describes tradition as our "socially embodied, interwoven, enduring practices." He believes the relationship between the people and their expression of faith is living and ongoing—an interplay of culture shaping tradition and tradition shaping culture. The job of the theologian is to assist in that dynamism.

Every Catholic is at the center of this give and take. Just as tradition is the assimilated wisdom of our ancestors, it will likewise be the repository of our story—our witness to this time and place. Tradition is not a theological abstraction or a bald set of rules, but a dynamic engagement of the past with the present while creating a map for the future. No one sets out on a trip using a map made long ago. Like maps, tradition must be updated and rendered relevant.

This living, breathing tradition is passed along through Church customs and practices, through prayers, beliefs, rituals, spiritual writings, insights, and understandings that guide us in day-to-day Catholic life.

The Analogical Imagination

Theology, then, is a very elastic word. It is the musty contents of ancient papyri, and it is Jesus looking down from corny billboards that pose the question WWJD? (What Would Jesus Do?) Most churches work hard to keep the concept confined, or narrowed, so that they can have greater control over it. Catholicism kept an impressive monopoly on theology for much of 2,000 years. And, lest we forget, the Church is still where Christian theology is anchored and assured of legitimacy; otherwise one is moving into a whole new sect.

On the other hand, in the postmodern Catholic world, theology is oozing out through the cracks in the structure. This brand might be less intense, more diffuse, more user-friendly, and even entertaining. It is a lively, multidisciplinary field of study that has been springing up in colleges and universities all over the country—often under the general title of religious studies. It includes poets, novelists, film directors, theologians, historians, anthropologists, Scripture scholars, religious educators, pastoral counselors, and more.

Students engage Catholic culture in a variety of ways: story, image, symbol, myth, just as an example. Tilley lumps these diverse pursuits together and calls the result the Catholic Intellectual Tradition. From the common vision of these creators, he sees a renegade new Catholic *tradition* being transmitted. It isn't always boxed neatly and tied with string. It's bigger than the rules or laws, but is true to Catholic principles. Tilley presents five principles he thinks form the infrastructure, transmitting conventional tradition while allowing creative cultural expression. I have paraphrased these, along with the essential Catholic character each transmits:

1. Principle: Catholicism works from the analogical imagination. Imperative: Move toward duality, seeing situations as both/and rather than either/or.

2. Principle: Catholicism is founded in hope extended toward everyone and everything. Imperative: Imagine all can be redeemed, and therefore treat everything as intrinsically redeemable.

3. Principle: Catholicism is inclusive. Imperative: Envision community as a process of gathering, not one of separating.

4. Principle: Although the Catholic religion is spiritual, it exists in the context of the world. Imperative: Don't limit it to one realm or the other, but see it as both.

5. Principle: Catholic imagination operates from both faith and reason. Imperative: Understand that everything comes as a gift from God. Human engagement can enhance or detract from what is essentially a good creation.

What Does an "Organic" Catholic Look Like?

In practice, Catholics are generally quite different from the image one might get from reading polemics and abstractions about the hierarchy, authority, and Vatican politics. Catholics do not arrive at who they are through theological discourse. Rather, the opposite is closer to the truth: Theology can be formed by observing Catholics living their lives in the familiar ways they have for generation after generation. The people's spirituality is steeped in "practice" and ritual, and for the most part it is integrated into day-to-day activities.

Catholics have an analogical imagination that focuses on how things relate rather than how they are different—as both/and, not either/or. For example: Life is both wonderful and full of suffering; we are both saints and sinners. The analogical imagination sees opposites as parts of a whole structure. God language becomes metaphorical, seeing God in all things: God is a summer day; God is a day with my old friend Sally.

Catholic analogical thinking experiences the world as sacred. Fr. Andrew Greeley, sociologist and novelist, describes this as *sacramental imagination* and locates it in Catholic "popular tradition." It is what I call the folks in the pew, who have a different relationship with Catholicism than does the hierarchy.

Sacramental experience is not dependent on logic or reason, yet it possesses both. It makes quantum leaps, finding divine grace and sacred presence in the here and now, in creation. A great place to explore this sacramentality is one's local Catholic bookstore. As Catholics splash holy water, light candles in front of statues, mark cookbooks with holy cards, touch rosary beads, or braid palm leaves, they "touch" God. By using analogical imagination, a scientist can accept apparitions of Mary as part of how Catholics are.

Catholics are characterized by an enduring sense of hope—existing in full recognition of the thin line between it and despair. In the words of poet Alexander Pope, "hope springs eternal." The unfailing arrival of morning light, the moon's cycles, the seasons of nature returning again and again for tens of thousands of years, all instructed the human psyche to expect resurrection. The sacramental life of today's Church uses the basic elements of air, earth, fire, and water connecting, across time, with the ceremonies of earlier indigenous peoples.

Some Christians have trouble with such an imagination. They are squeamish, for example, about linking Catholic ceremony to pagan ritual. However, the analogical Catholic has no problem. Logic is pushed aside, as is linear time, and the imagination takes over—the same imagination that leaps to God when all-too-human reason, left to itself, can see no God at all.

Censorship: Flexing Papal Muscle

If theologians fail to speak their truth, their integrity is compromised. But if they push the hierarchy too hard, they might be reprimanded in a variety of ways. The overriding current sore spot between theologians and Rome centers on the punitive use of papal power—especially the prohibition of discussion of controversial issues and the increasing abandonment of collegiality. This encroachment on the legitimate collective prerogative of the world's bishops is being described as creeping infallibility.

Case Study: Matthew Fox and Creation Spirituality

Matthew Fox, a former Dominican priest, founded the Institute for Creation Centered Spirituality, which advocated a pro-environmental Christian vision. He placed special emphasis on the imminence of Christ in the world, rather than on transcendence—a radical interpretation of the incarnation, but one that is steadily gaining followers. For a long time, Fox successfully danced on the cutting edge of what Rome deemed acceptable. His books and lectures were popular, and students of various ages traveled from all over the world to attend the institute.

In the mid-1980s, he crossed the Vatican line when he invited author, counselor, and self-proclaimed witch Starhawk, to join the faculty. Starhawk is one of the leading spokespersons for the neo-pagan movement, whose spirituality is based in honoring the Earth. She chooses to call herself a witch—a title used by the Inquisition to discredit herbalists, midwives, and women healers. Despite the uproar the name generates, she wants to redeem it from its false association with the dark arts.

Although the issue of Starhawk was never formally raised by Rome, it was seen by many, including the *San Francisco Chronicle*, as the core problem. Newspaper headlines declared that Rome silenced Fox for having a witch on the faculty. Officially, Fox was cited for calling God "Mother" in his books, and for being a "fervent feminist." He politely responded that Scripture, as well as the mystics, and even Pope John Paul II, had done the same. As for being a feminist, he reminded his critics "Jesus was a feminist." Fox issued an open letter charging Cardinal Ratzinger, head of the CDF, with being addicted to power, being unfaithful to the teachings of Jesus, being obsessed with issues of sexual morality, and infecting the Church with "creeping fascism."

Fox was officially silenced for one year. Both before and after his silencing, he continued to spar with Rome, making charges especially against Ratzinger. In 1999, he was asked to resign from the Dominican Order. In forcing Fox's hand, many feel that the Dominicans bowed to pressure from Rome. Fox had a reputation as a wildcard, and his theology colleagues didn't rally to his defense. They privately agreed, however, that many of the charges he voiced were well founded and resulted in forcing further dialogue.

Case Study: Charles Curran and Sexual Ethics

Charles Curran was a professor of moral theology at the Catholic University of America from 1965 until his dismissal in 1987 following the decision of Ratzinger's CDF that he was not suitable to teach at a Catholic university. He was popular and highly respected by his colleagues. At one time, some 600 theologians signed a letter of support.

Curran's removal was the culmination of a long and bitter dispute. On the surface, his case involved his disagreement with the Church's condemnation of artificial birth control. But it went much deeper: to a theologian's right to dissent from noninfallible Catholic teaching. Prior to the Church's birth control decision, Curran had published articles in journals calling for a reevaluation of the traditional position. He challenged the Catholic Church's sexual ethic in general, but specifically its treatment of masturbation and homosexuality as grievous sins.

The conflict between Curran and Ratzinger, both noted theologians who were ideologically diametrically opposed, spanned several decades and drew world attention. Ratzinger claimed that Curran's stand was a public scandal and therefore a threat to the faithful and that Curran was wrong in his argument anyway. Curran eventually proposed a compromise. During negotiations, he maintained that his views were mainstream, which were held by most of his contemporaries. Then, in classic Inquisitional style, Ratzinger asked for the names of those theologians and invited Curran to "accuse them" because the Congregation would be happy to investigate them, too. Their confrontation ended with Curran being offered one last chance to retract (shades of Galileo); an opportunity he could not take in good faith. Curran maintains that his dismissal was the result of politics, not theology.

The theological clampdown recently acquired a new wrinkle: the resurrecting of a practice long on the books though not enforced. Those teaching in Catholic institutions of higher learning are required by their bishop to sign a loyalty oath. Refusal is taken to imply disloyalty. This way, loyalty to the pope is made the measure of faith and a cornerstone of Catholic practice.

These "structures of deceit" (a phrase borrowed from the title of his recent book), Garry Wills asserts, are "fiddling the Church into intellectual irrelevance."

Case Study: Catholics for a Free Choice

In 1984, a lay group of theologians, teachers, and religious, calling themselves Catholics for Free Choice, ran an ad in *The New York Times* demanding dialog on abortion for the sake of religious pluralism. They also called for an end to sanctions imposed by Rome against those who spoke their conscience.

A few months later, the Vatican demanded a public recanting of the group's position. The citation said they were lacking in submission to magisterial authority. For the religious among them, according to Rome, refusal to comply would result in automatic dismissal from their communities. Some members of the group issued retractions, but the nuns would not, saying this would violate their moral conscience and the integrity of their communities. In this they had the backing of their superiors.

The Vatican also undertook reprisals against lay members of the group. Daniel Maguire, professor of ethics at Marquette University, received a demand from Rome to recant. His university did not fire him, but other Catholic colleges and universities began to cancel his scheduled lectures. Four laywomen academics received a summons from their bishop to discuss relevant matters of Catholic doctrine. Speaking and teaching engagements began to be cancelled. The list of scholars who received notices canceling jobs or lectures grew. One of the most prominent was Elisabeth Schüssler Fiorenza. Yet the group continues to be an active voice in the ongoing debate within the restless Church.

Power to the People: Liberation Theology

Liberation theology arose, seemingly spontaneously and out of nowhere, in Latin America, Africa, and Asia in the late 1960s. It stood traditional systematic theology on its head. The queen of sciences was replaced by a naïve confrontation with the human condition. A small number of innovators, who saw themselves less as theologians than agitators reminiscent of the Greek Socrates long before, began leading the people in asking questions. Why are we poor? How did we get this way? What can be done? Provocative questions for those in power, no doubt. Asking what can be done implied action, which soon worried a lot of people.

The movement had most success in Latin America, where the success of Gustavo Gutierrez's 1971 book, *A Theology of Liberation*, was a catalyst.

Colonizing Latin America began in the sixteenth century with the arrival of the Spanish Conquistadors. They came in search of a new world, including gold to take home to the folks, especially the monarch du jour. Arriving on the same ships were Franciscan missionaries whose goal was winning souls for Christ and the Catholic Church. Thereafter, the colonizers and missionaries made a common purpose—with disastrous secular and spiritual results.

Colonization brought devastation to the people and their civilization. The Europeans "enculturated" the native people by imposing European customs, language, and values. They used all means necessary to accomplish this agenda, including enslavement and massacres.

The mission of the Church was to baptize the natives. They justified the soldiers' cruel treatment of the people on the grounds that the natives were pagan and therefore not deserving of the same rights as believers in the true God. There were notable exceptions to these policies—times when the missionaries extended kindness and attempted to protect the people from the soldiers. However, they made no attempt to understand the local religion.

For the next 500 years, European supremacy would dictate unjust treatment of the native people. As recently as 50 years ago, a significant number of Catholic clergy were still involved in the age-old collaboration with the wealthy at the expense of the poor of Latin America. In this mutually beneficial relationship, the powerful rulers and landowners were assured of a ready work force by making certain that the poor remained poor. The Church cooperated by preaching a gospel message that promoted social inequality. The missionaries emphasized the special place Jesus has in his heart for the poor, reinforcing the practice of humility and patience in this life while waiting for a reward in the next. The clergy were rewarded by a privileged status that included personal safety and financial security.

Changing the Game

Liberation theology was created as a moral reaction to this poverty, suffering, and exploitation of the poor. Previously, the Catholic Church focused on private morality—what it took to get to heaven. Liberation theology reversed this thinking by introducing the idea of corporate or institutional sin.

Rather than concentrating on how the people weren't measuring up to what was expected of them by the Church, this new theology turned the spotlight on religion and politics—naming the societal forces that had been used oppressively against the people. This showed how collusion between the ruling elites conspired to keep the people poor—denying them education, health care, and even essential food and water—and how the Church consistently supported oppressive regimes.

A concerted effort by the Church and some governments has gradually grown to address these injustices. This was inspired not only by the second Vatican Council's emphasis on social justice, but also by an impressive body of earlier social encyclicals. A further major impetus was the shifts in political leanings of the 1960s. The pope and bishops from many countries sent thousands of missionaries to assist in digging Latin America out of the poverty imposed by hundreds of years of colonialism.

Liberation theology works at liberating everyone involved. It begins by helping the folks at the bottom, and it then gives the ones on top a chance to liberate themselves from the tyranny of imposing impossible and cruel conditions on others. Not everyone accepts the invitation to transformation—political retaliation often gets worse before it gets better.

As the people pressured the Church and insisted that it help in the struggle for justice, pushing bishops to take the bold but necessary option for the poor, the political climate heated up. The collusion gradually ended. The Church that had previously said its private prayers and looked the other way was now condemned by the universal Church for breaking the rules. But members of the ruling class had no intention of watching the system that operated so long to their advantage suddenly disappear. Coalitions between military regimes and immensely wealthy and powerful ruling families began a new reign of terror against the people as well as against clerics who now dared to side with them.

Taking a Stand

Archbishop Oscar Romero of El Salvador was one of the pastoral leaders who spoke out courageously for his people. The world was shocked in 1980 when Romero was assassinated as he celebrated Mass. Thirty thousand people gathered at the cathedral for his funeral. Romero's murder was followed by the killing of other clergy and workers. But a turning point had been reached and a new consciousness created. The blood of martyrs had yet again become the seed of faith. World pressure continues to chip away at the political injustices in Latin America.

Liberation theology has come under attack by conservatives in the Catholic Church who believe it is Marxist in nature—specifically that it incorporates concepts of class struggle and promotes revolution, that it politicizes the gospel message and undermines the authority of the Church. Pope John Paul has been repeatedly suspicious and critical of liberation theology. Because of his own earlier experiences under communism, anything that smacked even remotely of Marxist terminology was bound to arouse suspicion. Eventually, though, the pope admitted that liberation theology is both "useful and necessary."

More recently, theologians all over the world have begun to use the principles of liberation theology to identify social sin and demand accountability from their religious and political leaders. Action on behalf of the poor has long been part of Catholic tradition. Liberation theology brings a new dimension to this by the emphasis it places on the experience of the people, as well as by helping them find their voice.

114

It is biblically based in the Old Testament Exodus theme and in claiming the identity of Jesus as liberator. It has created a system in which people are empowered to demand that their leaders pay attention. It insists that Christian theory and Christian practice agree. Liberation theologies have now been written by Asians, Native Americans, African Americans, women, and ecologists. (See Chapter 11 for a discussion of base communities of Latin America, now being adapted into U.S. parishes.)

Feminism: A New Vision of Church

One of the most astonishing revelations of Catholicism is that it took 2,000 years for feminism to happen. This is a striking commentary not only on Christian theology, but also on the Church's power to control the agenda and keep people in their place.

On a worldwide scale, many more women than men "practice" Catholicism. In terms of work as opposed to mere decision-making, women keep the Church going. They just never have been allowed to decide anything important.

The men at Vatican II promised to promote women's "participation in the various sectors of the Church's apostolate." Not much happened in this regard, however. But voices began to be raised—especially the call for women priests. This wasn't exactly feminism. One could call it Theology 101, Christianity 101, prophecy, or plain common sense. This call continued to go nowhere—for theological reasons, the official magisterium of the Church said. Very well, then, some said to the Church: make a gesture, something symbolic; for example, appoint a few women cardinals. Although nearly everything went nowhere, something new was happening—discussion. Suddenly, a whole new role for women was not out of the question

In a short generation, feminism has grown to be perhaps the dominant issue in the slow-moving Church.

Work in Progress (Literally)

Feminist theology is described by Timothy G. McCarthy in *The Catholic Tradition: The Church in the Twentieth Century*, as "participation in and

115

critical reflection upon the Christian faith by persons (women and men) who are aware of the historical, political, and cultural restriction of women and who intend to retrieve the Christian faith in such a way that it promotes mutuality and equality."

"Feminist theology is a liberation theology," McCarthy writes.

Although still young and growing, feminist theology is already headed in many directions. At the most radical end of the spectrum is the separatist approach espoused especially by theologian Mary Daly, who essentially declares that the man-made structures are hopeless and women need to fashion their own new, utopian Christian community.

Another brand, described as reconstructive, is espoused by scholars Elisabeth Schüssler Fiorenza and Rosemary Ruether (see the next section). They want to radically dismantle and then reshape the Church so that by its very nature it would equally be an institution of women and men. More moderate than this is a "reformist" approach, supported by many mainstream liberals (if this is not an oxymoron), that would still shake up the old institution to an alarming degree.

At the other end of the scale is what some call "affirmative" feminism (perhaps another oxymoron), espoused by Phyllis Schlafly and others, that would promote women's interests largely by keeping them safe in the bosom of the traditional male Church.

Feminism is a work in progress, but it is also one of the most dynamic aspects of contemporary Catholicism.

Internal differences apart, some generalizations can safely be made. Women theologians view the Church as a community rather than a hierarchical structure. In creating their vision, they have no qualms about crossing denominational lines, and they exchange information with many different cultures. There is not yet a body of feminist theology as such; the term primarily describes the process. It does not focus on any one traditional belief or interpretation of the sacred, but is based on each woman's experience—through listening to stories, ideas about the sacred take shape, and a new understanding of the divine surfaces. The process of feminist theology is always open to new revelation.

Ruether: Connecting the Dots

Rosemary Ruether was one of the first to connect the ecology, women, God, and power, calling our systems and structures to accountability. Writing from the reformist tradition, she is not shy about challenging the system, but works within it to bring change. Ruether, who teaches at Garrett-Evangelical Theological Seminary and is the author of more than 30 books, is perhaps best known for *New Woman/New Earth: Sexist Ideologies and Human Liberation*—a book that gave birth to the eco-feminist movement.

Eco-feminism identifies those who work to end the exploitation both of women and the natural world. It sees how all the "isms" are really rooted in the same pot—a hierarchical ordering system that places Earth, children, and women at the bottom, resulting in the domination of people and the exploitation of nature.

Deep ecology is the result of ecology combined with feminism. It examines the symbolic, psychological, and ethical patterns of destructive relations between humans and nature. It also looks at how to replace these negative patterns with life-affirming culture. Eco-feminism calls for a comprehensive approach to theology, taking it out of the "church box" and putting it back in the ground where it can grow. It uses a multi-disciplinary approach, drawing on the work of historians, anthropologists, natural scientists, theologians, social economists, and others who share a concern about the exploitation of nature.

Working from a full analysis of how power is used and abused by the dominate culture, it sees the big picture—the interconnection of women's oppression, child abuse, the destruction of Third World people, and the rape of the environment. It calls for a new vision of the cosmos and of power. This new vision is one of awakened consciousness, understanding human relations in terms of cooperation rather than in competition for resources at the expense of the environment.

Ruether acknowledges that realizing this vision will be the combined effort of poets, artists, and liturgists, as well as revolutionary organizers. The vision requires crossing traditional lines—social, political, and religious—that have separated people in the past.

The following principles, paraphrased here from Ruether's book *New Woman/New Earth*, illustrate deep ecology, eco-feminism, and liberation of the earth and of the people:

- Life has intrinsic value that cannot be defined merely through its usefulness to humans. Diversity of nature is a value in and of itself.
- Creation, both human and nonhuman, is characterized by a fundamental goodness and generosity.
- Present human interference with the nonhuman world is excessive, and the situation is rapidly worsening.
- A radical transformation toward simplification and appreciation of life itself is called for rather than acquisition of goods.
- Theology must question human's assumptions regarding their place in nature in light of maintaining the richness and diversity of life, including economic, technological, and ideological systems.
- Awareness needs action. Policies must be realigned according to life values.

Creating New Models

For many years, the word *feminist* was like a battle cry that scared many, but the work of these visionary women is now making it into mainstream thought. Regular Catholics now recognize the significance of hierarchy and patriarchy; they understand why it is necessary to stop saying *man* when you mean men and women; they admit that God can be imagined as a woman just as easily as a man. I have always heard that the kingdom of God advances by increments. Little by little, inroads into a new consciousness about male and female is happening, as women theologians continue to speak their piece. (More on this topic in Chapter 7.)

Alongside feminist theology, a new discipline has surfaced, called womanist theology. It derives from novelist Alice Walker's book, *In Search of Our Mothers' Gardens: Womanist Prose*. Womanist is defined by Walker as "outrageous, audacious, courageous," and engages in "willful behavior ... wanting to know more and in greater depth than is good for one."

Womanist study has provided an image particular to black women, as they articulate their unique experiences and formulate their theology. Like feminist theology, it is a liberation model. It links and focuses on all expressions of oppression. Black women experience the prejudice of gender, race, and economic oppression. For many years, black women didn't feel comfortable in what they perceived as a white women's movement. The symbol of womanist has created an image that they can claim as their own.

Roots of Feminism: Historical Footnotes

Although new in many ways, some say feminist theology arrived in the "New World" with the Pilgrims or soon afterwards. Anne Hutchinson (1591–1643) was the first white woman on this soil to challenge the Pilgrim "fathers" and create her own religious sect. She began her public career protesting the concept of original sin. She went on to protest the authority of the male clergy and many of the restrictions they placed on the people, instead favoring inner guidance. At forty-six, pregnant with her sixteenth child, she was banished from the colony for her unorthodox beliefs.

A faithful follower of Hutchinson, Mary Dyer (1615–1660), was hanged in Boston in 1660 when she would not accept banishment for her Quaker faith. Dyer's real "crime" was that she chose autonomy rather than subordination to anyone—the government or her husband. Sojourner Truth (1797–1883) was born a slave and became a preacher, and she attended the second women's rights conference in Massachusetts. At the Ohio women's conference the following year, she spoke her famous words: "And ain't I a woman?" In her speech, Truth challenged white male ministers who were critical of the women's convention and saying women were intellectually, physically, and morally weak. Elizabeth Cady Stanton (1815–1902) published a feminist version of the Bible in 1895. She urged women to read the Bible carefully and to disregard any Scripture that detracted from women because it was not God's word, but the interference of men.

One can imagine that these women were not very popular in their hometowns. However, their work has become legendary. Without them, women wouldn't even be where they are. All these women, as well as many more, challenged authority, operating from an internal understanding that it was not God's will for people to be oppressed. They crossed color, gender, and religious lines. They didn't separate their work according to traditional categories, but saw political work as spiritual.

Today, as women confront the Church, challenging theology and refusing to be relegated to a lesser place, they stand in good company. When they refuse to be focused on personal sins rather than looking at the sinful conditions brought on through oppressive systems, the Church included, they draw on a rich tradition.

In Conclusion

Theology is a vital and creative discipline in which new thinking in the culture can be integrated into traditional Catholic teaching. Ideally, creative theology is used along with the teaching of the bishops and papal authority, offering new insight and a new sense of the faithful, into traditional Catholic teaching. Under the present pope, dialog has been virtually stopped and collegiality has been trumped by Vatican control. This restrictive policy and procedure include threats and retaliation by the Vatican against theologians who question noninfallible Church teachings. Many critics consider this a big step backward from the spirit of Vatican II—a clear indication that Rome is out of sync with the people of God. New ways of doing theology are emerging out of the Third World and through the efforts of women. These models turn the traditional tables and focus on corporate sin committed against the people rather than on people's personal sins.

Chapter 7

The Power of Image, Symbols, and Ceremony

Despite its claims, to say that the Catholic Church possesses "supreme authority" is to stretch the meaning of the words. On Earth, everything is, frankly, imperfect—a brick short of the desired load. That includes the Church. All too aware of our shortcomings, we give the name God to the 100 percent, totally supreme entity that only our imaginations can estimate.

Life, then, is a constant coming to terms. We try to rise above our limitations—cope with the missing brick—while at the same time we are drawn to the perfection that a full load implies.

In this pilgrimage to perfection, we are equipped to get by but not much more. Experts say that we use only up to 5 percent of our brain's capacity. When reason falls short, we top it off with imagination. Reason and imagination are supported along the journey by an impressive array of attributes. We can hear. We can count. We come equipped with a package of emotions that boggles the mind.

Despite the overtly male image that the Church projects, such as its all-male clergy and preference for male pronouns, many women continue to find satisfaction in its fold. One reason might be that women have long ago learned to bloom where they are planted. Another is the distinctly feminine presence that has survived in the Catholic Church despite all efforts to discourage it. This presence has been transmitted mainly through religious images and ceremonies.

As I discussed in the previous chapter, theology is a powerful part of Catholic tradition that uses reason to discover and convey ideas about

God and us. Now we'll explore imagery, symbols, and ceremony to see how these influence our quest. Sophia, the Old Testament wisdom figure, and Mary—the mother of God and the feminine character of Holy Mother Church—are among the powerful female images that restore some balance to an otherwise male-dominated institution, making it a bit more user-friendly.

Coming to Terms

We as humans are so complex that one solitary life is a wonder. Throwing us together in society ups the ante. Shepherding us into a Church of a billion souls calls for an ongoing miracle. So much is going on.

Historically, we have used most of our repertoire to cope with secular and sacred. We fail a lot, or we'd be perfect by now after all our striving. On the other hand, we have had our successes. If only we could get the brain up to 10 percent of its capacity. To supply the shortfall, we sometimes pray for outside help.

From Word to Picture

We are indefatigable in the search for new breakthroughs. Language was a big breakthrough, right up there with the invention of the wheel, but that was a long time ago.

Language has run the gamut. In early societies, it had a lot of freedom. Accuracy and specificity played second fiddle to poetry and grandeur. Wizened storytellers, around early fires outside caves, exaggerated and embellished without an ounce of guilt. This was imagination reaching out to imagination rather than syllogisms or spreadsheets trying to actually prove something.

As time passed, some people wanted more accuracy. Did Methuselah really live to be 969, was it 999, or was he just a really old guy? To say the corn is as high as an elephant's eye doesn't work in the corn futures market. True, on romantic evenings, Shakespeare or the Beatles still had the edge over hard facts. But overall, life was getting more taut. Science was useless if it wasn't precise; ditto one's bank account if it wasn't accurate. People increasingly demanded that the words mean what they say.

As this became a trend, the Catholic Church naturally followed the rest of the world. Indeed, the Church had long been concerned about language. Although an exalted subject like religion lent itself to verbal panache, Church authorities worried about theologians, saints, and others going overboard. An innocent-looking word such as *filioque* could give rise to an intense ecclesiastical tussle in the past. Works like Aquinas' *Summa Theologica* are excruciatingly accurate—and dry.

Practically from the beginning, the Church has been arbiter of what language is acceptable within its fold. Whoever controls the language wields the authority and keeps the flock on the same page. The urge to delineate, define, and circumscribe has seldom been more virulent than in the pontificate of Pope John Paul II. This has been a mixed blessing. Keeping people on the same page is in vain if it's a dull page without panache or prophecy. This takes us around by the scenic route to the sturdy old cliché that a picture is worth a thousand words.

Seated at the Right of the King

Say "God" in a crowded room, and then ask those present what comes to mind. Chances are it will not be a passage from Augustine, a papal encyclical, or any of the near-infinite words that have been so meticulously written. Chances are it will be a visual image. It might be from a painting by one of the old masters or from a simple holy card. Despite all the words written, something is in our composition, in our brain or in whatever magic box blends our past with our present at short notice—something that responds to the visual.

Religious images talk directly to our unconscious mind—overriding verbal communication even when the verbal message contradicts what is being expressed through image or symbol.

And not only visual images speak to us. Even if it came to us in words, the image that leaps from the page has more power than the words that merely go one-on-one with reality (the poetic image, in short). It has always been this way. Around those primitive fires, images rather than words came to life. In the most difficult times, in the days before leisure, poetry was making its mark on people. Poetry had power. In the old days in Ireland, the poet sat at the right hand of the king. Even when the Soviet Union of yesteryear was at its most oppressive, thousands of ordinary people would turn out—not on rare occasions, but constantly—to hear poets read their poems. On a monument on O'Connell Street in Dublin is the inscription: "Let others write a nation's laws if I may write its songs."

Because the image is more compelling.

Because, in some way we have not yet figured, the emotions are engaged. This is not to cast aspersions on the intellect, which is a fine thing, but it's not enough by itself. Nobel Laureate Isaac Bashevis Singer has remarked that although the Creator was somewhat tightfisted in both the physical strength and intellectual power he gave humanity, God was lavish when it came to our emotions. We have emotions to burn. Reason and logic have their own power, but if we want to caress or mess with the emotions, image and symbol have more power—nowhere more potently than in the realm of religion.

Wise Old Sophia

One of the greatest rewards reaped by scholars in recent years is the recovery of the wisdom tradition of the Old Hebrew literature—and for the most part, it is a well-kept Catholic secret. Although not as well known as other stories and characters in the Old Testament, Sophia gets more coverage than any other figure except God, Job, Moses, and David. Much of this material is found only in the Roman Catholic version of the Bible. Ecclesiasticus, Baruch, and Wisdom—texts that originated in the Hebrew tradition—are not included in Jewish or Protestant Scriptures.

No one knows who actually wrote the Book of Wisdom. Traditionally it has been attributed to Solomon, a "typical" wise man of Israel who instructed the people through his discourse. While many people have heard of the Wisdom of Solomon, few know that it refers to Sophia, a female character and aspect of God. Wisdom text was originally written in Greek about 400 B.C.E. for the Jewish people of Egypt. It belongs to the Greek Septuagint, the text of the Old Testament used universally throughout the early Christian Church.

Playing at God's Side

We know Sophia largely as wisdom in the Old Testament. Sophia's exact relationship to God is hard to pin down. She appears both as the Creator and the created. She is vitally involved in creating—somehow intimately assisting God one minute, and giving God directions the next. In *Wisdom's Feast: Sophia in Study and Celebration* (Sheed and Ward, 1996), authors Susan Cole, Marian Ronan, and Hal Taussig tell us of her many qualities: "Sophia is a co-creator with the Hebrew God, she is a heavenly queen, she is a messenger from God, and she is God's lover."

The human psyche carries the imprint of the Creator. Like a homing device, this guides our human journey, which often wanders off course. Carl Jung wrote: "It is the role of religious symbols to give a meaning to life …. Modern people do not understand how much their rationalism (which has destroyed their capacity to respond to the numinous) … puts them at the mercy of the psychic underworld." Thus, cultures fall prey to their own shortcomings; for example, manipulating the public imagination to meet a particular agenda. This has happened in the case of the Church, which inflated its male aspect while it de-emphasized female roles. Spiritual imagination, however, is immune to political or theological agendas. It instinctively knows that creation involves male and female. Theology and doctrine might continue to offer "proof" of God's overwhelming maleness, but wisdom, born of our lived experience, knows better.

In Proverbs 8:27–31, Sophia tells us of her part in creation:

> *When God set the heavens in place, I was present,*
> *When God drew a ring on the surface of the deep,*
> *When God fixed the clouds above,*
> *When God assigned the sea its limits,*
> *When God established the foundations of the earth,*
> *I was by God's side, a master craftswoman,*
> *Delighting God day after day, ever at play by God's side,*
> *At play everywhere in God's domain,*
> *Delighting to be with the children of humanity.*

The Great Mother

Theologians Elisabeth Schüssler Fiorenza and Elizabeth A. Johnson—
as well as many who practice earth spirituality, such as disciples of
"geologian" Fr. Thomas Berry or Matthew Fox's Creation Centered
spirituality—have begun to reconstruct the remains of the wisdom material, much of which had slipped through the patriarchal cracks, lying
neglected for thousands of years. Wisdom originated as an attempt to
integrate the existing goddess imagery into monotheistic Judaism. As the
Scripture is recovered, a picture emerges that reminds many of the archetypal Great Mother, an abiding image of the ancient cultures.

Her Earthly figure as she walks on the bottom of the sea tells of a
sacred presence in the course of creation. Sophia is God's spirit, inspiring
creation and taking pleasure in it. The slightly allusive quality of her role
keeps her just beyond our intellectual grasp, yet her importance in the
creative act is apparent. She is the ruah of Yahweh, the breath of God,
going forth creating, enlivening, inspiring, and maintaining life.

From Ecclesiasticus 24:3–5:

> *I came forth from the mouth of the Most High,*
> *and I covered the earth like mist.*
> *I had my tent in the heights,*
> *And my throne in a pillar of cloud.*
> *Alone I encircled the vault of the sky,*
> *and I walked on the bottom of the deep.*

At the time that Sophia entered the religious texts, pre-patriarchal
images of the divine feminine still existed in the cultural imagination,
yet Sophia's writers deferred to the monotheism of the Hebrew God.
The resulting ambiguity leaves us with many questions about her exact
relationship to God; however, there is no question of her importance.
She is one of the major spiritual characters in the Old Testament—
a significant female presence, bringing balance to the all-male image
of God the Father.

Perhaps it is Sophia who inspires the image of Holy Mother Church
as her spirit fills the faithful. Wisdom, often thought of as applied knowledge, comes to us through living the word of God. Holy Mother Church—
never an image of institutional power or buildings—is reflected in the

living experiences of the Church taking form through the people's lives and announcing the reign of God.

Mining the Past

Scholars go back to pre-patriarchal history to reclaim feminine images of the divine. They have uncovered images and themes that survived into Christian times. Archeologists, anthropologists, historians, and biblical scholars have begun to piece together fragments of history, and a picture is emerging. People of those earlier cultures expressed their beliefs in art such as cave drawings that told stories and celebrated their relationship to the sacred. Religious artifacts tell us these societies were primarily matriarchal.

There is almost always an assumption that matriarchy means the same as patriarchy only with women in charge. Indeed, this is why many men bristle at the idea of giving women power: They fear being placed lower on the ladder. But matriarchies are not built on the same social structure as patriarchies. They were not hierarchically ordered. Leadership was open to men and women—sometimes in shared partnership.

The Shift from Matriarchy to Patriarchy

The Hebrew tribes entered history about 4,000 years ago and began their long struggle to unite as a people under the one God, Yahweh. However, they were not the first humans on the horizon. Throughout the Middle East and many other areas of the world, people honored a divine being in the feminine form, and it is against the background of these cultures that the tribes of Israel began to define themselves.

For 25,000 years or more, people all over the world imagined the sacred in a female form. The symbol for her was the earth itself, and has been given the name Great Mother. The people saw how the earth produced new vegetation each spring, which appeared to die in the winter, only to reappear again the following year. The seasons of the year, along with the cycles of the moon, spoke of life, death, and return. The people buried their dead in the ground, placing the lost loved one back in the mother's belly, knowing that the body would be received by her and be reborn. Over many thousands of years, the human psyche was wired with this primordial rhythm—birth, death, and rebirth. Religious rituals were performed according to this pattern that are still the foundation of religious celebrations today.

Easter, for example, the biggest celebration of the Catholic Church, is determined by the spring equinox and the full moon: the first Sunday following the first Monday following the first full moon after the vernal equinox. December 25 was chosen as the date for Christ's birth because of its connection to the winter solstice—the return of light into the world. The ancient celebrations were organic—based on the movement of the sun and moon. They defined *natural* times of ceremony. They were first appropriated by Judaism and later by Christianity, acquiring added meaning for a new time and people.

Gradually, the cultures shifted to patriarchal rule. The divine changed from a feminine to masculine image, signaling a long slow shift to worshipping an exclusively male God. For more than 600 years, the Canaanite female divinity Ashtoreth (also called Astarte) stood side by side with Yahweh, and was worshipped along with him, before her temples were finally destroyed.

Ashtoreth was depicted as a serpent, a common image in the matriarchal culture, symbolic of woman's gift of prophecy—her wisdom. The Judeo-Christian creation story appropriated the symbol, turning it into the devil or tempter. The new story shows that the snake, woman's wisdom, tricked Eve into disobeying God. This was telling the people that they could not rely on their inner knowing. It heralds the coming of the male "sky" God, who exists outside of nature and who rules by external law.

One objective of the story of the fall was to show that man had assumed dominance over woman. It has successfully been used for thousands of years to justify male authority. In the hierarchical formula, God speaks directly to man, who passes instruction down to woman and child, who are spiritually, intellectually, and physically inferior. Man must exert control over woman (child and nature) because he is responsible *for* them, not *to* them.

The formula itself is inappropriate because it attempts to put distance between woman and God, making man the intermediary. This power inequity sets both men and women up for problems. Men, cast in a quasi-divine position, become overwhelmed by a simultaneous self-importance and inadequacy that often clash and erupt in violence. Culture, meanwhile, is denied women's wisdom.

Mother/Father God

Today, some theologians talk about God in both masculine and feminine terms. This is not radically new; rather, it's traditional. St. Paul called Jesus "Sophia," and the mystics often spoke of God in female terms. St. Teresa wrote that "Jesus is our mother." Female God imagery is again creeping into Catholic worship in some parts of the country. Some feel it is important to balance the patriarchal images of power and might with God's softer images of love and mercy. Change always meets resistance. Some believe this change of perception is sacrilegious. But the practice has not yet become widespread enough for many people to get hot and bothered about it.

Theologian John Wijngaards describes the difference between a masculine and feminine approach to God. The feminine way is a mystical approach in which we seek communion and participation; it is founded in our experiences of *union* with nature and union with our mother. The masculine approach is achieved through submission and surrender to God as *other* than self; it is based in experience of our own personality coming through relationship with our father.

Each approach uses a different power paradigm and emphasizes a different style of relationship. In the feminine form, power is mutual and described as partnership. Women experience God as naturally present within—in nature and in relationships. The male approach presupposes a struggle between two separate forces and requires an inevitable surrender of one to the other—winning through losing: winning coming as some manner of conquest. For men, God is experienced as "out there," and requires action on our part to get there.

Both approaches are valid and fulfill tasks the psyche must complete on its way to becoming fully integrated or fully self-conscious. Women and men have different challenges in their spiritual development. At the risk of reinforcing stereotypes, most people agree that women are instinctually more relational. Sometime during their adult years, women face the task of individuation—the challenge to experience themselves independent from others—in order to find balance. The opposite is true for men, who are naturally more individualistic. They face the challenge of discovering their relationship with creation.

Buddhist philosophy describes both processes as adjusting from different sides of the road. The task is to come to the middle, to find balance—expressed in the word interrelatedness that describes both individuality and connection. Sometimes our spirituality requires submission of our will and surrender; sometimes it requires strengthening and action.

Christianity has overwhelmingly depended on the masculine approach—strength and action. Correcting this imbalance means practicing surrender and submission. Ultimately, we need both the yin and yang of it.

Reclaiming Scriptural Images: Catholics Read the Bible

Prior to the Second Vatican Council, Catholics were not encouraged to read the Bible. Private interpretation was forbidden because the Church worried about deviation from its own carefully packaged doctrine. Reading the Bible was considered Protestant, which was enough reason to avoid it—Catholics pointed triumphantly to Martin Luther, who, as soon as he "fell away" from the Church, rushed to publish his own version. Catholics instead received their biblical message from the priest in Sunday morning sermons.

Thus, although Catholics had little direct contact with the text, they still acquired a good sense of biblical themes, characters, and stories. Two main biblical themes are salvation and liberation history. The Catholic Church preferred salvation history—almost to the exclusion of liberation history. But when people began to read the Scripture for themselves, they found, for example, that there were two versions of the creation story.

The one they knew from Sunday sermons was "The Lord God cast the man into a deep sleep and, while he slept, took one of his ribs and closed up its place with flesh. And the rib, which the Lord God took from the man, he made into a woman, and brought her to him" (Genesis 2:21–22). But the other version had a different slant: "God said, 'Let us make humankind in our image, according to our likeness' ... So God created humankind in his image, in the image of God he created them; male and female he created them" (Genesis 1:26–27). Women, especially, had their eyes opened by this egalitarian account. They began to question the idea of being second-rate creations.

Theologians and Bible scholars, including a new generation of women theologians, began to reinterpret the Bible in the 1960s and 1970s. Catholics soon discovered that St. Paul had more to say about a woman's position in the Church than keeping quiet and wearing a scarf. They discovered that he also said: "For all of you who have been baptized into Christ, have put on Christ. There is neither Jew nor Greek; there is neither slave nor freeman; there is neither *male nor female*. For you are all one in Jesus Christ" (Galatians 3:27–28). Phyllis Trible, a leading authority on Old Testament interpretation, has made the point that man's domination over woman is the *result* of the fall from grace—it describes the *sinful state* in which they now live, not the *ideal* intended by God.

Since that time, Scripture study has become a regular part of Catholic spiritual practice. This gives women, as well as men, a chance to see what the text actually says. Some of this reading has been both thought-provoking and life-changing. One woman recalled, "I can remember conversations about whether men had a missing rib on one side of their bodies; however, women being portrayed as inferior was not questioned."

Reading Between the Lines

In *Women and Christianity*, Mary T. Malone traces women's role in the early Church, dusting off the patriarchal interpretation that overlays and defines them. Malone maintains that early Christian men excluded women from the narrative on the strength of Eve's perceived role in the fall—specifically, her identification as disobedient and a temptress who dragged Adam into that whole mess. This justified confining woman to an obedient and subservient role. The outcome, according to Malone, was that Christianity was incapable of incorporating the prophetic dimension of the message of Jesus that inclusion of women would have assured.

The theme of woman as flawed resounded through every period of Church history. Malone and other scholars show teaching by the early Church was "prescriptive, not descriptive." But the very creation of laws to keep women from preaching and exercising authority in the Church hints broadly that women were performing such functions; otherwise, there would have been no reason to prohibit them.

Female scholars have developed a methodology and interdisciplinary approach to restore women to their place in salvation history. The first step is to acknowledge that women have been conspicuous by their absence. The next step is to ask what would have been a normal picture if Church history were not based exclusively on the male as normative. For example, when one reads St. Paul's remarks about women speaking in church, one might ask to whom and in what circumstances is he speaking. What is he correcting?

Little by little, women's names and stories are being found. A social framework is reconstructed, showing an average woman's life at a particular time in ancient history. Scholars go to journals, records, legal and religious documents, diaries, and letters, carefully piecing together an historical picture that will eventually be used to challenge traditional history. Although this is a slow process, inroads are being made. The new discoveries are gradually entering the mainstream of scholarship, and they will trickle down. In this way, a new history of Christianity more accurately representing women's lives and contributions will be written.

Virgins Rule!

A prevalent image of woman in early Christianity is the virgin. Malone sheds new light on what this actually meant to women—as distinct from how men perceived it. Far from being a companion piece to men's practice of celibacy, the virginal state preceded it by many years. Its significance lay in the fact that it presented a new option for women. Before, women had only one option: marriage. They passed from their father's rule to rule by their husbands. In such a patriarchal culture, marriage meant virtually a life of servitude, with no rights other than those granted by their spouse.

Marriage was a dangerous place for women and children. Mistreatment was a regular way of maintaining law and order in the household. One can imagine, then, the impact of the message Jesus preached, and one can understand why so many women left home to follow him. These women experienced the liberating message of Christianity, and were eager to share it. Continuing the early Christian communities was of paramount importance to them, and for a time following the death of Jesus women were especially active in the new Church. They held three main positions: deaconess, widow, and virgin.

Scripture suggests the role of deaconess included ordination. It seems likely that a widow typically performed the same services as a deaconess: home visits, praying, laying on of hands, teaching, and baptizing. Widows were considered part of the clergy.

However, as the status of male clergy was further defined and celibacy established, the role of women begin to diminish. The essential character of Christianity changed as women's influence dwindled. The Christian message had touched their lives, and they had been exuberant in their witness as they experienced freedom and joy in those early communities. Restricting their roles was undoubtedly a shattering blow.

Malone describes the removal of women from Church ministry as signaling the end of charismatic teaching. The female vision of Church was replaced by the more structured and logical teaching that has come to characterize Catholicism.

It seems evident that most male leaders of the early Church did not have the conversion experience women had. For the men, the new Christianity meant that they were losing the favored position they had held so long. Unable to imagine shared power, they were most likely threatened by what they thought the changes might entail. Feeling threatened, they blamed the women.

Furthermore, male distrust of human sexuality made a comeback. Although women might be deemed inferior, men were tempted by their very presence. Menstrual taboos were trotted back out, justifying restricting the woman's role in worship. After the relationship of male as superior and female as inferior was firmly established in Christianity, man measured his progress toward heaven by the distance he put between himself and woman. He rose to higher levels by reducing her status.

Despite their loss of official positions in the Church, many women chose to extend their freedom by not marrying, and devised a plan for doing that. Out of the loss of a place in the Church, the image of virgin emerged. Women began creating unique communities in which work was shared. They enjoyed meals together, sang, reflected on the Scripture, talked about God, and taught other women how to negotiate the singles world.

Their newfound freedom soon became the target of the patriarchal order. Woman was deemed dangerous and even evil. But the men were largely unsuccessful in dampening the spirit of these women, who had probably heard it all before. So the Church fathers eventually moved to co-opt the image of virgin and invented their own version—the ideal woman.

Patriarchy's Perfect Woman

The male leaders, operating from the belief that sex was detrimental to living the spiritual life, developed their own doctrine of virginity. At its best, this produced a sisterhood of which Christianity can be truly proud. As engineered by the hierarchy, however, it has often been a bumpy ride. At a certain stage, for example, this doctrine measured women's potential for "Godliness" against their propensity for carnality, based on whether they were married (which scored high on carnal, low on Godliness); widowed (less carnal), or virgins (best bet for heaven). Malone's figures give us the following scorecard:

	Godliness	Carnality
Wives	30%	70%
Widows	40%	60%
Virgins	100%	0%

The women were removed from the lives they had designed for themselves—communal celebration and joyful witness—and became theological captives of the hierarchy. That most women in the subsequent history of the Church freely chose this vocation must nevertheless be considered in the context of the spiritual ideals contrived for them by a frequently sex-obsessed hierarchy.

Enter Mary, Virgin and Mother

Out of this obsession with virginity, St. Jerome, a bishop and writer in the early Church, played a big part in fashioning the image of Mary as virgin and mother. He focused on obedience, humility, and purity. Nothing is said of her real role in delivering the original "good news." Rather than a woman of flesh and blood, fertile and willing to risk, she is cultivated for her passivity.

Despite the attempts of Church fathers to contain her, Mary is cele-brated in many different forms in every culture all over the world. Her image transcends patriarchal rhetoric and remains a powerful symbol for Catholics and many Protestants alike.

Morning Star and Arc of the Covenant

Mary stands barefooted on a global sphere, a snake beneath her feet, as stars swirl around her head and a crescent moon rises over her shoulder. She is the Mother of God. Although we may be in the act of worshipping her son, we know from this image how he got here—the intuitive mind is relational, not hierarchical. Tens of thousands of years of observing mother and child combine to create a spontaneous theology of feminine accessibility, of concern, and of wholeness. Mary's image communicates female power to all, but she is particularly important for women. Although women worship God the father, loving him with their whole hearts, seeking his council, and doing his will, they cannot fully *identify* with him. Deep inside, below conscious thought, women's psyche knows the male God as other.

Mary's stories developed especially in the Middle Eastern culture, where Artemis and other sacred representations of the female were active in the people's imagination. Now the mother and child captured the cul-tural imagination. Mary (with and even without her child) became cele-brated in poetry, song, art, and prayer. The Catholic Litany of Loreto captures Mary's many images: Mystical Rose, Cause of Our Joy, Morn-ing Star.

Mary's historical connection to the goddess raises questions for some people about whether she's Catholic. The answer is yes and no. Deep in the subconscious mind, in the soul of the race, religious stories all con-nect. Mary is necessary. Over and above her historic life on earth, she is an archetypal feminine form for the sacred. In the jargon of the day, she is God's feminine side.

Soul Sisters to the End

Eve, considered the prototype of woman, was given the tab for man's downfall, and hence, paradise lost. Daughter of darkness, she stands next to Mary, bringer of light—the two most prominent female characters in

Scripture. Woman was portrayed as either totally tainted or completely virtuous. In the religious imagination of the people, all women carry the stamp of Eve, and, as we've seen, this has been a problem.

But women are reclaiming Eve. Having mothered the human race, she is a symbol of women's fecundity. She is proactive. She makes her own decisions, exerting influence over the male Adam. Rather than being fooled into leaving Paradise, the revised thinking goes, there is the soul-stirring possibility that she took on life as an adventure and that she was willing to risk disobeying the patriarchal image of God, trusting her instincts.

We now know that women carry the mitochondria for the cells—literally, the body's intelligence. Women don't simply incubate a new life, they build the cells into which is placed the wisdom of the race. Jesus didn't just "book passage" through Mary; he received his human instruction from her. Whether Mary projects the image of virginal perfection, as Church fathers hoped, or whether she is the archetypal image of Great Mother, she continues to be a dominant religious presence testifying to God's availability, love, and concern. She is a living symbol. Jesus brought a new message of hope to the world, one that broke the established religious and social paradigms of the time. Mary carries on that message today, baffling traditionalists and progressives alike. She slips through the patriarchal barriers and appears in the most unpredictable places, to the most unlikely people, with seemingly pure spontaneity. She can still serve as an image of female empowerment, so long as one does not get tangled up in theological discourse and instead lets the image speak.

Catholic Ritual: Closing the Gap

Feminine qualities include feeling, emotion, mystery, darkness, receptivity, fluidity, spontaneity, intuition, symbolic understanding, relationship, and creativity. Catholic ritual itself is instinctively regarded as feminine—activating the feeling side of the brain through symbol. Ritual works internally and mysteriously—deeper than the written word. Although a whole congregation participates in a ritual together, each person is connecting to it personally, receiving a unique message. The Catholic mystical tradition is likewise an expression of its feminine side—not just because of its women mystics, but because mysticism itself is a feminine form. The mystic does not know God through logic, but descends into self, into the stillness of a mind disciplined by practice, and has an experience of the divine.

Ritual speaks directly to our subconscious mind, where time is not linear and where we experience relationship, namely our alikeness, rather than our differences. The roots of Catholic ritual go deep into the earth. They connect us to our origins among ancient tribal peoples for whom the elements of air, earth, fire, and water represented the presence of the Great Spirit in creation. Their spirituality, like that of Native Americans and most indigenous cultures, is holistic; it wasn't split in half by Western dualism.

Catholicism coexisted with those indigenous cultures for centuries, until many of the earth-based cultures were finally eradicated. Yet most of the ritual we still use today stretches back to the Middle Ages and beyond—only a blink of an eye in the big scheme of things. This ritual is a hybrid of earth culture and Christianity.

Sacred Presence in Creation

A long time ago, the hierarchy symbolically gave the earth to women, while men claimed the sky. This followed an ancient pattern, of Mother Earth and Father Sky. But there was a key difference: Ancient cultures did not take the sacredness out of earth and give it exclusively to the heavens. The ancients perceived one undivided whole because the human heart is attracted to wholeness.

Imagination goes deeper than written words. Despite an uptight logical regime of laws and doctrines, Catholics continue transmitting a sense of creation's wholeness—Father Sky and Mother Earth—through sacramental imagination. Regardless of theological understanding of God, Ritual conveys God's presence, both as male and female, throughout creation.

Although cultural variances are found among different peoples, the classical elements of air, earth, fire, and water are universal. These function symbolically irrespective of time and place. In *The Complete Idiot's Guide to Understanding Catholicism*, we wrote about the need to reconnect Catholic ritual with the earth and created the following chart to illustrate how the individual elements are used in the sacraments, connecting us to the sacredness of the earth.

Elemental Symbol	Corresponding Symbols	Symbolic Meaning	Implied Meaning	Catholic Beliefs and Practices
Earth	Winter; night; north; black	Death and gestation; nurturing; physicality; creativity; female	What appears to be dead is gestating and will be reborn; food and shelter; earth as sacred; physical body as sacred; wisdom; the mystery of life	Jesus' physical presence on earth; Jesus' birth in the manger; Mother Mary; Jesus' healing ministry (feed the hungry, heal the sick, raise the dead); Jesus' death on the cross and burial in earth; altar; holy oil; ashes (dust to dust); sacraments: Holy Eucharist, anointing the sick, marriage (procreation)
Air	Spring; morning; east; white; green	Birth; life and breath; new beginning; movement; promise; mind/meaning; male	The gift of life; hope; renewal; communication; thoughts as sacred	Incense; bells; prayers, songs, and chants; declaring the Word; Holy Spirit as dove; preaching and teaching; hope reborn; resurrection; sacrament: holy orders (as preaching and teaching)
Fire	Summer; noon; south; red; orange	Transformation; strengthening the will; in the action world; willing into being; fruition and abundance	Candles; sanctuary lamp; Holy Spirit as fire; zeal; missionary work	Catholic action (do the right thing); Christ's Passion; use of miracles; sacraments: holy orders and confirmation
Water	Fall; evening; west; blue	Inner depth; quieting; soothing; waters of the womb; emotions; female	Cleansing; initiation; reflection; fulfillment; universal solvent	Holy water; blessings; mediation; contemplation; intuition or doorway to wisdom; sacraments: baptism and reconciliation

Sacramental Connection: Air, Earth, Fire, and Water

When we pour water over the head of the one seeking baptism, that soul is cleansed because water is infused with God's saving grace. As the baptismal candle is lighted, the transforming spirit of the incarnated Christ is present in the fire. As the forehead, lips, and heart are signed, wholeness of creation is acknowledged and honored. A new spirit has been incarnated and is recognized and absorbed into the tribe.

To be human is to fail and to need forgiveness. In the sacrament of penance, words are whispered. The ruah of Yahweh, the spirit of God, once again comes forth from the mouth of the Most High. Our cry has been heard and answered. We are forgiven—told to go and sin no more. Retribution must be paid to the tribe for damages done, and we must be able to accept the forgiveness offered. Breath—elemental air— recreates us.

Eucharist reconnects us to Jesus by way of the sacred presence and nurturing spirit of earth. Fields of wheat ripen, bread is prepared—this is my body; eat of it. Grapes grow heavy on the vine where they are gathered and made into wine—this is my blood; drink of it. We are earth; we are spirit.

Confirmation evokes ancient coming-of-age ceremonies. As childhood draws to a close, more is expected of us, and we'll need strength. Oil anoints the body—and the creator's strength is drawn from the earth. Confirmation reaffirms our place in the tribe—the people of God. As the spirit came to the disciples on Pentecost, our will is now aligned with the divine will. We are called to be in right relationship with creation, and empowered to right action.

Marriage acknowledges sacramental union between man and woman—and their covenant relationship with God. Sacramental presence comes through the promise made by the couple. All who come witness the exchanging of wedding vows out of joyful expression of continuous creation—the tribe endures.

Holy orders follows ancient rites of shamanism where those with a special gift of ministry are anointed into the priesthood. Catholic ordination involves symbolic instruction by the bishop, laying on of hands, and anointing with oil—again symbolizing strength and consecrating fingers that will touch the consecrated hosts. The newly ordained then receive the primary "tools of their trade"—a gold paten and chalice to be used for communion. The physical symbols of ordination are of the earth—oil, gold, bread, and wine—representing Jesus' continued presence among us. In this way, the priest becomes the human symbol of sacred presence.

The final sacrament, anointing of the sick, offers healing, but it is also a preparation for death. The anointing is accompanied by confession and Holy Eucharist—a comprehensive care package. Throughout the Middle Ages, the people brought oil—probably made from comfrey or other healing herbs—to be blessed and used at home to anoint family members who were ill. Sometimes the oil, combined with prayer, brought recovery; otherwise, it strengthened the soul for its final journey.

In Conclusion

Although the Catholic Church projects an all-male image, other images lie beneath. Sophia speaks from the pages of the Old Testament, telling us that she breathed her femininity into creation. She might be the force behind the image Holy Mother Church—lending female savvy and wisdom to the people of God. Likewise, Mary continues to surprise those who would keep her in a theological box; she comes and goes in the world as she pleases. Women have begun to reconstruct Christian history through a variety of disciplines. The studies show women have always taken an active role in history, including the history of religion. Images speak louder than words, and the spiritual imagination of Catholics is a rich resource. Images transmit symbolic meaning and are understood intuitively. The elements of air, earth, fire and water—integral to Catholic sacramental life—connect us to our history as people of the earth and to a time when we knew no separation from creation.

Chapter 8

Sex and Power:
A Collision Course

Religion and sex are strange bedfellows. Religion is incorporeal, ethereal, and abstract—it's all about getting to the light. Sex is carnal, worldly, and tangible—it usually happens behind closed doors at night. They would presumably go their separate ways—except that they're bound together by their mutual humanity and must share life's journey. One seems to cling to the soul and the other to the body, but that is an artificial distinction our minds make. In real life, both need body and soul.

There is no other area in which religion and humanity bump and grind so discordantly as in the arena of sex.

The Facts of Life

Sex brings out both the best and worst in us. It can bring giggles, a blush to the cheek, or a spark of interest. It can override common sense, destroy a reputation, or create life. Andrew Greeley writes, "sexual pleasure heals the frictions and conflicts of common life and reinforces the bond between husband and wife." The gang on the *Jerry Seinfeld* TV show talked about "make-up sex."

Like it or not, sex is the engine that drives much of our culture. It is used to sell almost every product under the sun. It is glorified as a Holy Grail—compared with which most other values are trivial. The near-universal mantra that life's main aim is to have "fun" is code for sex in combination with various other extras from liquor to wealth to fame. Sex has a lot to live up to—and it often fails.

Life on earth is mundane by definition. Sex often means children—
to take a down-to-earth example—and that means bills, diapers, and perhaps college. Romantic sex is soon gone with the wind. Then it's time for
the disenchanted to take a harder look at how mundane sex fits into the
great scheme of things.

But where should one look? For much of our history, the subject was
kept cautiously under wraps. Call it restraint or prudery: People were not
comfortable with too much show and tell. Then all that changed, gradually at first. Novels such as D. H. Lawrence's *Lady Chatterley's Lover* or
Vladimir Nabokov's *Lolita* offended many sensibilities and caused a succession of minor sensations. But the dam broke for good in the 1960s
when the sexual revolution overwhelmed Western culture. The alleged
reasons for this upheaval range from a softening in traditional values to
the universal availability of artificial contraceptives. Morality became
more elastic. Both civil and religious restraints were relaxed. Neither
heaven nor hell seemed as immediate as in the ages of faith. The alternative assumption, that Earth might be our home, was a clarion call to
enjoy it. In such a climate, self-gratification seemed a good thing. Whole
industries geared themselves to support this ethos: from psychotherapy to
pharmaceuticals, from *Penthouse* to, more recently, pornography on the
Internet.

Not everyone rushed to the barricades for the sexual revolution. Many
people of goodwill—confused, angry, or fearful—looked to their religious institutions for guidance. It was not an easy time to be a church.
The Catholic Church, more than most, resisted jumping on the free-for-all
bandwagon. Whether this is a heroic stand for truth and virtue and human
dignity, as some see it, or the naysaying of out-of-touch celibate fuddy-
duddies, as others say, perhaps only the future can judge objectively.

Let's take a look at the history of the Church's relationship to human
sexuality, as well as how attitudes and behavior of the past contributed
to what is now widely seen as a gaping credibility gap.

Getting Off to a Bad Start

Over the 2,000-year history of the Church, its leaders have failed to heal the dualistic split between body and spirit. One casualty of this division of the person is human sexuality. Belief in the body's innate sinfulness permeated the relationship between man and woman. The recurring misogyny found in the early Church, and frequently thereafter, resulted in the union of marriage being more tolerated than applauded. Gradually a preference arose for celibacy over family life. Out of this same skewed dualistic thinking came the focus on personal sexual sin. This dualism, which is at the root of the Church's stunted vision, also seeped into and still continues to plague the whole of Western culture.

The outcome was constant ambiguity and inconsistency in relationships between men and women. Greek and Roman literature frequently exalted women and had a great time with sex. But literature didn't always reflect life. Women were often badly treated, including the all-too-common double standard with regard to sex. Both the Greek and Roman cultures subscribed to monogamy; but in practice, this was not always observed. Despite the greatness of Greek literature and Roman law and a host of other cultural triumphs, those were harsh civilizations, unfair and unequal, whose high-sounding rhetoric made little impression on the lives of the most vulnerable, which was usually the women and children.

Still, it was from the rhetoric of those civilizations that the most influential of Catholic thinkers later drew their inspiration. Sts. Paul, Augustine, and Thomas Aquinas, so pivotal in defining and delineating the philosophical and theological heritage of the Catholic Church, all drew upon the Greeks and Romans. Needless to say, there was no seminal classical feminist or liberation theologian back there to inspire a more female-friendly Christian philosophy for the ages.

During the years just before Christianity and for about 70 years after its arrival, a variety of Jewish spiritual communities were springing up in and around Jerusalem. Gnosticism was one movement whose popularity grew to the extent that some worried it might rival Christianity. Like the Greek culture, the Gnostic communities oscillated between pursuing pleasure and cultivating an aesthetic of shunning physical pleasure in order to search for spiritual truth. Perhaps as a corrective measure to Greek and Roman excesses, Stoicism became the dominant philosophical influence in the secular culture. The practice of aesthetic Gnosticism

143

was its religious counterpart.

The dualism prevailed, and so did the ambivalence. By the second generation, Christianity preached the rejection of physical pleasure in pursuit of spiritual gain. Yet the communities established by Jesus and his disciples involved men and women working together. Marriage was the accepted way of life and surely not condemned as an impediment to spirituality. Most of the apostles, after all, had been married. There are only a few references to celibacy in the New Testament, leaving scholars to conclude that celibacy was not presented as an ideal—much less a requirement. Before long, however, the early Church fathers were placing a superior spiritual value on celibacy, referring to it as a higher calling. This soon translated into thinking of marriage as a place for those who couldn't accomplish the celibate life.

Marriage Takes a Back Seat

No law was established in the first three centuries regarding celibacy for the clergy. Many priests, bishops, and popes were married and had children. Some second-century popes promoted marriage for clergy, whereas others promoted celibacy both for clergy and all believers. Clerical celibacy began to gain ground, growing in a quiet progression from custom to preferred path. At first, clergy were expected not to marry; or, if they had, to leave the marriage after ordination. Later, a meeting of bishops in Spain (about 306 C.E.) began to formalize the practice of celibacy—forbidding all bishops, priests, and deacons from having wives. Theoretically, there was to be no marriage after ordination, and married priests were to practice celibacy by abstaining from sexual relations. This practice was not adopted universally, and many priests and bishops continued to marry or keep women. At the Council of Nicea (325), the rules regarding celibacy were further defined—this time by papal decree—insisting that there be no marriage after ordination. And Nicea's decrees, lest we forget, carried the formidable endorsement of new Christian friend Constantine.

Many of the Church's ideals regarding spiritual life were developed in the desert during the second century, under the influence of St. Anthony (d. 356). Desert spirituality involved men and women living in separate communities in which they practiced celibacy and virginity, along with a life based on prayer and fasting. Augustine was impressed by Anthony and recognized the advantage of a community in maintaining celibacy. His encouragement influenced their further growth. In *Sex, Priests, and Power: Anatomy of a Crisis,* Richard Sipe makes the point that political, economic, and spiritual power began to build almost immediately as the Church moved toward celibacy as the model for priesthood, and these celibate communities became the primary source from which popes were selected.

At the same time, female communities began as a largely spontaneous phenomenon, as described in the previous chapter. They gradually came under patriarchal control, however. But the presence of the women—even in the innocuous role of white-clad virgins—grew ever more problematic for the churchmen in pursuit of celibacy. At the insistence of Rome, the women were moved farther and farther from the centers of power—the communities in which men were presumably being prepared for Church leadership.

Subduing the Flesh

Although attempting to create a new vision, the early Christians remained dualists in a dualistic culture. They believed spiritual transcendence depended on subduing the flesh. The practice of celibacy was rooted in an attitude akin to abhorrence and rejection of the body. The same distortion affected the sexual relationship in marriage. The Church drew its primary rationale for both celibacy and marriage from Augustine. Despite his renown, this was an abysmal mistake.

Augustine grudgingly upheld the marriage institution, but an exaggerated dualism prevented him from going the extra mile. He put the damper on sexuality, reserving intercourse for the purpose of procreation only. The whole matter of procreation was a problem for him because he thought original sin was transmitted through sexual union. At the same time, he realized that reproduction was necessary and inevitable.

Caught though he was on the horns of that dilemma and admittedly tormented by his own unresolved lust, Augustine became the primary source by which the Church's standards for sex and marriage would be determined for much of the next 2,000 years. Although others writing

145

at the same time expressed a much more moderate and human view on sexuality, Augustine's ideas dominated the theological landscape and eventually grew from custom to papal decree and were encoded into Church laws. For good or ill, but definitely forever, Catholic understanding of sexuality, although supposedly determined by the *Holy Spirit,* would bear a striking resemblance to Augustine, Stoicism, and Gnosticism.

A considerable collection of Church documents points to the hierarchy's fixation with sexuality and celibacy. These reflect both hate and fear, which are often projected onto women. Marriage, a necessary but second-class life, was seen as a lesser state primarily because it relegated man to the inferior world of the female. In *Sexuality and Catholicism,* Thomas C. Fox describes Church writings that refer to the "horrors" of marriage and "the constant anxiety about the uncontrolled and uncontrollable aspect of orgasm ... and always, for men, the dangers of becoming effeminate."

Highs and Lows of the Middle Ages

In the first part of the Middle Ages, the Church's energy was spent coping with the barbarians, eventually baptizing most of them and accepting them into the fold. This mission spread Catholicism throughout Europe. A rich cultural exchange went on through assimilation of the many tribes who inhabited the continent. This is reflected in the rich sacramental life of Catholic rituals and ceremonies.

During the Middle Ages, Church art, music, and architecture flourished. Every city and town built a cathedral—each more splendid than the next. A convenient alliance was struck between Church leaders and secular rulers. This brought relative safety, and the Church grew rich under secular protection. In turn, the Church repaid kingly kindness with Church offices and guaranteed salvation. Construction of cathedrals and the opulent lifestyle of the clergy constantly drained Church resources, making the constant extraction of money from the people a necessary part of Church practice.

"Necessity" invented the practice of selling Church positions as well as granting salvation through selling indulgences, relics of the saints, and other sacramentals, and a flourishing business was born. We call it simony. But entrepreneurship wasn't the best thing for the Church. Internally,

Christendom was in a state of moral decline, having fallen prey to wealth and power. Its priests and bishops were becoming increasingly more worldly (usually a code word for having sex). Many were married; others had "open marriages," which meant that they kept women. Some historians contend that it was the matter of too many offspring claiming inheritance rights against Church property that finally drove the pope to tighten the celibacy regulations.

The Church's Little Black Book

The Church continued to maintain the position that the marriage bed was reserved for procreation only. No attention was paid to the development of a spirituality of love, marriage, child rearing, or community life. The habitual "worldliness" of its priests and bishops was creating a growing concern in the papal home office regarding inheritance. Candidates for the office of bishop who had wives and children were required to sign a statement protecting the Church from any inheritance claims. Still finding it impossible to enforce celibacy, a papal document decreed the illegitimacy of priests' sons. The hardship this decree inflicted on women and children, now pushed out of the financial loop, seems to have gone without comment.

The particulars of sexual intercourse and sexual sin continued to be the overriding concern of the Church. Definitions of exactly what act resulted in which sin became increasingly detailed and were cataloged in a handy booklet called a *penitential*. In addition to identifying and describing sexual acts, a penitential also recommended appropriate penances to be prescribed by the confessor—depending on the intention, frequency of the act, and the established moral weight of various transgressions. Thomas C. Fox depicts the Church's excessive concern for sexual transgression by describing the penances imposed, such as fasting on bread and water for up to 10 years for practicing contraception. Anal and oral sex were considered unnatural because procreation wasn't a possible outcome, and resulted in penances such as fasting for up to 15 years— a more severe punishment than for murder.

In 1018, Pope Benedict VIII took measures against the general decline in Church policies and instituted stronger laws to support clerical celibacy. This move was further supported by Pope Gregory VII (1073–1085). His enforcement of the existing rules is regarded as the first effective implementation of clerical celibacy. According to theologian Hans Kung, Rome required unconditional obedience and the renunciation of marriage, which resulted in a virtual witch-hunt of priests' wives in the rectories of the day. The Second Lateran Council in 1139 seems to provide the first written law that made it impossible for a cleric to get married. At that time, all pre-existing marriages of priests were declared invalid, wives were declared concubines, and children became Church property and effectively became slaves.

Aquinas's Natural Law

Thomas Aquinas (1225–1274)—a Dominican friar who first incurred the wrath of Rome for his innovative theology, but later became a Doctor of the Church—continues to be held in high regard to this day. Aquinas introduced a sacramental view of marriage, essentially bestowing the blessings of the Church on human sexuality. His theory allowed for a bit of marital pleasure in the bedroom, but he continued to uphold the earlier teaching on indulging in sexuality for procreation only. Aquinas's scholastic thought, based on the natural law theory, became the new basis for the development of moral theology.

This theory maintains that natural laws exist governing all creation, including the activities of animals and humans. By observation and reflection, a person can determine a correct moral response to every situation. The Church used natural law theory to arrive at its conclusion that there can be no artificial interference in sexual intercourse. Natural law was not without its limitations, and its further application allowed the Church to deduce that although fornication, adultery, incest, rape, and abduction were serious sins, they preserved the "natural order." However heinous these actions were, they had the potential to include reproduction; thus, they were classified as lesser violations of the moral order. Greater violations listed by the Church included masturbation, sodomy, homosexuality, and bestiality, because the potential for pregnancy does not exist. These theological conclusions became the source of manuals used in the education of priests.

Moral discernment and the development of theology were exclusively under the direction of priests and especially monks. Regardless of whether they were observing celibacy or merely writing about it, their day-to-day involvement in people's lives was minimal. They did not see the whole picture of marriage as a complex set of relationships between human beings based on love and caring for one another. Rather, they viewed it as a series of sexual acts—disconnected from any context other than procreation. Marriage continued to be regarded as secondary to the clerical state: necessary for the continuance of the species, and, begrudgingly, as a way of containing lust. This attitude defined human sexuality and marriage for the next 300 years.

A Bad Day Was Had by All

In 1484, a document called the *Malleus Maleficarum* (the Hammer of the Witches), written by two Dominican Monks, Heinrich Kramer and James Sprenger, was published. The book had been commissioned by the pope to be used as the working handbook for the Inquisition—the Church's ongoing method of working with dissenters. As mentioned in Chapter 5, the Inquisition was a "court process" designed to rid Christendom of heretics and infidels—specifically Jews, Muslims, leftover pagans, gypsies, and women.

Millions were killed during this 300-year period. Galileo and Joan of Arc were two of its more famous victims, and Martin Luther barely escaped being roasted over a papal fire. It is relevant here because of the profoundly distorted sexual views of the *Malleus Maleficarum*—in its description of women, the crimes of which it accused them, and the terrible sexual tortures imposed on them. *Malleus Maleficarum* alleged that women possessed supernatural powers granted to them through sexual intercourse with the devil. They were accused of flying around at night, causing disease and crop failure, and of mating with animals. Girls at the age of 9 and boys at the age of 10 were considered fair targets. Arrest brought on certain rape and years of sexual torture. Confined in hidden cells, no one was allowed to visit them other than "zealous Catholics"—their male persecutors.

Church accounts tend to minimize the Inquisition and to downplay the Church's participation, passing blame along instead to the secular courts. Critics of the Church have been accused of erring on the other side—

making too much out of it. Regardless of the exact details, most commentators agree that this unfortunate chapter in history has gone largely unacknowledged by the Vatican. In *The Women's Encyclopedia of Myths and Secrets* (Harper and Row, 1983), Barbara Walker includes the following passage taken from the *Malleus Maleficarum*:

> The accused witch must be *"often and frequently exposed to torture. If, after being fittingly tortured, she refuses to confess the truth, he [the inquisitor] should have other engines of torture brought before her, and tell her that she will have to endure these if she does not confess. If then she is not induced by terror to confess, the torture must be continued."* If she remained obdurate, *"she is not to be altogether released, but must be sent to the squalor prison for a year, and be tortured, and be examined very often, especially on holy days."*

The state of moral corruption within the Church reached a critical mass in the early 1500s when a Catholic monk named Martin Luther nailed his list of complaints to the cathedral door at Wittenberg. Luther attacked the practice of selling indulgences. His disagreement with the Catholic understanding of faith and grace became the focus of the Protestant rebellion. Luther's stand was on salvation by faith alone, whereas Catholic tradition insisted faith without works is dead. The mess, and the suggested solutions, however, were much more complicated than that.

Luther also challenged the Church's theology regarding sexuality, strongly advocating marriage for all Christians, including clergy, believing it was a cure for the temptations of lust. Luther was excommunicated and went on to form his own well-known church.

The Council of Trent: Mopping Up

The Council of Trent, as you might recall from Chapter 5, was called by the Church in 1545 to deal with the wreckage of the Middle Ages. The birth of Protestantism resulted in many Catholics changing sides. The Church was in a state of chaos of its own making. The Council of Trent lasted for 18 years, with interruptions. The Church emerged revitalized—with the emphasis back on the sacramental life—and focused especially on the Eucharist. It promoted a rigorous spirituality of prayer. It also endorsed an authoritarian approach to moral discipline, with the pope in complete command. Like generals going into battle, bishops were charged with policing their dioceses and rooting out any and all transgressions.

On a softer note, Trent for the first time made the connection between love and marriage, but it upheld the traditional position that sexual intercourse was only for procreation. It likewise confirmed that the celibate state was of more spiritual value than marriage and reaffirmed it as a mandatory requirement for priesthood. The council did admit that celibacy was a Church law, not a biblical mandate.

Additional trouble loomed on the horizon as the freethinking people in the seventeenth and eighteenth centuries questioned Church teaching. There was a slight murmur among Catholic theologians, implying sexual intercourse might have its own excuse for taking place. Reaction to the rise of critical rationalism and liberalism sparked much theological debate. Response to these new philosophies spawned the reactionary Jansenist movement—in essence, revisiting the Augustinian understanding of sexuality, original sin, and a general sense of our doomed nature. Following the view of a Dutch theologian, Cornelius Jansen (1585–1638), it reaffirmed keeping a stern attitude toward sexuality and a pessimistic understanding of the relationship between human nature and grace. In that regard, it dangerously flirted with predestination. Jansen was accused of tampering with papal business and of Calvinist leanings, and his theology was condemned as heretical.

Vatican I: The Birth of Infallibility

In the years following Trent, the Catholic Church found itself in a culture clash of major magnitude. Protestantism took its toll, as did the Enlightenment and the French Revolution. Science was beginning to answer questions about existence that once belonged to the realm of the Church. The political structure of Europe changed. As monarchies fell, Catholic power frequently eroded. The spirit of liberalism and free thinking introduced by German Catholics threatened the rusty Church mentality. Pope Pius IX responded with his *Syllabus of Errors*—in which he essentially condemned progress and much of the modern world.

At the First Vatican Council (1869–1870), Pius IX sought to recapture the power he had lost in the political world by proclaiming himself infallible. The Church then turned its back on the world and remained in cautious retreat for almost a hundred years, until Vatican II.

The Power to Forgive

Not even in its muscular Holy Roman Empire days did the Catholic Church wield such power as that which it quietly exercised over the consciences of its members century after century as it claimed for itself sole authority to forgive sins in God's name.

Jesus had been big on forgiveness. The Father would forgive up to seventy times seven times, he said. This sure was good news. The only stipulation was this: Don't sin any more. The Church formalized this practice, declared it a sacrament, and buttressed it with rules and regulations. It was and is called penance or confession. The confession of sins must be made to a priest (or higher-up). Although the priest has emerged from the wooden confession box since the reforms of Vatican II, the sacrament is private and intimate. Sins traditionally fall into two categories: mortal (severe offenses, usually premeditated) and venial (lesser transgressions). Mortal sins must be told, however embarrassing or serious; otherwise, there is no forgiveness.

Looming in the background is hell. Although recent theology and practice have underlined the positive and therapeutic aspects of this sacrament as reconciliation, it had for centuries been a sinister and intimidating ritual. One's eternity rested on it. If one were lucky enough to die on leaving the confessional box, one's soul would go straight to heaven. If one died without confessing all mortal sins, one went straight to hell. Purgatory was a paltry cushion of insurance between these two extremes.

And lest there be any doubt, the horrors of hell were driven home to Catholics at every opportunity: the fire, the pain of loss, and the regret at opportunities missed. Hellfire sermons were *de rigueur* at certain times, such as parish missions, or for certain people, such as sex-starved teenagers.

This was not a game of gotcha by cruel priests in certain backward localities. It was the universal teaching and practice of the Church. To older Catholics, it is old news; to most younger people, it is probably new news because most have not been exposed to its more virulent manifestations in the post-Vatican II era.

Sex was the crux. Confessing Catholics threw in peccadilloes such as talking during Mass, but eventually there was no avoiding what penitent and priest were building up to—the sex sins. Everything was mortal here. In the area of honesty, one had to dig deeply in a neighbor's pocket to reach mortal sin status. In the case of sex, the sinner was automatically in the big leagues.

Lucky was the penitent who hadn't died before reaching the box. To protect against this dire eventuality, sinners could save their skins by an act of perfect contrition. This had to be so sincere in order to be effective that Catholics tortured themselves not only in reaching for that great sorrow, but also in wondering afterwards whether they had pulled it off.

It was not just kids who worried over eternal damnation. Century after century, the Catholic Church successfully instilled this fear of God in the faithful. As people grew older, often they worried more. No one was exempt. The pope himself goes to confession to this day. High ecclesiastics have to confess, and, unless they are deep-down unbelievers, they presumably still fear hell.

At least in theory. The fear seems to have evaporated a little. Word is out that maybe not every sexual thought, word, and deed is deadly. Maybe masturbation will not land one in fire and torment, as it once so assuredly did.

And just as the Church, from the very top down, condoned this fearsome exploitation of guilt, so today it quietly—but never officially and explicitly—condones the relaxed morality that refuses to inflict such fear on so many vulnerable people. And not just the ignorant—everyone believed it because it was the faith of the Church.

But what power it was. A pope—who could decide good and evil, just by decree; who could decide who should be forgiven and how (some sins were "reserved," usually to the bishop, but on occasion even to the pope when he had a bone to pick with the world)—could get nearly everyone to do nearly anything.

Those who flirt with "creeping infallibility" should perhaps be thankful that not all universally held and enforced doctrines of the Church, at any given time, are necessarily the last word on the subject. Few go to confession nowadays.

Catholic Sex Comes to America

In the 30 years between 1830 and 1860, the U.S. population increased 800 percent. A disproportionate number of these immigrants were Catholic. Many brought with them a Jansenist, puritanical tradition from Europe. The great majority settled in national ghettoes in big cities. They belonged to national parishes. The local pastor was their protector, promoter, and disciplinarian; and the flock was grateful, docile, and obedient. The Church had enormous power, the people had a new and relatively successful life, and Rome was far away.

Catholics Get Rhythm ... and Lots More Children

The success and spread of Protestantism brought new theologies. One big innovation was a different relationship to power and authority. In the twentieth century, Catholic and Protestant thinking took different paths regarding sexuality. In 1930, the bishops of the Church of England removed their ban on birth control and recognized a separation between the procreative aspect of sexual intercourse and its potential to provide comfort and pleasure.

The pope responded with an encyclical reaffirming the Catholic stand that removing the sexual act from its natural power of procreation constituted a violation of natural law, and thus was a grave sin. A slight concession was made toward validating the personal value of human sexuality, when the pope supported the rhythm method of family planning. To paraphrase Charles Curran's description of the Church's teaching on sexuality midway through the twentieth century, from his article "Roman Catholic Sexual Ethics: A Dissenting View" (www.religion-online.org):

1. Genital sexuality can be expressed only within the context of an indissoluble and permanent marriage of male and female.

2. All sexual acts must be open to procreation.

3. Natural law theory results in an absolute prohibition of artificial contraception and other acts deemed as "unnatural," such as masturbation, homosexual genital relations, and all premarital and extramarital sexual relationships.

4. Virginity and celibacy are higher states of life than marriage.

The Contraception Controversy

In 1960, the birth control pill was approved by the Federal Drug Administration, and it was an immediate success. A climate of change was sweeping through the culture, challenging traditional norms in the social, political, and religious arenas. A new global awareness raised concern about the rising world population. People were looking for solutions and asking questions. The birth control controversy reached deep into the core of Catholicism, especially in the area of papal power. Nearly everything the Church had been teaching about human sexuality and authority for the previous 20 centuries came into question in just a few years.

Pope John XXIII had already expressed concern for world population. He also expressed awareness of the pain the Church's position on birth control was causing Catholics. Both academics and clergy publicly questioned the Catholic position, claiming the pill offered a morally responsible alternative to the rhythm method. One of John's first acts as pope was to assemble an advisory commission to study the issue.

The pope died before the six-man advisory group met, but they went ahead under the direction of Pope Paul VI. They failed to arrive at a conclusion after the first round of discussion, so more members were added. Over the next five years, they met many times. Each time, new members were added: scientists, sociologists, priests, professors, medical doctors, theologians, married couples, nuns, single men and women, and finally 14 cardinals and bishops—bringing the total to 72 participants.

During the long, arduous process, even the teaching of Aquinas and natural law were called into question. Some argued that famine and disease were also natural, yet science is allowed to intervene. But Church authority was at stake. How could it admit to being wrong on this matter without calling *all* of its teachings into question? Attempts were made to find a way around the sacred cow of tradition. One member suggested that perhaps Church thinking could be *reformulated* rather than changed.

Members of the council called for a new understanding, allowing that Church thought evolves over time. This was a fairly radical proposal in 1962—one that has been further developed since the Council. Although many questions were raised and much debate followed, they located one point of agreement: Love between a husband and wife was primary and should not take second place to any other consideration. In this the council finally cracked the age-old philosophy of Augustine and put a sizeable dent in dualism.

By the end of the process, the group issued two documents—a majority and a minority report. The majority report included the following points:

1. Artificial contraception could be allowed in some cases, while insisting that sex and marriage are properly oriented toward the procreation and education of children.
2. The priority should be what is good, overall, for a marriage, rather than focusing on the sex act alone.
3. Artificial contraception is not inherently evil, but its morality must be judged as it applies to specific situations.
4. These new conclusions were consistent with previous Church teaching because the focus continues to be *protection of the value of having and educating children* (which would be secured in either decision).
5. The attitude of entering marriage without any willingness to raise a family continued to be condemned.

The minority report moved to uphold tradition, maintaining that the Church *could not have erred* in previous declarations. Fearing a crack in the dam, the minority report stated concern that *if* the Church could err, the authority of the magisterium in other matters would be questioned and the trust of the faithful compromised, particularly regarding further sexual teachings.

Closing the Bedroom Door on the Pope

Shock reverberated throughout the Church when Pope Paul VI's encyclical *Humanae Vitae* was published. It rejected the majority report of the pope's own papal advisers and upheld the Church's ban on artificial birth control. *Humanae Vitae* didn't sit well either with the folks in the pews or with theologians all over the world. Although Vatican II forged a vision of bringing people together, the encyclical significantly widened the gap between Rome and the faithful. Conservative and progressive Catholics now set out resolutely on different paths. Polarization increased both among the laity and Church hierarchy. The always precarious relationship between theologians and the Vatican has grown more toxic since that time.

Humanae Vitae signaled a rejection by the pope of the emerging vision of Church as community. It dealt a serious blow to collegiality, and initiated the buildup of papal power that has characterized the last 40 years. In acting autocratically, the pope essentially invalidated many years of difficult work by the committee appointed to advise him. It was a cavalier misuse of power and a setback for mutual respect. Andrew Greeley's Chicago-based National Opinion Research Center reported a dramatic loss of credibility and of financial contributions as a direct result of this decision. It is estimated that the Church lost one-third of its membership.

Although the issue of birth control has great personal importance for all married couples, on a global scale it takes on even more significance. Over the last 40 years, the survival of whole populations of African people has become a serious challenge as they confront the rapidly growing AIDS epidemic. The Catholic hierarchy, both to maintain face and preserve the myth that it is never wrong, is forced to continue to oppose contraception even when confronted by the AIDS catastrophe. This is seen as a scandal by much of the rest of the world. It casts an even greater shadow on Catholic credibility than changing Church teaching would do.

Catholics have a deep respect for the clergy. Despite the lingering aura of papal grandiosity, people still hold the pope in high esteem, even if they personally disagree with some of his theological positions. But universal education and spreading democracy have removed some of the

157

awe. The defining crack in people's unquestioned loyalty to their Church leaders came with *Humanae Vitae*, when Catholics firmly locked the bedroom door on the pope.

From the Moment of Conception

The Catholic Church supports an absolute ban on abortion. Most Catholics are against abortion in theory; but many realize that in a less than perfect world, there might be mitigating circumstances. Since 1973, when the U.S. Supreme Court upheld a woman's right to control her body over the right of a fetus, Catholics have been the major voice opposing this law. Where some Catholics disagree is over the absolutism of the Church's ban, which includes cases of rape or saving the life of a pregnant woman. This stand is based on the belief that the soul of a new human is present *from the moment of conception.*

Although experts still disagree about exactly when it could be assumed that the life of a new soul has begun, as opposed to the potential for a new soul, the Catholic Church's "Declaration on Procured Abortion," written in 1974, states: "In reality, respect for human life is called for from the time that the process of generation begins. From the time that the ovum is fertilized, a life is begun which is neither that of the father nor of the mother; it is, rather, the life of a new human being with his or her own growth. It would never be made human if it were not human already."

Some theologians call for a more person-centered approach to moral decision-making and more sensitivity toward the complexities people face. Sadly, the credibility lost by the Church in the case of contraception has dulled the clarity of its voice in the complex issues related to abortion.

A Womb of One's Own

Beverly Harrison, professor of Christian ethics at Union Theological Seminary, believes the real agenda behind the Vatican's ban on abortion is not merely preserving life, but controlling women's sexuality. She points out examples in the laws of the Church that excommunicate a woman for having an abortion, whereas murder—including nuclear holocaust—does not carry the same penalty.

Harrison charges that lack of discussion on abortion betrays the Church's negative opinion of women—feeling that the Church's position makes the fertilized egg the legal moral peer of a woman. Harrison, as well as many other men and women, see the Catholic prohibition as another result of being under patriarchal rule—in this case, men who are many times removed from women's real lives make decisions for them. The idea of celibate men who have a history of misogyny focusing so much energy on women's reproductive life to the exclusion of forming any other relationship with them seems bizarre and disturbing to a growing number of Catholics. Harrison adds that the Vatican attitude is based on the assumption that women cannot be trusted to make honorable decisions and that only male-made laws and male-controlled funding can make women responsible and moral about their reproduction. (For more on this topic and other ethical issues, go to www.religion-online.org.)

Riddled with Inconsistency

Daniel Maguire, professor of moral theology at Marquette University, finds the Vatican's absolutist approach to abortion "abhorrent." He takes the "male-dominated liberal Catholic press" to task for not doing their job in reporting the degree of dissension around the issue. He believes that this has resulted in the appearance of a monolithic Catholic position on abortion, which he says isn't the case.

Maguire points out that the Catholic Church has the ability to influence elections and legislative and judicial decisions, including specific instances such as denying abortion funding for poor women. The general public is affected in those communities in which Catholic hospitals are the only health care facilities. The reproductive rights of people living in such communities are curtailed when their hospital is restricted by the Church's *conservative* view on abortion and other reproductive issues such as tubal ligation and contraception—views that reflect a particular politic.

Maguire believes that only a minority of Catholic theologians would argue that *all* abortions are immoral, though many will not speak out on the subject for fear of losing their academic positions. He objects to the absolutist tone of the abortion declaration and compares it to the Vatican's statement on the possibility of ending the world through nuclear war: "Distinct moral options coexist as legitimate expressions of Christian choice." Even the issue of nuclear war, Maguire remarks, is framed with the possibility of different Christian approaches—a nuance severely lacking in the Church's position on abortion.

The Seamless Garment

In 1983, Cardinal Joseph L. Bernardin of Chicago proposed linking many moral issues into a consistent moral ethic to be applied across the spectrum. This would involve abortion, capital punishment, modern warfare, euthanasia, and socioeconomic issues of food and shelter for all people. His approach honors the interrelationship of human social concerns and the need for life to be respected at all junctures. Bernardin believed a Catholic ethic could not support contradictory responses to different issues, such as saying no to abortion but yes to capital punishment or war. His theory is called the "consistent ethic" or "seamless garment" approach—a reference to Christ's garment that was said to be seamless.

Most Catholics probably find themselves in agreement with other mainstream religious traditions in wanting as few legal abortions as possible without treading on women's rights and without making it necessary for them to risk their life by attempting self-induced or back-alley abortions. Most recognize that abortion is not a good solution to unwanted pregnancy. However, given the limitations of our current personal and societal development, it might be the best we can do right now. Those working for a solution look at the larger social picture and realize that women face a variety of experiences different from one another and different from men. Economics, coerced sexual relations, or rape—even within marriage—are among the many factors that enter into the process of discernment.

If society removes the choice of abortion, it must address the other conditions that make abortion an imperative. Issues around the workplace, such as hiring and firing practices, job advancement, insurance and health care coverage, and child care are just some of the aspects that must be confronted. If society were to remove abortion as an option, it must first resolve the problems that make abortion a compelling choice in our culture. A comprehensive moral and social strategy would take into account not only how the law treats fetuses, but also how it treats mothers.

Although the pro-life movement agrees that helping the unborn requires helping mothers, the difficulties in effecting this ideal in this culture have not been resolved. Making unwanted pregnancy, abortion, and related issues a primary focus and creating the dialog to move society toward making deep changes will be a long-range task. Some pro-life people say that society won't make the necessary changes until the abortion option is closed. Pro-choice proponents say deep societal problems accompany the abortion issue and must be addressed first. The basis for agreement is present—both groups want to see better conditions for mothers and children and eliminate the *need* for abortion. Without their mutual cooperation, any satisfactory end to the social conflict over legal abortion is hard to envision.

The Right to Dissent

According to Charles Curran (see Chapter 6), the main challenge moral theologians face today in forming a Catholic sexual ethic is the right to dissent. Sexual ethics did not get the expected overhaul at Vatican II. Church teaching still relies heavily on the natural law principles of Aquinas, and is still influenced by Augustine, drawing on some very antiquated ideas about gender and biology. Because the Church has declared its position on key problems without allowing for debate among the bishops or consulting theologians and ethicists, and because dissenters are being openly disciplined, the matter is as good as locked in the Vatican vault. The question then becomes: Is it possible for the hierarchy to allow dissent in these areas? Can these decisions be changed?

Reasons cited by Curran for Rome's reluctance to change official teachings or allow dissent are the "patriarchal nature" of the Catholic Church. Its teaching on sexuality has excluded women from any kind of significant decision-making role, although the issues have the most direct effect on women. Curran believes that the Church's desire to control others, and its unease with sex in general, also contribute. However, the strongest impediment to the hierarchy changing its mind is its understanding of the magisterial role as teacher of *the truth*.

The Vatican bases the authority of that teaching role directly on the guidance of the Holy Spirit. Curran asks: "Could the Holy Spirit ever permit the hierarchical teaching office to be wrong in a matter of such great import in the lives of so many Christians? The role of the Church and of its officially commissioned leaders is to mediate the salvific word and work of Jesus through the presence of the Spirit. Could the hierarchical teaching role actually hinder and hurt the people it is supposed to help?"

The Church, then, is fearful of losing credibility by changing its mind. So it tries to silence dissenters. Ironically, it is the dissenters who are actually attempting to rescue the credibility of the Catholic Church by helping it modify its position. Curran reminds all that "the primary teacher in the Church remains the Holy Spirit—and no one has a monopoly on the Holy Spirit."

Prayer: A Potent Aphrodisiac

In light of the previous discussion, it might seem logical that Catholics would be terribly inhibited about sex. The popular cultural stereotype is indeed that Catholics and repressed sexuality are synonymous. Not so, says Andrew Greeley in his book, *Sex, the Catholic Experience*. His studies show that many Catholic couples have enviable sex lives, surpassing their Protestant neighbors in every aspect he measured.

So what is the difference between the hierarchy and regular Catholics? How can Catholic couples enjoy a guilt-free marriage bed while Church authorities are still sleeping with St. Augustine? One reason is that everyday Catholics don't depend on Rome for their sexual instruction or moral decision-making; they rely on their instincts and private consciences. Another reason is that attitudes about love and marriage are transmitted through what Greeley calls "popular tradition," which is derived from family and culture, stories, gatherings, rituals, and ceremonies that accompany marriage. And, of course, the sacrament of marriage itself connects to ancient and subconscious patterns in the culture since time began. Greeley describes some such customs as barely Christianized versions of paganism—such as blessing the bride, groom, and marriage bed to assure a vigorous and pleasing experience.

Greeley notes a positive correlation between couples who share prayer life together and the sexual satisfaction of their marriage. The couple's love reflects their personal relationships to God. To paraphrase Greeley, intimacy with God creates intimacy in marriage. Daily prayer then becomes the difference in sexual fulfillment—given that the image of God is a loving and warm image.

In Conclusion

All religions tend to define morality for their followers, creating a code of behavior that meets the norm established by the community. However, a couple of patterns began to develop early in Catholicism that haunted it throughout its history and continue to be the source of difficulty between leaders and people today. Many such issues arise from the dualistic understanding that pits the life of the spirit, or Godliness, against the life of the body—looked at as the source of evil. This false understanding of creation then gets played out in many ways. One way is through the disturbing focus the Church places on personal sexual sins, to the exclusion of many other agendas. Understanding history and an awareness of culture depend on a process of reflection. It isn't fair to hold the practices of one time in history responsible for the practices of another time. Although the Church is in the business of reflection, it continues to repeat the same thoughts over and over, with no adequate new interpretation or insight. This defective practice gets passed off as infallibility informed by the Holy Spirit. Overall, Catholics get along very well when it comes to sex, and they do it by not paying too much attention to instructions from Rome.

Chapter 9

Midnight in the Garden: Cultural Patterns of Abuse

The treatment of children might be one of the great double standards of all time. On one hand, everybody loves children. They're cute, winsome, and innocent. Adults shed their reserve and inhibitions when a child appears on the scene. They make nonsensical, childish sounds—the adults do—and pass the child around; and their cooing is a vote of confidence in love, marriage, and the future of the world. Even after the cooing stops, the child is treasured just for being a child.

Once upon a time, old people were revered for their wisdom, but too often modern civilization—particularly in the United States—is eager to get them out of sight, relegating them to nursing homes. But the child is treasured just for being young. In a world where nearly everything is measured by money, being young is still a value—a reason to be cared for. This is not only because of pervasive love, but also the child's potential, his or her promise for the future of the family and the race. To the extent possible (and often to excess), food, clothes, time, effort, and especially love are lavished on our children. That's on the one hand.

On the other hand, a dirty little secret of the ages is how badly so many children are treated and how hierarchical power affects those on the bottom rung of the ladder.

An Enduring Legacy

Volumes of documentation reveal a history of worldwide child sexual abuse. Although public opinion told us there was a universal taboo on incest, there has been instead a near-universal practice of it. The further back in history the research goes, the more crushing is the evidence of wholesale cruelty to children, including infanticide, ritualized beatings, and sexual abuse by parents and caretakers.

Progress toward a social ethic that would protect children from this horrendous plight is both very recent and also far from universal. Almost from the beginning of recorded history, children have been bought and sold. But this is not just ancient history: Trafficking in children is now almost a global business. Populations—that are victims of war, of economic sanctions, of greedy dictators, of social breakdowns—are constantly forced, in our time, into life-and-death situations in which sacrificing one's own children to sexual or other slavery is the price of survival. Such decisions, however reluctantly made, assure the daily killing, maiming, molestation, and starvation of children all over the world.

Sexual Abuse of Children Today

Such abuse does not happen only in faraway places. The U.S. Department of Health and Human Services not long ago released a survey estimating that child abuse and neglect in the United States nearly doubled during the seven years between 1986 and 1993. The report estimated that the number of abused and neglected children increased from 1.4 million in 1986 to more than 2.8 million in 1993. The statistics do not make clear whether increases signify a rise in abuse or new and better gathering of statistical data.

In the United States and Canada, scientific studies, based on lengthy interviews, report that 30 percent of men and 40 percent of women remember having been sexually molested during childhood. (Molestation is here defined as actual genital contact, not just exposure.) About half of these were directly incestuous, with family members, whereas the other half involved caretakers in at least 80 percent of the cases. Figures were based on the conscious recollection of memories only (that is, details were recalled without psychotherapeutic assistance, which some experts find questionable).

Children fare much worse in non-Western nations. In India, for example, masturbation of children is an accepted practice—a means of inducing sleep for the child or of venting parental frustration. Sexual intercourse between parents and children, as well as siblings and extended family, is still believed in some cultures to be necessary to curb the extreme sexual appetites of children. Laws against the long established tradition of child marriage were passed as recently as 1929, over opposition by men who insisted early marriage was necessary because girls were perceived to be particularly sexual and must be married early lest they seduce adults. Indian mothers often supported early marriages to protect daughters from incestuous attacks by the father and male siblings.

India and Asia

According to the New York City–based Institute for Psychohistory, throughout the Indian subcontinent, incestuous marriage between fathers and daughters, between mothers and sons, between siblings, and even between grandparents and their grandchildren is still practiced. At about the age of 6, children are often placed in sex dormitories where they are initiated into intercourse by older youth and men under threat of gang rape. They then spend the rest of their childhood in such an institution.

The same report shows similar institutionalized rape occurs in China, where pederasty, castration of boys for use as eunuchs, marriage of young girls, and widespread boy and girl prostitution are common. The ancient practice of foot binding, only recently abandoned, was performed for sexual purposes—the girl for years underwent extremely painful crushing of the bones of her feet because men found the aesthetic benefits of such mutilation sexually arousing. Girls who did not undergo this crippling practice were not considered as sexually pleasing, were therefore less acceptable for marriage, and were often condemned to a life of prostitution.

Childhood in contemporary Japan still includes masturbation by mothers to put crying babies to sleep—a practice prevalent in England until modern time. Japanese parents often sleep with their children, having intercourse with them—in some cases, from early childhood until the child is 10 or 15. One recent Japanese study found daughters over age 16 sleeping with their fathers more than 20 percent of the time (Institute for Psychohistory).

The Near East

The sexual use of children in the Near East is as common as in the Far East. Institutionalized forms of pedophilia are extensively documented, including child marriage, child concubinage, temple prostitution of both boys and girls, parent-child marriage (among certain sects), sibling marriage (common among Egyptians), sex slavery, ritualized pederasty, and child prostitution. Masturbation in infancy is said to be necessary to increase the size of the penis, and older siblings are reported to play with the genitals of babies for hours at a time. Mutual masturbation, fellatio, and anal intercourse are also said to be common among children—the older boys using younger children as sex objects.

Age-old devaluation of females results in higher numbers of girls being used incestuously than the number of boys. One report found that 80 percent of Near Eastern women surveyed recalled having been forced into sex by older brothers, cousins, uncles, and teachers as early as three years of age. The girls rarely complain because protests usually result in severe punishment. A recent survey of Egyptian girls and women showed 97 percent of uneducated families and 66 percent of educated families still practiced clitoridectomy—the cutting off of all or part of a girl's clitoris as a social custom or right of passage—and this practice is increasing, according to United Nations reports. It is estimated that as many as 74 million females have undergone genital mutilation.

Many psychologists and other experts in human sexuality believe clitoridectomy and circumcision are both sexual mutilations, and categorize them as incest. The experts base this on circumcision ceremonies that are often accompanied by orgiastic dancing and intercourse following the ritual. Ceremonies are presided over by a traveling circumciser, who is sometimes accompanied by prostitutes, as it is widely understood that observing the ritual results in sexual arousal.

If one accepts the position that circumcision is sexual abuse, one is forced to conclude a practically universal form of incest is taken for granted. Its religious roots are in Judaism, but it is practiced routinely in Christianity as a medical procedure. Circumcision has recently begun to be questioned in the United States, with increasing skepticism expressed by medical practitioners who testify that it is seldom required.

This lends support to the claim that it has been unwittingly practiced primarily as a form of ritual abuse. There is no indication that the practice of clitoridectomy is anything but sexual abuse.

A Horrific Menu of Abuse

Many societies practiced child sacrifice in one form or another from antiquity until quite recently. In a large cemetery discovered in Carthage, more than 20,000 urns had been deposited between 400 and 200 B.C.E. These contained the bones of children sacrificed by parents who often would make a vow to kill their next child if the gods would grant them a favor. Some urns contained the bones of stillborn babies along with the bones of two year olds, indicating that if the promised child was not born alive, an older child was also killed to satisfy the promise.

Early Christianity

History supplies ample evidence that Greek and Roman children lived in the constant shadow of sexual abuse. Greek stage comedies routinely included scenes of little girls being raped. Plutarch (*c.* 45–125 C.E.)—a priest at the temple of Delphi, as well as a renowned philosopher whose works were widely read in Rome—published an essay that included suggestions on the proper kind of person to whom a father should give his son for the man's personal purposes, which were widely understood to include sodomy. Young boys between the age of seven and puberty were regularly handed over by their parents for the pleasure of male friends. Child brothels offering sex slavery prospered in nearly every city in antiquity. Petronius (*c.* 66 C.E.) produced a literary portrait of first-century Roman society, including the practice of adults fondling the private parts of boys. And Tiberius, a second-century Roman emperor, was said to have taught children, whom he called his little fishes, to play between his legs while he was in his bath.

Christianity gradually succeeded in eradicating the most serious practices of child abuse, but others endured. With the advent of communal Christian life, children were sent to the local monastery or nunnery to be used as servants, which often meant sexual service as well. The business of selling children prospered. The refusal of parents to raise their own legitimate children continued through the nineteenth century.

Children were routinely abandoned to foundling homes at birth. Some-times they were picked up by their families at about 5 or 6 years, but many died before that age. Despite advances toward ending direct killing of children, most other childrearing practices of antiquity continued in the Middle Ages. The sodomizing of boys—even in monasteries—continued to be widespread, and seemingly accepted by society.

Child beating continued throughout the history of Christianity, often taking on religious overtones as it was feared children suffered demonic possession and might be "changelings"—a belief held by St. Augustine and expounded later in the *Malleus Maleficarum*, which noted that changelings could be recognized by their howling. Thrashing children was common; instruments for "beating the hell" out of them abounded. Whippings contained more than a hint of eroticism because they were often focused near the genitals. The practice went almost without dissent; attempts at reform were directed only toward prevention of death.

"Spare the Rod and Spoil the Child"

By the thirteenth century, the practice of giving away young children to monasteries had ended. The first disapproval of pedophilia found its way into childrearing tracts. There was no longer the worry that children might be innately evil, but the understanding lingered that they should be carefully watched. "Hitting" and other less intrusive practices were employed for the purpose of "breaking a child's will," an integral part of proper childrearing.

An underlying eroticism continued to be played out—often in the form of punishment and often directed toward natural functions such as toilet training, bedwetting, and masturbation. Pediatrics and educational philosophy born of the Enlightenment promoted kinder treatment of chil-dren. The humanistic, religious, and political revolutions we associate with early modern times brought reforms. However, "spare the rod and spoil the child" remains standard procedure in many parts of society even today.

Nineteenth-century reformers who opposed the abusing of boys in schools were often found suspect by parents who believed such treat-ment hadn't hurt them and therefore wouldn't hurt their children either. Early attempts at child labor laws directed at lessening atrocious working conditions met with strong resistance. Those who thought children could be raised with kindness were considered everything from unrealistic visionaries to socialists.

Today, it is widely accepted that childhood trauma can have serious consequences. Adolescents with a history of sexual abuse are much more likely than average to engage in sexual behavior that puts them at risk for HIV infection. There is typically an increase in drug and alcohol consumption, as well as crime, and beyond that the likelihood of continuing the cycle of abuse into the next generation.

The penny has finally dropped. The wisdom of tackling child abuse is apparent in statistics that show trillions of dollars spent annually on the effects of social violence in terms of law enforcement and other consequences.

Today, there are an estimated 60 million survivors of childhood sexual abuse in the United States. The task of reversing this pattern is huge. But there is a growing body of information to show that education works.

Perceptions and Misconceptions

Although during the whole history of humankind no one seemed to want to study child abuse, a wide range of new efforts is now afoot to study the psychology of pedophilia. Many theories are being explored to understand what happened in the past and how to prevent it from happening in the future.

A logical step toward clarifying the problem would seem to be to profile a "typical" sex abuser. But such a profile is elusive because there are many contributing factors. Furthermore, the shame and contempt surrounding the subject results in reluctance on the part of perpetrators to reveal much about themselves even to a therapist. Experts say, for example, that people who have been abused as children frequently become abusers as adults. Yet not all who have suffered abuse go on to abuse. Studies have found inherited conditions exist, which affect hormone levels that then play a part in creating the physical and psychological profile of an abuser. Some studies suggest that no correlation exists between sexual abusers and levels of education, religious preference, vocation, or income. Other research shows, however, that would-be child abusers tend to pursue vocations that would give them access to children.

Tribal Laws

Similarly, there is disagreement about the subtle role religion might play in supporting abuse. For example, authoritarian religious systems that promote unquestioned male authority are known to contribute to a power inequity that easily crosses the line into abuse. Many experts say such a power dynamic is itself abusive.

This problem, as we've seen, did not leap full-blown into existence to make headlines in recent years. Our Old Testament ancestors dealt with it. There is, for example, the shocking little story of Lot and his daughters in Genesis 19:30–28. It seems unlikely that the daughters would conspire to get their father drunk and sleep with him in an attempt to become pregnant.

Not every culture coped with sexual abuse in the same manner. Indigenous American cultures handled sex abusers swiftly and decisively, according to Lakota author and lecturer Charlotte Black Elk. In a presentation in San Francisco called "Stories of Our Grandmothers," she talked about the inherited culture before European values began to affect tribal practices. The tribe had an accepted way of handling sex abuse, as well as the abuse of women. Before being awarded adult status by tribal elders, women were trained in every skill necessary for tribal survival. As the young women matured, they were awarded different knives, each of which had a specific function. When the elders decided a woman had achieved all the other prerequisites, she was awarded a special knife and charged with a unique responsibility: protecting all children and women from abuse. If she saw any man violating the tribal laws in this regard, she was obliged to kill him. Tribal wisdom taught zero tolerance.

Australian aborigines likewise had their way of handling child sexual abuse, particularly between a father and daughter. When a girl entered the sexual time of her life, there was a ritual enactment of incest in which both recognized that such thoughts and feelings exist and, at the same time, that they cannot be acted upon. The ritual involved the whole clan as witness. The young girl lay on the ground with her legs spread apart, and the father drove a lance into the earth between her legs. The ceremony acknowledged the impulse that arises from the unconscious mind and simultaneously insisted on the absolute tribal taboo regarding incest.

Child Sexual Abuse Study Is New

The scientific study of sexual abuse is relatively new. Because much of the research began as recently as the early 1980s, it isn't yet clear whether sexual abuse of children is increasing in the culture or whether awareness of it has increased.

Unfortunately, it seems to be the nature of sexual abuse to perpetuate itself. Most experts agree that abusers don't usually stop with one episode of sexually acting out, but usually repeat the offense with multiple victims. The current estimate is that each child abuser averages sexual contact with 117 victims. If it is true that having been abused contributes to the likelihood of passing the abuse on to others—which is the belief of many in the field of psychology and counseling—and each abuser infects an average of 117 children, child abuse is bound to become an ever-bigger problem unless dramatic steps are taken.

Incest has traditionally been defined as sexual activity between two people too closely related genetically for such a relationship. That emphasis on the genetic aspect fails to consider the severe emotional and spiritual consequences of the act. Today, experts broaden the definition to include sexual activity between a child and adults in a position of trust similar to the parental relationship. In her address to the U.S. Conference of Catholic Bishops in June 2002, "The Experience of the Victim of Sexual Abuse: A Reflection," Mary Gail Frawley-O'Dea described the current violations against the young by priests as incest: "Make no mistake about it: The violation of a child or adolescent by a priest is incest." It is all the more grievous because it is inflicted by "a man whom the child is taught from birth to trust above everyone else in his life, to trust

173

second only to God."

Sorting Out the Terminology

Terminology is often used carelessly both in private conversation and the media. Pedophilia is the term most often used in describing adult sexual activity with a prepubescent child. We lack precise terminology to describe having sexual relations with 15- or 16-year-olds—which is considered abusive and criminal. The term that comes closest is pederasty—however, pederasty is archaic and usually describes sexual activity with males only. This has led to the term often being used (incorrectly) to describe homosexual activity.

Ephebophilia describes the attraction to boys at the time of puberty. In recent reporting of sexual abuse of children by the news media, most have tended to lump all the variables together under pedophilia. This is not wrong in the strictest sense. However, when an adult has sex with a 16-year-old, society levies a different judgment than when the crime involves a much younger child. Treatment follows a different protocol, and recovery of the young person and also the abuser is different than with the more conservative definition of pedophilia. Sexual abuse at any age has devastating effects and requires treatment. When sexual abuse begins at a very early age, the results are more damaging; recovery is more difficult and takes a longer time. Adults engaging in sexual activity with prepubescent children—particularly the very young—seldom are treatable. That is not the case with pubescent children up to adult.

There are two types of pedophiles. One is exclusively attracted to children; the other is attracted to children as well as adults. There is same-gender pedophilia—a man attracted to boys or a woman attracted to girls. There is also opposite gender and bigender pedophilia.

According to available statistics, the sexual abuser is 10 times more likely to be male than female. And the abused child is six times more likely to be a female than a male. Sexual abuse is simply and broadly defined as any use of a child for sexual gratification. A five-year difference in age is usually applied when defining sexual abuse between siblings. Sexual exploration between children of similar age and experience is a normal and necessary part of growing up as a healthy sexual being.

When adults "catch" children in sexual exploration and treat it insensitively, it can be sexually abusive and result in psychological trauma, but does not necessarily make that adult a sex abuser in the way we have come to understand it.

Some experts say that many men are attracted to adolescents but don't act on their impulses, and that does not necessarily imply they are pedophiles. The lines of distinction between what is normal and acceptable sexual activity blur as a child matures and reaches the age of legal consent. According to Catholic Church law, the age of consent for heterosexuals is 16 rather than the legal age of 18 that is the common standard in this country.

Shrouded in Secrecy

Most cultures publicly agree that sexual abuse of children is deplorable. It is, therefore, usually shrouded in secrecy and misunderstandings. For many people, it is incomprehensible. Some deny that it even exists— sometimes even believing it to be the fabrication of children's imaginations. Others attempt to distance themselves from it by insisting that it exists only among certain ethnic groups or particular socioeconomic categories.

Those who have worked closely with children know differently. Teachers, parents, psychologists, counselors, police, and ministers (to name just a few) know about the widespread, nondiscriminating nature of pedophilia firsthand as they experience assisting individuals and families—and no family, high or low, is immune to its devastating consequences.

"How is it possible to have been abused and not remember it until you're 30 or 40?" many people ask. Amnesia surrounding trauma is nature's way of protecting children from a shock or shocks that would overwhelm the central nervous system. Sexual abuse is one such trauma that often results in temporary amnesia—usually lifting sometime during adult years. At the time of the abuse, the brain releases epinephrine—a stress hormone that creates a trance state and amnesia. In the trance state, the child can experience a sensation of leaving the body—even actually seeing the incident from above. The hypnotic state provides a degree of anesthesia. Epinephrine also creates amnesia—although nothing is ever really forgotten. The memory resides in the subconscious mind and will be recalled at a later time. The results of the trauma, however, do manifest and persist throughout childhood, teenage years, and adulthood. The results are devastating, and recovery is a long, slow process.

How Could We Let It Happen?

The history of child abuse is a sad indicator of how slow human progress has been toward basic human decency, not to mention Christian charity. Much of this cruelty took place even as a variety of world religions were supposedly devoting all their energies toward elevating this life on Earth to make it worthy for eternity. Hinduism, Islam, Judaism, Christianity, Buddhism, Sikhism, and a handful of others have transformed the world in many ways. Yet, they seem to have done little to tame raw human nature.

Most of all, perhaps, religion has failed thus far in protecting the most vulnerable of life's pilgrims. The focus here is primarily on Christianity.

The Church: A Window to the Cultural

Jesus Christ, who loved everyone, had a special fondness for children. "Suffer the little children to come unto me" (Mark 10:14) is the classical New Testament rendering of his attitude. This, it turns out, was no guarantee that children would be treasured—he loved women, too, but that does not seem to have much improved their lot either inside or outside the Church in the centuries that followed. Still, if one is looking for an endorsement for children, Jesus is as good as endorsements get.

Although it is risky to generalize, Catholic preaching, teaching, and theorizing has not concentrated much on children for their own sakes. Overall, they were viewed rather as an appendage of the family or the community. Theology seemed willing to protect them rather than cherish them. The overwhelming role played by celibates and virgins in the Church might have something to do with this.

Yet that's not the whole story, either. No organization on Earth, ever or anywhere, has done as much for children as the Catholic Church. It has looked after orphans since it first got organized. It has protected and rescued the most vulnerable, helped feed the hungry, and educated the poor, as well as the rich, from the barbaric Dark Ages to today's inner cities.

Sure, the Church regularly fell short. It was always tainted by the mores of the times. Tales abound of what the mean sisters did by way of corporal punishment to little angels (possibly yourself) not so long ago. Yet there existed and persevered an enormous energy and will to good, amid otherwise drab lives, and the world would have been an intellectually, emotionally, and even physically more impoverished place were it not for Catholicism.

Much of this was taken for granted in good times and forgotten in bad times. Yet it was appreciated deep down. Most people respected and many loved the local nuns and priests (bishops and higher-ups were usually too remote for such sentiments). Above all, people trusted their Church ministers. In a frequently double-crossing world, the Church was a refuge, even an oasis. The young priest or nun was a friend who took kids camping. Catholicism had a decidedly sunny side.

It's not hard to understand, then, that people would be incredulous when pedophilia stories began to surface; that they would give the priest and the Church the benefit of the doubt. To its dishonor, the Church played on this incredulity all too long. But it could not keep its dark secret away from the daylight forever. Once the floodgates opened, there was no stopping the torrent of anger and recriminations heaped on the priest pedophiles and the prelates who covered up for them.

Yet there is an odd anomaly here. The miles of newsprint and interminable hours of television seldom bother to mention that priests commit pedophilia only about as much as others do. Occasionally, cases from other denominations get mentioned, but the victims don't seem to sue as much as Catholics do. This might be because the Catholic Church has deeper pockets. The scorn directed at the Catholic Church might have something to do with previous arrogance—real or imagined. At an institutional level, Catholicism has a rich heritage of triumphalism and self-righteousness, and people do like to see the high and haughty get their comeuppance.

What few in the media seem to bother to investigate or report is the pandemic proportions of child abuse in the general population—in this country and nearly everywhere else—at this time and always. This is the great untold story. If there can be a silver lining to so dark a cloud as clerical pedophilia, it might yet be the uncovering of the enormity of child abuse in society in general.

Not Only the Children, but Women as Well

For several years, complaints drifted around the world—from what used to be termed mission countries, but are now called developing nations and from Latin America to Africa—about a novel manifestation of sexual abuse. From almost two dozen countries, there were stories of priests using their power and status to demand and gain sexual favors from girls and nuns.

Detailed reports had been brought to the Vatican, which for years had done nothing about them. The reports circulated privately from country to country; then other reports were added. Mostly, they were compiled by sisters who were faced with a fierce dilemma: They would bring down great wrath on themselves, their communities, and their mission work by going public with their scandalous story; but by staying silent, they would be allowing a great wrong to go unattended. Eventually, the *National Catholic Reporter* and other media made the scandal public.

In Africa in particular (on other continents, there were and are variations on the theme), Catholic priests, many of whom practice celibacy only in name, were fearful of getting AIDS from the prostitutes who traditionally met their sexual needs. One of their strategies was to persuade or pressure local sisters to have sex with them. The sisters were presumed to be "safe."

Even more safe were secondary school girls. They were often naïve and easily intimidated by the prestige and authority that a priest represented in such a culture. And sometimes they were in a special, ironic bind. A girl who wanted to became a nun (in many African countries, there is presently a surge of vocations to the religious life) needed a letter of recommendation from her local priest. The priest was happy to oblige, but only if the girl would do him a favor in return. If the girl then became pregnant, not only would the religious community reject her, so would her family and village, and she would be left to raise her child as a disgraced outcast.

Even more shocking are the many cases of rape by priests. As was the case with the recent sexual abuse cases, when the crimes were re-ported to bishops and to Rome, they fell on deaf ears. According to a young African nun recovering from a rape by her parish priest three years ago, AIDS is not the whole problem. In an April 6, 2001, article by Pamela Schaffer, the young woman goes on to say that the problem is the African culture, where men have rights over women, including sexual rights. Often illiterate, women are completely dependent on men—in this case, the priests—for money. The Church has not changed these patterns. Nuns are not educated and do not study theology. Therefore, they have to rely on whatever the priest tells them. The article goes on to say that bishops are no better than the priests—they control all the finances, and whoever has the purse strings decides everything.

Power inequity and sexual abuse is an age-old problem. For the girls as well as for the religious communities, the problem was compounded by the fact that talking about such matters was virtually taboo. There was no one for a girl to turn to. The nuns had a similar problem. In a March 16, 2001, article, John L. Allen states that documentation of sexual abuse goes back to 1988. In a 1994 report, a leadership group comprised of diocesan women was rejected by the local bishop after complaining that 29 sisters had been impregnated by diocesan priests. With the help of a group of missionaries, a report was sent to Rome in which the women's cries for help from the constant harassment by priests went unheard.

When a sister became pregnant, she was usually dismissed from her congregation. The priest was merely moved to another district.

In one particularly macabre case, a priest insisted that the nun he impregnated have an abortion. She died from the procedure. The priest officiated at her requiem Mass.

Sexual abuse of women by priests has been uncovered in 23 coun-tries, including the United States. The majority of cases are in Africa. It is extremely important to point out that not all priests are like this, whether in Africa or elsewhere. It is also important to point out that, despite years of reports and pleas for help, Rome was doing nothing at all about this mega scandal—until the story broke. Now, several Church bodies are looking into it.

Sex, Celibacy, and All That

Stories such as these, however sad, should also be reminders of the altruistic and often heroic work that dedicated priests, nuns, and bishops do all over the world. But now, it is midnight in that garden as well.

The hierarchy of the Catholic Church has taken the position that celibacy is not the problem behind the clergy sexual abuse scandals. It maintains that priests are no more likely than other groups of people to engage in this kind of misconduct. Priests are, however, the only pedophiles who profess to practice celibacy. This is an odd wrinkle. As the focus on the sex scandals refused to go away, mainline Catholics began to question the integrity of the practice of mandatory celibacy. When news of the scandals focused on the Boston archdiocese in early 2002, the people's intuition screamed to look at celibacy. When one hears of the bishops' refusal even to look at celibacy, intuition is joined by suspicion.

Author Alice Walker's audacious "womanist" woman, who is always "wanting to know more than is good for her," can then be heard knocking at the door. "Why would you approach a problem as devastating and complex as pedophilia by closing some of the doors?" the womanist question goes. Because the majority of priests involved were in good standing in the Church—which means that they were presumed to be practicing celibacy—and because they were nevertheless having sex with young boys, celibacy is surely part of the mix. To rule it out raises suspicions. A more responsible approach might be: "We're going to take this organization apart and look at every aspect of it until we find out what's going on."

Celibacy is an awesome ideal that fascinates some people and confuses others. It's the mandatory aspect that seems most bothersome. Many single people are celibate, but this doesn't earn them a special place in their community. On reflection, then, imposed celibacy raises questions of power—who's forcing the celibacy, and why?

Canon law has this to say about celibacy:

*Clerics are obliged to observe perfect and perpetual conti-
nence for the sake of the kingdom of heaven and therefore are
obliged to observe celibacy, which is a special gift of God, by
which sacred ministers can adhere more easily to Christ with
an undivided heart and can more freely dedicate themselves to
the service of God and humankind (Canon
277 #1).*

The definition still embodies the implication that those who practice it
are better Christians than those whose hearts might be divided—between
loving a *person* and loving Christ. This might be valid if love were a limited resource.

If a person is called by God to lead a celibate life, we've heard from
Augustine and others that he or she will be given the grace to do it.
But when celibacy is demanded by the Church, is it the Church or God
bestowing the grace? This is just one of a long litany of troubling questions about clerical celibacy when it's not optional.

The Church responds with formidable arguments from Scripture, tradition, and canon law. The arguments are often impeccable. When persuasion breaks down, the bottom line remains: No one is forcing anyone to
become a priest. This cogent but ultimately ruthless response fails to take
into account the great numbers of men and women who don't feel particularly celibate, yet feel the urge to serve God and humanity within the
Catholic Church because few comparable opportunities are available for
doing so (never mind that there might be a supernatural vocation from
God into the bargain).

Logic might win the argument. What is needed is not a change of
mind but a change of heart. And in that department, intuition says that
the Church doesn't even come close.

The Priest Caught in the Middle

After the children, it is the average priest who has most suffered from a
celibacy burden he did not create and can't readily shake off. It is important to remember that the priests who have been so ignominiously paraded

in handcuffs on television were all old men. They entered the Church in a different era from ours. Most went into the seminary directly from high school, and many even went to seminary-type high schools. They embarked on this formidable life journey all afire with idealism. When flesh raised its rowdy voice, older priests assured them that grace would prevail. The older priests were heroes then—men who had labored through the heat of the day. If they could do it, it could be done. With God's help, everyone added as an afterthought—which must have made God wince every time he (or she) heard it. Thus, with more idealism than experience and with minimum psychological or spiritual preparation, yesterday's priest went to meet the beguiling, flattering, and tempting "outside" world in which girls could scarcely hide their admiration for this or that clerical "hunk" who had the true grit to give up everything and serve God alone.

Only when these young men left in droves did Church authorities take another look at their dysfunctional structures. Seminaries were transformed and then moved to the cities—where candidates could rub shoulders with temptation to test their mettle. Swarms of psychologists left no libido unturned.

Above all, the age of the candidate was adjusted. Let the young man joust with the world first. When he's an older young man or a younger middle-aged man, he will be in a much better place for evaluating God's call, which, truth to tell, is usually a faint call and nothing like that legend of St. Paul getting thrown from his steed.

The older vocation solution is too recent to evaluate its ultimate efficacy with confidence. But there are murmurings of concern. What was it about the world that made the late vocation want to turn his back on it, sort of? Why was he not yet married and more engaged with life? Might the priesthood be a refuge from some of life's vicissitudes? Might he be gay?

The Church is in a bind of its own making here. The gay issue is, at least, a public relations embarrassment waiting to happen. Centuries of its own theology and tradition forced the Church to the position that homosexuality is somehow a "disorder." On the other hand, a high proportion of new candidates to the priesthood are gay—in this and similar intimate areas, exact statistics are impossible to find. At one level, the hierarchy has no problem with homosexual priests—it is an open secret that there are gay bishops and cardinals right up to the highest echelons of the Church. There is also general agreement, without relying too much on stereotypes, that the gay temperament is well suited to the ritual, lifestyle, and caring ministry of the Church.

But at another level, there is the inconsistency of calling such men morally disordered. There are also widespread complaints about the emerging clerical culture, whether gay or straight: that it is fastidious and effete, snobbish, theologically and socially conservative; that it is ambitious and careerist.

The Church has deftly ducked most questions about these matters. But at the June 2002 meeting of bishops in Dallas, Bishop Wilton Gregory, president of the U.S. Bishops' Conference, did finally worry aloud lest the clerical culture become or be perceived to be a predominantly gay culture—a situation that would discourage others from embarking on the priesthood.

No matter what the Vatican might say to discourage the discussion of married priests or women priests, these considerations remind us that the priesthood is, as it has always been, a work in progress.

Best of Times, Worst of Times

Not for the first time in history, priestly morale is low. If some young priests are on the make, others are sincerely trying to fashion a life of integrity, service, and compassion. Older priests, who put in their hours year after year and who served and persevered, are haunted by questions of identity and whether the Church to which they gave such allegiance might turn out to be a house of cards. When all else fails, many resort to the hope that the Holy Spirit will take care of things, but who can be sure that the Spirit is not looking over its shoulder at those early days when a bunch of women first discovered that Jesus had risen from the dead and rushed off to update the men, who at the time were just fellow disciples and not yet a hierarchy?

More Than a Hint of Good Old Boy-ism

Typical Catholics are similarly puzzled. For one thing, they're not keen to put their hard-earned money in an envelope on Sunday knowing it will go, by a tortuous route, to pedophilia victims and armies of lawyers.

Typical Catholics look at the Church educating men—but not women—for 20 centuries to be something special: men who often speak several languages, study philosophy, theology, and the arts, often in the world's best universities; who enjoy a refined standard of living; and the respect (until now, at least) and even love of the community. Furthermore, these men are supposed to be privy to the whispering of the Holy Spirit. Yet they have not cracked the dualistic code of so long ago, haven't resolved elementary ways of being in the world, haven't resolved, for example, how men and women should be together in the world, or how priests and children should be together in the world.

The Church should scarcely be surprised, then, if many see priestly celibacy as an expression of the good old boy system that has long been a source of domination in society. This implies a wink and a nudge to the effect that celibacy isn't really mandatory in practice; that sex is forbidden only in theory; that chastity is an ideal toward which everyone is working, but of course no one ever gets there.

If there is a hint of truth in this suspicion, trust takes a beating. If the Church, that great ship of idealism, is leaking, all the other human efforts to make life better become suspect as well.

A Kinder, Gentler, Firmer Future

This takes us back to basics—as any discussion about religion must repeatedly do. The Church exists on Earth because civilization has advanced enough to allow religion to do as well as religion does; but it also exists because civilization isn't yet good enough to make religion superfluous. "Grimed with smears," as Francis Thompson wrote, we "stand amid the dust o' the mounded years." If so, we need to be able to embrace a broken-down, wounded Church because there will never be a perfect one.

So our lives as Church members become a balancing act. We need to cut the Church some slack—because, for one thing, we *are* the Church.

Liberal Catholics, especially, are like liberal Democrats: We expect too much from central government instead of taking destiny on our own shoulders and climbing the hill with it. In that case, we need to cut the priest (and the bishop and pope) some slack as well, plodding humans all, as unsure as the rest of us, behind all the posturing, about what is the right thing to do and what reception awaits us the first time we open our eyes after death.

To complete the balancing act, we must hold certain feet to the fire—first our own, the feet over which we have most control; then others, including bishops' and popes'. Happily (we might conclude), this is not just an indulgence on our part, but an obligation—part of our project to perfect the world.

There is no one magic way all this works in practice. But it seems safe to say that we will never regret giving others the benefit of the doubt. It is one of life's anomalies that the least fortunate are least likely to get the benefit of the doubt. Most of the denizens of death row don't get it—most were rejects from the start. Right now, not many pedophilia priests are getting it. This is not to condone what they did or feel less sympathy for their victims. Yet, behind the head-lines, the Catholic Church to which the whole cast of characters belong has always taught redemption and forgiveness.

It turns out, many pedophilia priests were themselves sexually abused in their youth. Willingly or not, they have made others pay a heavy price for those past traumas. They have in turn been dragged through shame and will pay a great price for years to come—it is said that even in prison pedophiles are regarded as the most degenerate inmates and treated accordingly by other inmates. The child molesters have also dragged the Church through shame. Some would say it dragged itself. Either way, it is a damaged institution.

It has been damaged before, people of faith respond. Yet it has survived: risen like a phoenix time and again. Some say that the Church is slow to learn lessons from its experience. Yet it has transformed itself over and over.

Like most human entities, the Church has been most successful (to human eyes, which are the only eyes we have) when it had humility to go with its great, multifaceted power. It might be better if its mission returned to bringing hope and help to those who suffer, with less emphasis on higher offices and bigger buildings. Presently, the Church has plenty of reason for humility. It has sinned against the community and needs to do penance. The Church has been a great defender of children before they are born. There is a huge opportunity, and obligation, to expand this mission: to the woman during the years before and after the conception; to the child during the precarious years after birth all the way to the grave.

Including Women Is the Safety Net

Several years ago, a bishop was asked why the Church didn't put more energy into working for peace and justice, and less on the private sexual lives of its members, especially its female members. He replied that until a child was safe in its mother's body, no other issue had any importance. This is devious rhetoric without logic. There are millions of ways to respond to it. Many children are not safe in their mother's womb because their mother is malnourished, overworked, or beaten. The child will enter that world of violence, possibly be sold into some kind of slavery, and the mother, more often than not, is powerless. She will be impregnated again and again. The safety of the mother's womb has not been secured in many parts of the world. It would be a worthy mission for the Church to make it so, everywhere.

It's been said that the sex scandals don't bother Rome much because the future of the Church is in the Third World. There is diabolical cynicism in that view, and one hopes that it isn't true. But it raises questions about the future of the Church in developing countries where millions are waiting in hope. What is the agenda of the Church as it casts its nets in the Third World? Is it going to convince those people that their bodies are something to be ashamed of? That women are inferior and must be kept in their place? And that children must obey, must be silent and invisible? Will these celibate men preach about the sin of birth control and demand more babies out of overburdened female bodies? Runaway population increases, AIDS, worldwide child pornography, trafficking in women and children on the black market, and always the gnawing poverty—one hopes the Church has plans to change all that.

Perhaps, in a new papacy in a new century in a new millennium, the Church might look in the cosmic mirror with bowed head, muster the will, and pray for the grace to redeem itself yet again.

There is plenty to do. The horrific accounts of child abuse with which this chapter began would be an obvious, worthy, and belated mission to undertake. The justice it would bring about for the silent, unseen, terrified, enslaved, and betrayed children of the wide world would then be poetic justice.

In Conclusion

The global history of child abuse paints a dismal human picture. The cultural context of early Christianity did not encourage it to become a great champion of children, except maybe in theory. Napoleon noted a long time ago that the education of children began 20 years before birth with the education of the mother. Conversely, the abuse of children begins with the abuse of women. The subsequent performance of the Church is deficient in its concern for the deplorable conditions of women and children, and it does not indicate any awareness on the part of the Church fathers that anything is amiss. The recent sexual abuse scandal has created an opportunity for reflection regarding what part the Church has played by its beliefs and practices—specifically obligatory celibacy, an all-male power structure, and emotional distancing from the people it serves. The Church is now faced with vital options. It could become defensive, or it could grasp the opportunity and challenge that this scandal offers and become a true champion of vulnerable women and children.

Chapter 10

Creative Crises:
Invitation to Transformation

It's been said that there are no problems, only opportunities. Some say that this is an old Chinese saying, others say that it's Indian, but it has probably been said everywhere people have confronted challenge, not to mention catastrophe.

We're programmed to react with almost endless optimism in the face of adversity. Enduring became our triumph. If this sounds grim, it sometimes was. But we learned to dance and sing through it. We learned humor as a coping mechanism. We found contentment and fulfillment a thousand ways climbing the steep hill. It was never lasting bliss, and that was another thing about us: our hope that it will get better later. We ride hope like a wild stallion. The mountain we know we could never climb changes miraculously from problem to opportunity.

Our imaginative literature is full of us overcoming. According to the myth, Sisyphus kept pushing the rock up the hill the more it kept falling back on him. Almost every movie ever made began with a problem that needed to be overcome. People complain that nothing is on television but bad news. But no one wants to hear that all the trains ran on time. The one that crashes grabs our attention because we are programmed to focus on problems or opportunities.

So it came to pass that in the year of the Lord 2002, a problem spread across the land, nay across many lands, and the problem was twofold: clerical pedophilia and Episcopal cover-up. There was great wringing of hands and gnashing of dentures. Money changed hands. A number of wretches went off to jail. But the really important persons talked their way out of trouble. It was a major crisis. It cried out for our attention.

Seeking to Understand Strange Behaviors

Many attitudes and behaviors of the Catholic hierarchy are as old as Church history, yet they never stop puzzling us. The patriarchal structure is far from most Church members' ideals of Christian community, yet it continues. Although our need for creative solutions, guided by moral and ethical principles, has never been greater, our most creative thinkers—theologians in particular—are muffled by the pope. Rather than engage in meaningful dialog, Rome responds to the day's big questions with theological platitudes and frequently shuts off discussion altogether.

In attempting to understand this puzzling behavior, I am turning to *Stages of Faith*, by James Fowler, director of the Center for Faith Development at Emory University. Elements of Fowler's faith development scale can be applied to the Church in search of deeper understanding and improved communication. Describing levels of faith presupposes that every human being has the potential for such transformation. Just who is called to deeper levels of faith, as well as when and how one's potential is engaged, remain a mystery.

Fowler's development scale describes six stages of faith. I'll de-scribe the movement from stages three to five—using it as a springboard for further analysis. According to this theory, the Church hierarchy displays the characteristics of stage three faith, which he calls synthetic-conventional. It is an adolescent level of faith and understanding of the world—characterized by a core identity of *conformity* to a particular perspective or faith system. Believers live *inside* and *through* a faith story or set of symbols, which they have internalized and concretized. Their very literal understanding becomes the sole measure of reality. Everything must be converted into the perspective and terms of this belief system in order to be understood.

Believers who are at stage three lack critical reflection. Therefore, they are faithful primarily out of a need to belong to the group. There is little need to understand what that faith incorporates or calls the believers to. At this stage of faith, all who are outside the group are seen as *other*—"not like us." In stage three, power is seen coming from the top down.

We'll explore these five elements—conformity, literalism, lack of critical reflection, relation with others, and authority—to see how they apply historically to Church leaders. This should provide some insight into today's baffling Church behaviors.

The Conformity Imperative

From a very early stage, the Church has insisted on conformity. This imperative is reflected in the inordinate control needs of the leaders. It is currently expressed in the Church's absolutist approach to theological questions about infallibility, celibacy, abortion, birth control, and women's ordination.

When theologians talk about moral discernment, they mean nuance and tone—distinctions and circumstances in the real lives of people that must be included in the formation and application of moral laws. They work from an understanding that we are imperfect creatures living in an imperfect world and that although we work toward important ideals, we find ourselves falling short despite our most sincere attempts. In the larger picture, ideals stand face to face with the realities of life and must be negotiated. However, conformity to the "faith" has always been emphasized by Rome as the overarching value. More often than not, Rome has assumed an all-or-nothing attitude. The Catholic is *either in or out.*

Priests, who are pastors, are often caught in the middle, expected to be faithful to Catholic ideals yet seeing the need to help parishioners in their struggle to live the faith in the real world. They see the need for a human approach rather than conformity at all costs.

The faithful, too, are caught in a double bind when the circumstances of their everyday lives are discounted and they come up short of leaders' expectations. Such a no-win situation often results in reduced commitment. Many drift away. Those who remain search for a way that does not amount either to forced compliance or compromise.

As I've mentioned, the trend in Rome over the last 40 years has been back to the authoritarianism of the pre-Vatican II Church. Rather than following the recommendations of the council, which the people assumed had been consolidated into canon law and new Church structures, leaders have instead reversed some decisions and watered down the impact of others. Pope John Paul II has veered toward wrapping much of canon law and Church tradition in a vague cloak of infallibility. This is not in accord with traditional Catholic teaching.

Conformity has become the measure of faith, and those who disagree with Vatican policy are pressured and punished for their views. The papal office has repeatedly undermined collegiality, conferring less and declaring more. The tradition of bishops' participation in Episcopal appointments has been reduced to a token submitting of names. As a consequence, the pope has gerrymandered conservative bishops into key locations where the population is more progressive, thus subverting rather than representing healthy diversity. Papal preference for conformity has resulted in a curial staff guaranteed to agree. Conformity at all costs should not be confused with unity. The Church grows more distant from the people.

Literalism and Concretized Symbols

Stage three faith is literal. At this level of understanding, symbols become concretized, and are "taken on." We can see this happening in the early years of the Church as it shifted from a movement to a structured institution. Scripture tells us that Jesus promised his followers he would remain with them and guide them. So, the early followers gathered in homes to celebrate his presence and re-enact a ritual meal like the one the apostles shared with him. The *communities* were the *living* symbol of Christ's presence among the people.

As the structure of the Church developed, the leaders began to concretize the symbol in the institution of the hierarchy. The office of the pope, a symbol of the Church's unity, began to regard *itself* as the symbol of Christ's presence. The pope's title, Vicar of Christ, shows the appropriation and internalization of Christ's symbolic presence. Belief in Christ became equated with belief in the Catholic Church and soon progressed to belief that no salvation existed outside the Church.

The institutional Church, meanwhile, took on the characteristics of the culture, not the characteristics of the communities of Jesus and his followers. Leaders began placing more importance on maintaining the institution than ministering to its people.

Symbols are numinous; they draw power from interaction with our imagination. When the Church fathers concretized the symbol of Christ's presence in the institution, they shut themselves off from its numinous, transformational power and began to function in their own right.

Today, literal thinking is evident in the importance leaders place on apostolic connection to Peter. Peter has "the magic," and the literal mind *believes* it has to maintain this direct line, whether or not it can be established. The institution attempts to reduce the magnitude of Christ's presence in the world by placing it in one person. This misses the point of the incarnation—Christ's total availability.

Literal interpretation shows up in recent statements by Rome regarding women's ordination: for example, that women don't *look* like Jesus and therefore can't represent him. Such a factual interpretation begs such ridiculous questions as: Should all priests be Jewish? Should all wear long hair? Should there only be 12?

Lacking Critical Reflection

Stage three faith lacks the capacity for critical reflection, which is the ability to stand outside the self to achieve a degree of objectivity and thereby gain perspective. Through such reflection, we see ourselves in relationship with history (time) and with the larger world (space). Ultimately, this stance allows us to relate to God as a universal symbol and not merely as the object of one's personal faith. As this is accomplished, the believer understands that divine grace is capable of speaking through more than one symbol—meaning that the Judeo-Christian God can validly coexist with other faiths' representations without conflict.

Critical reflection also describes the process of assessing new information in light of our own body of knowledge—our experiences of reality—and integrating it. This constitutes an interactive exchange between what we already know and new insights received. The Church thwarts the development of critical thinking when it insists that *tradition* be upheld as essentially unchangeable. Although consistency is valuable and even necessary, blind adherence to previous positions thwarts new development and growth.

Reflection is dynamic. We are informed by revelation—but at the same time, the transmission of revelation is subject to our personal limitations and also our creativity; thus, we inevitably leave our thumbprint. Time brings new understanding, and in light of this previous revelation is then reinterpreted in an ongoing process. Revelation can be beyond our ability to comprehend, and we can sometimes outright refuse to hear it. However, if we insist that our body of knowledge can't be tampered with, we will impede the revelatory process and lock ourselves out of it.

Without critical thinking, we have little or no ownership of our beliefs. Consequently, theory and practice often lack consistency—and the inconsistency often goes unnoticed. For example, many have claimed to be Christian while failing to operate in the world with Christian principles. I'm not talking about failing to be perfect and knowing one is missing the mark, which is the human condition. Rather, I'm talking about the failure even to perceive inconsistencies—moral dilemmas—and hence missing the impetus to raise moral questions.

Many American Catholics experience this lack of alignment between belief and practice in the Church's failure to tackle social and political conditions in light of the gospel, both in our own country and worldwide. When religion fails to connect its principles to the societal and cultural level—addressing Christian principles to issues of world hunger and lack of health care, for example—and instead remains focused on the level of individual morality, religion loses relevancy. This is what many call Sunday morning faith. Contained within the walls of the Church, it has no existential connection with the world. At this point, the Church runs the risk of being reduced to selling raffle tickets and paving the parking lot.

Vatican II issued a strong and inspiring directive that the Church's mission was to work for peace and justice in the real world, as well as preaching the word and celebrating the sacraments. Although aimed at every member of the people of God, the hierarchy was charged with implementing this responsibility. Yet Catholicism has remained ingrown and privatized. Critical reflection is directed at the people, not the institution. An obvious example is the hierarchy's habit of measuring the morality of the faithful in terms of personal sexual sin while overlooking its own institutional sins. This double standard has been applied almost from the beginning. A recent striking example was the U.S. Catholic Conference's inflicting of zero tolerance on individual pedophilia priests, while neglecting to even address the institutional American Church's years of sins of omission in this same area.

When the Church uses Scripture without critical reflection, the result is likely to be no more than finding texts to prove one's point. The devil can cite Scripture for his purpose, Shakespeare said—taking a line or two and applying it without historical context. Enough inconsistencies exist in Scripture to assure that as quickly as someone hauls out a line in support of one argument, someone else can haul out two lines to say the opposite. We have seen how the writing of Paul can be used against women's full participation, relegating her to a lesser position in the Church. At the same time, Paul can be quoted to show the equality of all members of the Christian community.

Improved scholarship has corrected mistakes in translation and pro-vided more accurate interpretation of Scripture. Yet, healthy disagreement still exists. There are legitimate differences in what we believe Scripture is saying, and it does say different things to diverse people at various times in life. However, the *principles* of Christ's message can best be gleaned through a general understanding of his relationships with his fol-lowers and how the early communities functioned. There is less disagree-ment among Catholics when Christ's life and example are the focus rather than reaching for lines of Scripture. Critical reflection helps put this big-ger picture in perspective.

Relationship with the "Other"

For many years, Catholics identified anyone who wasn't one of them as *non-Catholic*. Vatican II sought to improve ecumenical relationships between Catholics and other Christian denominations, as well as interfaith relations with other traditions. It attempted to help Catholics be-come more neighborly instead of dividing the world into "us" and "them." It specified that the term *church* applied to all Christians, not just to Catholics—a big concession for many.

But the conservative post-Vatican II leadership has not continued to foster such pluralism. Rather, it has veered back to an identity of Church suspiciously like that of the pre-modern world. An example is the recent attempts to promote papal infallibility—a position not only unpopular with many Catholics, but a more painful sore spot with the world community of believers.

The matter of relationship and global interconnection is particularly crucial today. Much of the tension between Eastern cultures and the Western world originated in unresolved religious conflicts between the Christian and Islamic traditions going back centuries. Damaged relationships between Christians and Jews likewise go back to Christianity's claim that the Jews were responsible for Christ's death—a teaching that has been officially discontinued only recently. However, this image of "perfidious" Jews has persisted throughout history, and similarly ongoing disputes regarding Rome's handling of Hitler's Holocaust have never been settled.

Evangelizing means spreading the good news that we are all invited to share in the love of Jesus Christ. However, only the most naïve reading of history reflects anything but the opposite practice by the Christian Church. Christianizing has most often been an excuse to subdue and even plunder whole societies. That was notoriously the case in the Americas. Recent reports of clerical sexual abuse in Africa (see Chapter 9) are not likely to help this tarnished Catholic image.

One of the most blatant examples of Catholic *otherness* is the persistent sexism of the hierarchy. As entrenched curial officials continue to wallow in the duality of the ancient world, belittling woman in the outdated belief that she is of a lesser spiritual dimension than man, they foster a deep separation among their own people. As a result of this skewed dualistic mentality, they squander the potentially immense contribution of women. And into the bargain, they are all too often cut off from their own feminine nature—a condition that leaves author Jason Berry to conclude in *Lead Us Not Into Temptation: Catholic Priests and the Sexual Abuse of Children:* "Celibacy, as political and theological model, has failed to give maternal grace her rightful role in ministry."

Authority as a Top-Down Phenomenon

The growing alienation between the folks in the pews and their Church leaders isn't usually about dogma or doctrine. Mostly, it is about the Church's use of power.

The Catholic Church is by no means the only exponent of top-down authority. Had another model been popular when Catholicism was getting itself organized, chances are that's what we would have now. (The rest of the world might have moved on to other experiments, but everyone knows that Rome moves slowly and would still be arguing to keep the old status quo—whatever it was.) But top-down has endured. To this day, from nations to corporations to football teams to rap groups, the buck usually stops at the door of one person—all too often a man.

There have been differences in how that person got there. His (or her) title was often a clue. A king and a dictator traditionally arrived by different routes—a president by yet a more popular route. The one with whom the buck stops does not always have the same amount of power. In the United States, the power is shared with the other two branches of government. In corporations, too, there are various means of getting there—and, as we have recently seen, various ways of cashing in when one gets there.

In other words, leadership is still a work in progress. Even in such small societies as the family, there has traditionally been one boss, woman or man depending on the times, though families have become more democratic lately. Not that democracy means that everyone rules—it has more to do with how the ruler got there and the spirit in which the ruler rules. Round and round the paradigm goes. There have been back to nature movements—everyone getting together under a big tree and deciding the common good—but that doesn't work when the population gets big, diverse, and complicated.

A Vague, Utopian Dream

There is always the vaguely utopian dream that we could all find a way to decide things communally—as in the early Church, we sometimes say. Except that, even in the early Church, some—such as Peter and Paul, and maybe even Mary—were more equal than others. More recently, the Communists gave communal role a major try. Unfortunately, too many of them turned out to be corrupt. Soon there were very definite top dogs who were killing their so-called equals by the millions and more. Human nature always butts in.

Nearly everyone agrees that Catholic leadership is one of a kind—top-down, without a doubt. But it isn't a monarchy, the pope insists, nor even a dictatorship. In fact, he's elected. Yet it isn't a democracy, either. The Holy Spirit is in the background, too, as well as other mysteries to contend with.

Although the military, for example, appropriately runs on a strict up-down authority system, as do most large corporations, many believe this exercise of power doesn't fit a religious system. The antiquated arrangement is encrusted with long-standing tradition. Because of the stage three faith of the leaders, they cannot imagine it differently. Also, many Catholics believe they need absolute Church authority to keep them in line—they have grown dependent on it. Others are finding the traditional system less tolerable.

Meanwhile, leaders, firmly entrenched at the top, reinforce people's dependency. Rather than moving to a higher level of faith, one based on inner authority, continued reinforcement promotes passivity in the members. This self-feeding pattern tends to lock both hierarchy and the people at this stage of development.

We see this reflected in civil society as powerlessness in the face of company policies and political decisions with which people are in mass disagreement but cannot muster a significant show of strength to derail. The usual consequence is apathy in the practice of democracy—a system that depends on vital engagement for effectiveness.

Another reason Catholic authoritarianism continues to survive is the large number of Catholics who simply don't pay that much attention to Rome, particularly regarding matters of morality. This tends to make of the pope a mighty and beloved symbol but an entity without moral leadership for the long haul. This could have serious ramifications, such as making the Church, one day, into a club without bite but also without benefit.

The Reality of Papal Position

While television cameras focus on Rome, it appears the pope plays a bigger role in the lives of Catholics than is probably the case. Most

Catholics over 50 grew up paying much less attention to Vatican politics than is common today. For 500 years, the Church had turned away from the world—in retreat behind Vatican walls. It began to resurface in the public consciousness for a number of reasons about a generation ago.

During John F. Kennedy's presidential race, public attention was drawn to the relationship and especially the loyalty of Catholics to Rome. Kennedy famously articulated what most Catholics agreed with: that loyalty to the Catholic religion was not centered in Rome; and that he would uphold the primacy of the U.S. Constitution over all concerns. Kennedy magic, captured in the image of Camelot, continued to keep Catholicism in the news. The Church also made headlines during Vatican II, propelled especially by Pope John XXIII's generous charisma. And for the last couple of decades, the world travels of Pope John Paul II, also a charismatic man, have continued to keep the spotlight on the comings and goings at the Vatican.

At the same time, the pope's anti–birth control decision in 1968, combined with a more highly educated Catholic population, clearly point toward independence from papal authority among U.S. Catholics. Figures showing that birth control and abortion are as common among Catholics as they are among the general population support that idea. Even more significantly, Catholics who make independent moral decisions nevertheless remain in the Church and continue to receive Holy Communion. Thus, they dodge the conformity issue associated with stage three faith.

As the people openly disagree with the Church regarding personal sexual morality, the Church has an opportunity to refocus Catholic energy on spiritual solutions to worldly concerns. Most Catholics are eager to engage their faith at much higher levels than the present leadership seems willing to contemplate. In other words, many folks in the pews reflect a higher stage of moral development than their leaders. But this in turn might be a matter of public perception. It might mean that the leadership is waiting to be led by its people.

The Perfect Storm

Faith development is by definition mysterious. Insofar as we can fathom it, faith grows and transforms lives if given a healthy environment. It also benefits from spiritual direction or religious education designed to help people discover more about themselves.

Spiritual transformation can also result from unfortunate events that serve as wake-up calls. Life-threatening illness, unexpected death in the family, or situations that challenge our deep convictions: These can become opportunities.

I'm calling this the perfect storm. Perfect storms threaten to sink the boat. Water rushes in over the sides and through the cracks. We're sure that the world is coming to an end. Noah had a highly publicized encounter with a classical perfect storm. But just about the time he and the Mrs. were ready to give up, the dove circled back bearing the little green branch.

There are times when, through no effort of our own, fate, grace, or sheer luck brings the exact mixture of variables into our path and creates a perfect storm. We start asking all the right questions, but the old answers are inadequate, maybe even ridiculous. We ponder, as surely the Noah's must have done—sitting out on the deck under their umbrellas—waiting for the dove to return. At those times, it seems as if our beliefs unravel before our eyes. Extreme cases are described as the dark night of the soul. But in the light of dawn, we often find ourselves rooted deeper in our faith.

The elements of such a storm occurred in the case of the Church's pedophilia crisis. Confident or complacent Catholics were shocked to discover the bishops had prior knowledge of widespread sex abuse happening among their clergy and had been sitting on it—pondering on it for a full 15 years. That incomprehensible time lapse, combined with the severity of the charges, jolted many twenty-first-century Americans. The reaction was so intense that a perfect storm was created.

The notoriously lethargic bishops then practically leaped into action. Their June 2002 meeting in Dallas, usually a sleepy, routine gathering of the club, became a landmark event in modern U.S. Catholic history. For the first time in memory, the bishops were not waiting for instructions from Rome; rather, they forged ahead in seeming tension with papal and Vatican signals to be prudent and go slowly. For a couple of dramatic days, the meeting reflected a fresh image of Church as bishops listened to lay victims, lay experts, and even women. Their leaders faced the media and expressed sorrow for the past and resolve for the future. It was unprecedented.

Skeptics might say that a perfect storm does not make for a perfect shipwreck. Whether the Dallas meeting, and the many other gestures and resolutions, add up to a true change of heart or are merely window dressing under pressure, only time will tell.

Iconoclasm: Opening to Transformation

When a subject is just outside human grasp—as matters of faith usually are—we often reach for metaphors. One of the problems between the Church of the East and the Church of the West was over the use of religious images. Opposition to using icons was expressed by going into the Church and breaking them—referred to as iconoclasm. The metaphor serves to describe challenging beliefs about ourselves that we cling to even when they no longer fit. Maybe deep down we have not truly believed them for some time. By challenging them, we give grace a chance to transform us.

Sometimes challenging or discarding an old icon feels like freedom, and those are easy to let go. But sometimes fear of change is so great that it overrides the process and we shut it down. Yet, as any iconoclast will tell you, choices have consequences. What we choose (and failure to choose is a choice, too) will have a ripple effect in our lives and in the history of the world. So philosopher John Paul Sartre said a mouthful when he reminded us we were condemned to freedom.

Those who grew up when Soviet Communism threatened to snuff out both democracy and the Catholic Church might relate to a sermon at the children's Mass in my parish. The priest graphically described scenes of armed soldiers breaking down our classroom door and demanding that we renounce the faith. Those who capitulated would be spared, but would know that they were traitors to the faith of the martyrs. Those who refused to deny their faith would be killed. Those brave souls would go immediately to heaven. I can vividly recall knowing in my gut that I would renounce my faith! It wasn't my time, or so I console myself.

Grace does not always come to the front door dressed in white and carrying flowers. It is very likely to be delivered in a strange, unseemly, or scary package.

I suspect that the wounds of the recent sexual abuse scandals might be harboring grace. I do not mean to imply that God is sacrificing young people so that we can learn or gain something. Yet the innate duality of life allows us to find grace in our despair. The Christian religion is built on the spiritual truth that in death there is resurrection—not just once upon a time but on an ongoing basis.

Crying for a Vision

Vision quest is a Native American spiritual practice of prayer and fasting to prepare to receive a life-transforming vision. The Lakota people use the word *Henblecheya*—crying for a vision—to describe the experience. It represents the human endeavor of going as far as one can go with the information and other capacities at one's disposal. In the Native tradition, one meets this challenge by prayer and fasting, followed by a time spent alone in nature sitting before the Great Mystery, waiting for that personal vision.

To receive such a new vision, you must be able to let the thinking brain rest and go deeper. A vision quest or a more typical spiritual retreat that would include time for meditation, prayer, and talking with a spiritual director is helpful. You will most likely receive insight that will help you progress on your spiritual path.

We each have particular icons that must be broken in order to progress on the faith journey. Paradoxically, we can't locate our personal icon without interacting with something outside of the self. In this instance, we'll use the Church as the means of that reflection. We'll review some of the areas we identified earlier in the chapter to see what icons might need to be challenged in order that we might move on. Nearly everyone has personal convictions about what needs to go and what needs to stay. The following are perhaps typical samples.

Breaking the Conformity Icon

The conformity icon holds the hierarchy virtual prisoners in the Vatican. It confines leaders in what they think Catholicism is all about, separating them from the awesome variety, flux, and potential of the Catholic people.

If they were to break the conformity icon, the leaders might discover the many different ways God works—how destiny uses the most unlikely people and situations to deliver the word and transform the world. Making certain that one billion people all march to the same tune is exhausting and, finally, futile.

Without the burden of the conformity icon, the hierarchy could practically enjoy life. The real world is diverse, which keeps life from becoming too bland and boring. Conforming to rules is a necessary concession to the human condition—it stabilizes the tribe—bestowing a degree of safety, but risking believing we're all God's children can go one better.

As we break the conformity icon within, we must be willing to live our truth even when it means disagreeing with others. We don't have to leave the Church over differences—staying can mean being open to transformation. At the same time, if we need to go elsewhere to get spiritual needs met, we have the responsibility to do it. As we break this icon, we move past seeing ourselves as other. That can mean surrendering prejudices and renouncing judgments we hold about "those people."

Such iconoclasm calls us to be tolerant of differences, even when feeling threatened by them, and choosing to place faith in God rather than in human theories.

There is freedom in following inner guidance—trusting our ability to discern truth—and responsibility as well. Finding one's truth takes more time than agreeing for the sake of agreeing. In breaking this icon, we're signing on to incorporating prayer and meditation in our daily life and to finding a community with whom to reflect. As confidence grows, we are less threatened by differences—it allows more interaction with people who don't hold the exact same definitions as we do.

As our inner sense of self gets stronger, the walls we put up between us and others are needed less and less. Transformation increases community. Through open engagement with others, possibilities increase.

Breaking the Magisterial Icon

The magisterial icon drags along with it the icon of rational thought. Here iconoclasm heralds the return to common sense! It means getting creative again. The early Church writers were free of this icon and wrote spiritually imaginative messages that are still an inspiration today. They didn't have to stay inside the lines because many of the lines hadn't been drawn yet. Those who study theology, philosophy, and even literature can sometimes get so respectful of ideas from the past that they forget many of those same ideas were considered outrageous, even heretical, when they were first written. Creativity is like that—it blazes a new trail.

When we break our magisterial icon, we get to let go of needing to be right and can listen to other viewpoints respectfully. We have to become responsible for keeping actions consistent with belief. This includes being willing to be wrong when we are wrong; and equally to take the responsibility for being right when we are right—even when it separates us from the pack. To do this requires great clarity, surrender to God's will, and courage. In those moments, we have no need to convince anyone of our truth, and we become truly useful.

This transformation sounds like a lot of work—but we will probably find ourselves singing more often!

Breaking the Church's Power-Tower Icon

As the tower of authoritarianism grows taller, it moves dangerously away from the ground. Tall towers fall hard. The good news for the hierarchy is that, when the power tower is toppled, they will get to come back down to Earth where they can smell the flowers, listen to the wind howl, wade in a cool stream on a hot day, and walk on the beach at sunset.

When the Church breaks the double-faced icon of patriarchy and hierarchy, it can rejoin the community of regular people. Granted, that means having to find a parking place just like everybody else, but the rewards are worth it. As the icon of male superiority is broken, everybody wins. There will be a lot less competition, which means that leaders and would-be leaders won't have to spend so much time jockeying for position. They won't have to separate themselves from their feelings and emotions. This might mean a lot more laughing, some crying, but more authentic and real human relationship.

When we break the hierarchical and patriarchal power tower in our head, we too can heal the dichotomy of mind and spirit that has separated us from our selves and from God's creation—we can come home.

Making this leap of faith qualifies the leaper to live with paradox. The known world seems to crack open and fall away—and almost as quickly a new construct emerges—one that has our name on it.

Life takes on both mystery and knowing what we need to know at the same time. The result is more complex, but infinitely more interesting. For example, we're able to go behind the symbols and touch the reality of what they represent—I have it on good authority that when we do
this we find we're mostly about the same thing.

It's where Chief Seattle and Jeremiah talk the same language and where White Buffalo Calf Woman of the Lakota people, Sophia, and Jesus all meet for lunch. The sacred meal might be bread and wine, bagels and lox, or fry bread. And we realize: God is with *us*, here, now.

A Chorus of Midges

The term *holiness* is a close relative of *whole*. We have an inborn drive toward wholeness; it is our spiritual destiny. If this is true, why is it we often find ourselves settling for less?

There are, no doubt, many good answers. One answer has to do with how we receive revelation—or God's instructions that keep us moving along our path. Revelation connects to our instinctual knowing. It is the indwelling of the Holy Spirit. It awakens our deep truth. Yet, even when truth has been spoken, many find themselves unable to hear it. What stands in the way of responding creatively? How can we be sure what sounds like good news *is* good news?

Sometimes our inner world is so cluttered with the voices of *others* it's like being enveloped in a swarm of midges. In such times, we can't decipher what is authentic and what is false prophecy. In her poem "Transcendental Etude," poet Adrienne Rich describes this as a time "when we have to pull back from the incantations, rhythms we've moved to thoughtlessly." It calls us to silence—in which we sort through the "oratory, formulas, choruses, laments, static crowding the wires."

Obviously, some people hear a louder chorus than others, but no one escapes. The chorus yammers away, repeating every little instruction, true and false, that we've ever been given. It reminds us to eat everything on our plate. It tells us we're not smart enough, good-looking enough, tall enough, small enough, and if we don't follow instructions we'll end up under a bridge.

Sometimes we have joined the midges, and can't tell our own voice from the swarm. We shut the door on our own truth. Always, if we continue to sing in the chorus, even when it's singing gibberish, we're getting paid off in some way. The paycheck isn't always money. We will sacrifice our truth to earn love or to fit into any number of artificial roles or cultural boxes if we need to belong badly enough. In those cases, we need a bigger bump—one they call a defining moment. Defining moments are big enough to silence the chorus long enough for us to make a choice. Then we finally become teachable.

Again, Rich describes the process:

> *We cut the wires, find ourselves in free-fall, as if*
> *Our true home were the undimensional*
> *solitudes, the rift*
> *in the Great Nebula.*
> *No one who survives to speak new language can avoid this:*
> *the cutting away of an old force that held her*
> *rooted to an old ground ...*

This new language announces new vision—it is definitively creative. Culturally imposed differences fade, and we are exposed to the bigger picture. Put in reign-of-God talk, it is when we understand justice on the larger scale—not just justice for "our" people. We see that everybody's baby needs food.

Sometimes we have over-Christified religion—made it seem as if it's all about being saved *from* life, not about *living* life.

Throughout history, visionaries have grasped the bigger picture—the Old Testament prophets, for example. Isaiah sets us right in the midst of creation:

> *For thus says the Lord,*
> *The creator of the heavens,*
> *Who is God,*
> *The designer and maker of the earth*
> *Who established it,*

Not creating it to be a waste,
But designing it to be lived in:
I am the Lord, and there is no other (45:18).

Leaving Room for Glitches and Grace

There are so many ways the world could have been designed—everyone wishes that the Creator might have made some better choices.

With regard to the current topic, Jesus could surely have set a vastly different Church in motion. The stable, for starters, didn't augur well for fame and fortune. The angels singing and kings visiting were more stylish, but he didn't follow up on that aspect. He obviously was a fine speaker, with great powers of persuasion, but frankly he could have done better. Anyone who could raise the dead could surely have put the fear of God in more people, including the uppity Romans. Use it or lose it— he not only could have cured the occasional sick soul, he also could have leveled the mountains, brought water to the parched places, made sad hearts happy, put food on every table, and discovered America before breakfast.

If only we could have given him a list. Sure, we would all have different lists, but he could have helped us iron out our differences. St. Peter's, the Vatican, and bishops' rings might not have been on every list. But we could make compromises. At the end of the day, the Messiah might have opted for popes exactly like the ones we've had—or gone for greater variety.

But that was then. Jesus missed the opportunity. This is now. Hope springs eternal. And problems, including the pedophilia scandal, are in fact opportunities. This pope or the next one could still do it our way. He could call another council and invite us all. Sparks would fly. Or Cardinal Ratzinger could invite our favorite experts to spruce up the old paradigm and get everyone on board: Hans Kung, Joan Chittister, Richard McBrien, Mother Angelica. They would still have trouble from the right wing, or the left, unless infallibility were spread around to the satisfaction of everyone—or, failing infallibility, goodwill; or something more crazy and ethereal, like charity.

And even then, only time would tell. After the analysis, come the propositions—and one must then sit back and wait for reality to react. There might be an earthquake or a hijacking or a schism. And after that, one still has to worry that the unpredictable Holy Spirit might throw a divine wrench in the works. There would always be problems. Or if you prefer, opportunities.

A very wise teacher once told me that a much bigger plan is unfolding than what any of us can imagine. And it is unfolding despite our attempts to hold fast to our chunk of reality. In the end, we will be dragged kicking and screaming, nails scraping the ground, to our destiny. At the risk of challenging other wise people, my teacher said that we're as saved as we need to be—and we'll all sink or swim together. He suggested that we go out and enjoy ourselves because time is short. Radical, yes, but it does allow the breath to come and go a bit deeper. I have heard the question raised that if we are already saved, why did Jesus need to come? I don't pretend to know, but what if he came to spend some time with us and see what it was like to be human? I like to think that is possible. Like many of us, he had some bad luck. Not because he or we are bad, but because that is how it works.

In Conclusion

We've seen how both Church leaders and people are at a point of faith transformation. These critical junctures are presented at various times in life—it's when the birdcage door opens and we have the chance to fly. When God opens the door, the invitation is there if we choose to accept it. Risks accompany this opportunity. However, to refuse is to stay on our perch and close the cage door—and our spirit suffers. If we take the leap into transcendence, we are rewarded beyond what we can imagine. Choosing to fly means living by our instincts, trusting that God has a plan for us and that instructions will be forthcoming. You don't throw away the good stuff you've learned, but you see how it applies in a bigger way—not as an either/or but both/and. The prophets of the Old Testament foretold this time, as did many others. So maybe it's no accident.

Chapter 11

Pilgrims and Prophets

Catholics need not be alarmed to wake up some morning soon and find that Catholicism has changed dramatically while their backs were turned.

It will probably happen early in the next pontificate. Not only will the new pope present Catholicism with a new face, he will also gather new people around him who will have little appetite to fight the same old battles. These newcomers will be formed and motivated by different interests and crises from their predecessors, excited by different challenges. They will not be locked in vendettas with yesterday's warriors of the right or, especially, the left. There will be new concerns to worry about—over and above the hardy perennials. With a bit of luck, the sun will shine through those Vatican windows and show that many old bones of contention have crumbled to dust.

This change was not, we will then realize, an overnight sensation. With hindsight we will see it was germinating, hatching, and quietly happening even as the old regime dug in and blustered and occasionally reprimanded a high-profile theologian. If we look closely, we will then see that the new scenarios, recently so hotly disputed, were quietly gaining ground in books and articles and expounded at conferences, for some time now. We will realize that the authors are not being hauled in any more—as if the good men of the Roman Curia threw up their hands and said "we give up." (That raucous sound you hear in the background is the rest of the Church shouting "Alleluia!")

This transformation will have happened so imperceptibly that the faithful scarcely noticed or seldom talked about it. Such changes of communal consciousness are a common occurrence. One childish example in the Church is the inclusion of altar girls. A very short time ago, some pastors and bishops would have drawn their swords to protect the sanctity of the sanctuary. Now the girls are yesterday's news.

Most of the changes are bigger and more far-reaching. Many are less visible than the altar girls—born of the head and heart and often played close to the chest. The majority are about the very things discussed in this book, especially about power and how it is used and by whom. Although obscure doctrines lurk unresolved in the background of Church life, the quiet perceptual shift is down at the level of daily life and down in the neighborhood—where the average priest is moving close to retirement age, where so many of the parishes are priestless, and where women, who only a generation ago could not touch the chalice, are now running parishes from sea to shining sea.

They're not priests yet—Rome wasn't built in a day, Cardinal Ratzinger will tell you—but they are only one small decision away from that. And if the stories are true, women have already become priests. The women priests are, or were, off at a safe distance in Eastern Europe. (If they were in the rambunctious United States, that would be a worry and everyone would know about it—but the clandestine ordinations happened underground in Czechoslovakia.) The sky didn't fall when word seeped out. A rearguard action by the Vatican denying validity received only passing attention. Progressive people—the ones who usually break old laws and change the Church—were getting used to the idea. Thus, when Rome eventually says yes to it, lays hands on some female heads, and maybe even insists that it was the Vatican's idea all along, public opinion will already be on board. This is just an example of the changing Church.

Shaping Tomorrow's Church: Religious Freedom

Since the day it started, the biggest question facing the Church has been "What is the Church?" Obviously, it's not an easy question to answer because the Church itself has wandered all over the place in search of the answer: from persecuted little band awaiting doomsday all the way to mighty empire. In more recent times, two concepts have played tug of war: the Church as institution and the Church as its people. The institution, always a necessary component, has fought fiercely to be the main event. Since the first Vatican Council, though, and despite every effort at restoration, it is losing ground to the human component. Quietly, but relentlessly, the people of God are asserting their individuality and freedom of conscience.

Rarely, if ever, has it been clearer: We are a pilgrim people. We are, furthermore, a Church in progress, not the proverbial *fait accompli*. We are not merely people in the pew, nor merely bishops and bureaucrats, but prophets as well. Our journey is toward a vision of the reign of God. The amazing difference is that we no longer look so exclusively to the hierarchy for answers, but rather into our hearts to examine our consciences for clues that only we can provide.

As we stand on the edge of tomorrow, we're doing what we're supposed to do—actively engaging the faith and asking legitimate questions. The Vatican is doing what it feels is right—preserving the faith. The need for conversation is apparent.

The struggle among Catholics centers on the right to follow inner guidance—or dissent, as the hierarchy calls it. The good news is that where there's a struggle, there's life. The old method of sitting listening to the "experts" isn't working for a significant number of Catholics who are ready to take more ownership of their religion—and even move on if they must. This new conversation must be a *dialog*, not the traditional monologue in the top-to-bottom method.

Catholics face the future both fearful and full of hope. In this final chapter, we explore some emerging or re-emerging concepts that should be included in the new dialog because they will go a long way toward shaping tomorrow's Catholicism. These include: freedom of conscience, faith based communities as a promising new model for the Church, and a change in consciousness that is being born through the union of faith and science in hopes of healing the duality that has plagued us for so long.

The Right to Dissent and Freedom of Conscience

Many Catholics find themselves in genuine conflict with decisions handed down by Church leadership. Once, people gritted their teeth and carried on. Today, many who differ over particular teachings are choosing to remain in the Church and receive the sacraments. They are skirting the boundary between institutional authority and personal moral choice, defining new turf. Some use the slightly pejorative term "cafeteria Catholics" to describe these seekers. But established Catholic traditions guide such pilgrims and prophets as the journey leads them into new territory.

St. Thomas Aquinas taught that personal conscience is the ultimate guide in all moral decisions. The thirteenth-century theologian, still considered one of the Church's leading moral teachers, maintained that even an erroneous conscience was morally binding. A haphazard hunch or the most convenient answer is not, therefore, the proper moral solution. One is free from fault once every effort has been made to form a right moral judgment. Aquinas regards conscience as the primary vehicle for receiving God's direct instruction and places it above any earthly source, including the teaching of the magisterium.

Progressives maintain that the doctrine of freedom of conscience and the teachings of Thomas Aquinas clearly resolve dilemma regarding relationship between conscience and authoritative teaching. According to Thomas, official Church teaching would serve conscience in decision-making by providing information and moral guidance.

This model changes the noun faith into a verb, "faithing," emphasizing its proactive quality. In a new and vital faithing process, all the people who struggle to live the truths of the Church would, along with the hierarchy, lend their insights and experience.

It's in the Catechism

The official Catechism of the Catholic Church has this to say about conscience:

> *Deep within his conscience, man discovers a law which he has not laid upon himself but which he must obey. Its voice, ever calling him to love and to do what is good and to avoid evil, sounds in his heart at the right moment. ... For man has in his heart a law inscribed by God. ... His conscience is man's most secret core and his sanctuary. There he is alone with God whose voice echoes in his depths.*

In *The Catholic Tradition: The Church in the Twentieth Century*, Timothy G. McCarthy defines conscience as "a permanent natural disposition that summons us to seek the good and to avoid evil." It is not, therefore, an "impersonal oracle" or a divine whisper in one's ear.

Conscience is found within us. We are expected to question ourselves and be present enough to hear God's direction. This inner voice guides us in perceiving and "doing" morality. Conscience directs us to take responsibility for wrong action, seek forgiveness, and start doing right—thus cultivating virtue.

Conscience works through reasoning and in conformity with the true good willed by the Creator. The catechism reminds us that a well-formed conscience is sincere and truthful and also must be informed, which is a lifelong task. Three things help guide the process: assistance from the Holy Spirit, witness or advice of others, and guidance from the authoritative teaching of the Church.

Faced with a moral choice, we must always seriously seek what is right and good and discern the will of God expressed in divine law. In this process, we must apply prudence—as experience is reflected on in light of the times. Certain conditions must be applied in all situations of moral discernment, especially the following:

1. The end does not justify the means. Evil may never be pursued so that good may result from it.
2. The Golden Rule must be applied: Do unto others as you would have them do unto you.
3. Charity toward others must be expressed in our choices. This presupposes awareness of how our choices affect others.

Not Without Controversy

The Catechism is a compendium of Catholic teaching prepared by a papal commission of 12 cardinals and bishops under the direction of Cardinal Joseph Ratzinger. It was first proposed as a teaching guide for bishops—to assist them in their job of instructing the faithful. It quickly acquired clout as the last word in the Church. A thoroughly institutional document, it is ironic that it should itself be so controversial.

The recent rendering of this document was published with the approval of Pope John Paul II, but was found too vague by several cardinals. The commission submitted the revised text to the world's bishops in 1989, where it was criticized for its failure to reflect recent scholarship in theology and biblical studies. The commission made more revisions based on the response of the review board, but a major conflict over the use of inclusive language further delayed publication. All this maneuvering goes to show that even the Church is not immune to the ambiguities and dilemmas of applied Christianity.

A similar rift occurred later in the same year when the Congregation for the Doctrine of the Faith ruled against using the New Revised Standard Version (NRSV) of the Bible for liturgical and catechetical purposes. The NRSV was the result of the cooperative efforts of an ecumenical group sponsored by the National Council of Churches, and had been officially approved by the U.S. bishops and the Vatican three years earlier. In rescinding approval, the Vatican again stated that the use of inclusive language had distorted essential truths contained in Scripture.

Critics of Vatican policy point out that the use of inclusive language was applied only to human imagery, not divine. In other words, God as male was not being challenged—simply the use of all male pronouns in describing humans. Vatican insensitivity and tactics were interpreted by many, including bishops, as misuse of power.

Announcing the People of God

Over the last century or more, much of the world has grown increasingly pluralistic. As old and new nations learned how to live with their differences and changing fortunes, the Catholic Church had to reconcile itself to coexisting with other religious expressions. For a Church that believed it was the only game in town and the sole repository of all truth, this was particularly humiliating. The growing liberal attitudes spawned by the Enlightenment and other historical forces were moving toward a diversity that made the monolithic Catholic dinosaur uncomfortable.

Popes have usually been reactive rather than proactive. One of the juiciest examples was Pius IX, confronted by a precarious future in the tiny Vatican state, declaring himself infallible in 1870. He had already set the tone in 1864, when he published the *Syllabus of Errors*, which told the world what was wrong with its thinking, and by implication stipulated how and where the truth was to be found for the future—at the Vatican, of course.

It is very important to remember that Pius IX is a hero, at this very moment, to great sections of the Catholic population, and precisely for the reasons hinted at—the pontiff had a firm grasp on right and wrong, and he knew he had it. (Not everybody, then, is raising the flag of surrender and leaving the old battles behind, as hinted at the beginning of this chapter.)

One tenet of the *Syllabus* was to reclaim the Church's once-favored position as the state religion—in all states.

Pope Pius's statement was considered by many to be, at least, excessive. The French Archbishop Felix Dupanloup successfully created a way around the papal faux pas by proposing that the Church should uphold the pope's statement as an ideal while recognizing that there are times and situations that make the ideal impossible—such as the up-and-coming, free-thinking superpower called the United States. The whole Pio Nono brouhaha was a grand effort at papal face-saving, and an end run around tradition. As Garry Wills comments, it managed to "paralyze (Catholic) thinking for a whole century."

But it didn't, entirely. What Pope John XXIII referred to as the signs of the times were making themselves felt. People no longer feared that every thunderclap meant God was angry at them. Indeed, God had been declared dead by Friedrich Nietzsche and others. And even if most people still believed, few thought God still stuck his finger in the pie every time a decision had to be made on Earth. Civil leaders were seen as quite hu-man functionaries, not mouthpieces of the divinity as of yore, and even the pope was a less credible mouthpiece than once upon a time. Huge adjustments were taking place in the way people and groups related to each other. Authority was up for grabs—as was its counterpart, religious liberty.

An American Priest Makes His Mark

Fr. John Courtney Murray (1904–1967), an American Jesuit, made religious liberty his mission in life. He went back and back again, trying to get to the root of things. To debate whether civil society or religious society came first is probably as futile as the conundrum about the chicken and the egg. But what Murray writes about civil society in *We Hold These Truths: Catholic Reflections on the American Proposition* (Franciscan University Press, 1993) applies neatly to both: "Civil society is a need of human nature before it becomes the object of human choice. Moreover, every particular society is a creature of the soil; it springs from the physical soil of Earth and from the more formative soil of history. Its existence is sustained by loyalties that are not logical; its ideals are expressed in legends that go beyond the facts and are for that reason vehicles of truth."

Looked at thus profoundly, any society will seem a tough nut to crack. So much idealism, pain, promises, broken promises, surprises, and setbacks—who would want to tamper? Yet, Murray contends, tamper we must. Argue and critique we must. "The distinctive bond of the civil multitude is reason, or more exactly, the exercise of reason which is argument."

So Murray jumped into the Catholic argument. And for his pains, he was silenced by the Church in the 1950s. But as so often happens in the Church, yesterday's outcast is tomorrow's prophet. He was rehabilitated in time to attend Vatican II as an expert. Of all the documents that emerged from the Council, none belonged to the inspiration and courage of one man as much as the Declaration on Religious Freedom belonged to Murray.

In a 1966 article on authority in the Church, he hinted at the diplomacy and skill which must have been required to guide the Vatican document through such a maze of opposition and conflicting interests. The hierarchy has one essential function, he writes: to unify the very multidimensional Church. This the leadership should do by dialog and consultation—and not, therefore, by decree.

This unifying function has two aspects. The first is to direct the Church community according to its nature, tradition, and aims. This, of course, includes discipline because the Church is a free-spirited organism in an unruly world. But the second unifying aspect is corrective. Because the Church is human and even sinful, it will forever need adjustments to keep it on course and achieve its mission. This second aspect seems a brilliant ploy to placate the die-hards who say that the Church can't change a thing it has said or done in the past lest it be perceived as less than infallible.

Murray's argument for religious liberty stated that the Church's freedom would best be secured in a pluralistic society such as the United States by adhering to the constitutional protection of religious liberty. He further warned that attempts by the Church to create a state religion would result in a devastating backlash, doing even more harm.

To make this point, he had earlier introduced an unaccustomed but authentic use of the word *conspiracy*. It means "breathing together," he pointed out, and therefore union, accord, and unanimity. This leads to its meaning of united action for a common end on which the parties agree. He traces the word back to the Stoics and Cicero, thence to the Scholastics who helped form the Western liberal tradition. "Civil society is by definition a conspiracy," Murray concludes. "Only by conspiring together do the many become one."

The success of Murray's argument rested on his care not to condemn earlier Church teaching—thus avoiding direct challenge to Rome's authority. He paved the way for change by endorsing the Church's previous stand, reasoning that at the time people were not ready for self-direction and needed the Church's paternal government. He maintained that *education and awareness* made people more capable. His presentation affirmed the Church's position and at the same time required that the *original teaching develop further*.

He received some criticism at the time for tap dancing around papal politics rather than taking a more straightforward run at it. However, his approach was vindicated with the 1965 Declaration on Religious Freedom, insisting that the dignity of each person and freedom of faith are the foundation stones of religious liberty.

Securing Religious Liberty

The Second Vatican Council's document *Lumen Gentium* (light of nations) removed the restrictions on Catholics reading the Bible. It also removed the restrictions placed on the intellectual freedom of theologians by eliminating the mandated anti-modernism oath. Unfortunately, an updated, watered-down version of this has been reintroduced in recent years.

Another Council document, *Gaudium et Spes* (*Joy and Hope*), declared it is only in freedom that we can do good—because without freedom, there is no choice. It affirmed that human dignity requires acting according to one's knowledge.

The Church was directed by the council to reflect on its role in the world. Social action must begin with theological reflection on the people's real-life experiences, not with the abstractions of a pre-established tradition or biblical basis. Real-life experiences are then looked at in light of Scripture to determine correct action by the Church on behalf of the people.

Gaudium et Spes also called for continued development of themes found in the social encyclicals, decreeing that a social justice mission is as important as the Church's sacramental or teaching life.

Gaudium et Spes thus became the foundational document guiding Catholic theology on peace and justice during the 1970s and 1980s. It inspired a vital social engagement within the Catholic Church. It secured *freedom of conscience*. And it determined that theology and other religious scholarship allow for balance in the relationship between the pope and the bishops—in this way *giving voice to the laity*. As a result of the lively debate at the Council, the traditional identity of the Church as hierarchy shifted to its identity as the People of God.

However, censoring of theologians by Pope John Paul and additional strictures placed on Catholic universities have undone some of this good work. This is unsubtle enough to remind Garry Wills of the McCarthy years, and caused former Notre Dame University President Theodore Hesburgh to voice concern that the freedom of the university to seek and teach truth is in danger of being compromised in favor of narrow religious indoctrination.

Probabilism: When in Doubt, Don't

Probabilism is a little-known seventeenth-century moral system allowing for legitimate dissent regarding Church law about which there is reasonable doubt. Reasonable doubt occurs either when an individual has serious personal doubt or when five or six theologians have expressed doubt about a particular teaching. It maintains that one can follow the opinion favoring freedom from obligation even when the opinion favoring obligation or the law is more probable. Probability flows from the universal understanding that *a doubtful obligation is no obligation.*

Written on the Heart

The following are some suggested considerations in applying probabilism:

- Intrinsically: This guideline is based solidly on insight. If a person finds, following prayerful reflection, that his or her conscience is in dissent from the hierarchically supported view, probabilism can be employed.

- Extrinsically: Probabilism can be used when five or six theologians of recognized status hold the dissenting view—even though all other Catholic theologians, including the pope, disagree.

- There is no moral debate that falls outside the scope of a probabilistic solution. There are no exceptions to its application once good probable reason has been found for the lawfulness of an action in a particular case. Even when contrary reasons might be stronger, one can act in accord with one's inner-guided reasoning.

- It is not based on permission, and it cannot be forbidden. Church discipline requires that a priest hearing confession, who is aware that a probable opinion exists, let the person know it even if the priest himself disagrees with it.

- Probabilism is rooted in the Old Testament declaration, "I will place a law within them, and write it upon their hearts" (Jeremiah 31:33–34). It is echoed in the New Testament scriptural teaching of John and Paul to the effect that spirit-filled persons are taught of God, and again by Thomas Aquinas's doctrine that the primary law for the believer is the grace of the Holy Spirit poured into the heart. Aquinas further states that all written law, including Scripture, as well as the teachings of the popes and councils, is secondary.

Probabilism carries a degree of risk and requires caution, but is thoroughly Catholic.

Probable and More Probable

For several centuries, two opposing groups of theologians fought a battle—each group advising priests how to handle doubtful matters in the confessional. The Jesuits, upholding individual conscience and taking a more pastoral approach, taught probabilism—saying that in doubtful matters, people could follow the probable opinion of a competent minority of theologians.

The Dominicans, advocating a more traditional approach locating authority in the Church, disagreed. They said that when doubt existed, the more probable opinion of the majority of theologians was to be followed. Their system was called *probabiliorism* from the Latin word for "more probable." Eventually, the Jesuit understanding of probabilism prevailed. Credit for this is given to St. Alphonsus Liguori, an eighteenth-century moral theologian, who was declared a Doctor of the Church in 1871 and aptly named the patron saint of confessors and moralists by Pope Pius XII.

Hierarchy Has a Problem with Probabilism

Some Church officials say that probabilism cannot be applied on a clear teaching of the magisterium. They invoked this restriction twice in recent history: over the Church's ban on birth control and again over its ban on sterilization, both issues of personal sexuality.

Critics say that this position would be valid only if the magisterium had never made an error in an authoritative teaching. Because errors have been made, there is a probable reason to believe that further mistakes could occur, and, therefore, probabilism could be justified. Dissenting theologians insist that Rome is out of order in any case because probabilism by definition implies that there are no situations to which it cannot be applied (see the third and fourth points in the earlier list).

Although some Catholics continue to look to the Church to provide all the answers, the Vatican Council stated: "The Church does not always have at hand the solution to problems." If one were to follow this reasoning, one could conclude that the bishops no longer have a monopoly on authoritative teaching.

Rapidly developing areas of knowledge such as biological engineering and political developments—as well as sociological and anthropological discoveries—make it impossible for bishops to always stay ahead of the game. It is only reasonable to assume that they'll need to be assisted by professionals in many academic fields. Many bishops welcome the possibility of more inclusion and appreciate an educated laity that insists on taking responsibility for its personal destiny. Many, as always, are nervous.

Today, competent theologians disagree with several authoritative (but not infallible) teachings of the magisterium. Catholics are justified in using these writings to inform their consciences. Probabilism has a biblical foundation, a scholarly one, and a history in the Church. However, the caveat remains that probabilism should not be employed without due cause and sincerity of purpose.

Grass-Roots Christian Communities

There has always been a tension between private faith and public commitment. Church teaching has usually been more comfortable with people cultivating personal piety and nervous when people wanted to get organized and make their faith matter in the world. It's a control thing, the cynical might say. It's also quite human: Leadership always believes it has an obligation to guide the members and believes it knows best what needs to be done. Thus, during the years between the Council of Trent and Vatican II, the faithful were encouraged to be pious and loyal, and any further initiatives would be undertaken by the hierarchy.

There was, however, another tradition: of reaching out, especially to the poor, sick, and disheartened; of the Christian obligation to improve life on Earth rather than wait for a happy hereafter in heaven. This crusading attitude was paramount in the early Church and often afterwards when people got a chance to express the compassion that was a key characteristic of Jesus Christ. The Second Vatican Council did much to restore this outgoing aspect of Catholicism, and it was usually summed up as the pursuit of peace and justice.

This urge to Christian action manifested itself dramatically and independently in some of the world's poorest countries about the same time that the ferment that would become Vatican II was growing in mainly First World nations. It is still too new for its name to be a household word, but its local manifestations are called base Christian communities. Although priests and other professional religious might have supplied the liberation theology framework on which base communities were built, the movement was and is overwhelmingly a lay expression of Christian life.

The Church in Movement

Base communities pose the biggest challenge—or opportunity—to come along for a very long time in the established Church.

They are small groups of people who gather for faith-sharing through Scripture reading, reflection, and worship. Scripture and reflection are used as a means of working through real-life problems both on a personal level and through engaging social issues when such action is called for. These communities are a spiritual invention of the Third World and have spread throughout Latin America, Africa, and Asia.

Base communities are a grass-roots movement. There is no one-size-fits-all blueprint. They reflect the character of the people and culture in which they form. Each functions independently of other base communities (although usually not independently of the Church), echoing the diversity of the people they serve. They reflect the variety of early communities of the Church: Each evolved in a way that worked for itself, yet all strove for the same ideal.

Indeed, design and implementation play a big role in becoming a vital and unified community. In her book *Base Communities: An Introduction*, theologian Margaret Hebblethwaite makes the point that "base communities are not movements within the Church, they are the Church in movement." She describes these communities as cells of the Church—the living body of Christ.

Building a successful community requires keeping the group small enough for a true sense of connection and intimacy—ideally about 15 to 20 families. The multigenerational factor is important as it more closely reflects family. Groups meet once or twice a week to share problems and generate solutions inspired by the gospel. First and foremost, they are religious communities.

Although the wealthy are not excluded (wealth need not refer to money alone), base communities are mostly composed of poor people in poor areas. At this most basic level in society, they become a voice of the disenfranchised. In addressing the conditions that contribute to their poverty, the groups often engage the political structures. However, a political agenda is secondary—a result of the previous spiritual and religious discernment.

These communities are transforming the Church, reconnecting it to our origins in apostolic time—announcing the reign of God. It is a process of empowerment. Sharing stories, members participate in the unfolding of a new creation—the core of a new/old Christian vision.

Living the Gospel and the Living Gospel

There is a creative tension between the faith aspect and the political agenda that often results. This reflects the early Church, which was prophetic, challenging, calling for a new world order, but at the same time Eucharistic. As religion takes root in the heart, principles are lived. The living gospel is politicized—not by intent, but as a natural result of *living* the faith in the world. Liberation theologian Leonardo Boff makes the observation that action without faith is not enough, nor is faith without action.

In their desire to be Eucharistic, base communities face the challenge of priest shortages. By necessity, the focus often shifts from Eucharist to exploring other ways of coming together for meaningful worship. Prayer services in which consecrated hosts are distributed are one way. Another is through celebrations of the *Word,* where imagination finds fresh expression. As each individual community finds its spiritual voice, liturgy rises directly out of the people, and Eucharist returns to its origins as the living presence of Jesus Christ among us.

Northern Exposure: Base Communities in the First World

The base communities of Latin America are a model for many U.S. Catholics seeking more authentic engagement with their faith. These are often mainstream Catholics who feel dissatisfaction with the Church for a variety of reasons. As a result of their involvement, members are renewed in faith and begin to take more of an interest in parish life— somewhat to the surprise of critics who feared the Church would lose energy to them.

Although it is early to draw too many conclusions, at first glance they are serving a vital need. They face the challenge of staying true to the forms developed in Third World countries—such as action for justice, while at the same time being true to the time and place in which they crop up. Many Third World people instinctively have a highly developed sense of community, whereas the cultural perspective of the European American is the opposite—one of individualism. This cultural difference is reflected in more frequent Latin/Hispanic membership. American Hispanics come together easily and naturally, whereas European-American communities must work through their ingrained ethos of independence.

Pot-Luck Community

The base communities in Latin America emphasize organization and leadership as integral to the process of liberation. Groups don't just happen; they don't just come together spontaneously; they are started by someone who has studied the process and knows how to bring a group together without taking it over—a delicate and vital combination of skills.

After the rudiments of a community are established, that leader must step back and allow the people to go through a process of self-organizing. Likewise, leadership is encouraged, but must rise up out of the group. This formation stage is integral to the community identity as is the setting of agenda, which must flow freely from the group.

These factors are what ultimately make the group its own invention. If a base community isn't nurtured and supported, it tends to disintegrate. Paradoxically, breakdown can also be the result of being successful in accomplishing some of its goals. When the impetus of need is reduced, sometimes the community begins to unravel. This is why the focus must be on the spiritual as well as the political agenda. The main identity should be in coming together for worship and reflection, and action is a result. If it is the other way around, the community loses its essential ingredient.

My first experience of a U.S. base community was during my internship at the Catholic community at Vanderbilt University in Nashville. One of my duties was to assist in coordinating a weekly potluck gathering of graduate students—most of whom were married, stretched for money and time, and in various states of fatigue and stress. The meal was central to the evening and was followed by a Scripture reading and reflection. The students left renewed. They did not bring the same experiences as the Third World communities who face poverty and often political danger as a regular part of life. Yet the experience had spiritual meaning and led to action.

The mission of the Catholic community was focused on social justice—at times providing the only visible sign of social action on campus. Reflection unfailingly focused on world conditions and finding Christian responses to our neighbors. In the course of the two years I spent there, various groups of students traveled to Nicaragua, instituted a hunger drive on campus, were active in the creation and maintenance of a family shelter, worked in a halfway house for people coming out of prison, and hosted monthly Amnesty International meetings. The group had the benefit of an experienced and skilled priest and nun—both of whom had a strong commitment to social outreach, and were able to nurture this in the students as well as provide the necessary resources and connections in the community. This points to the need for good leadership skills in establishing base communities.

Growing a New Church

According to survey figures in *The Catholic Experience of Small Christian Communities*, Bernard J. Lee reports that at least 37,000 small Christian communities are currently meeting in the United States, with a membership of more than a million adults and children. Numbers are said to be rising. Approximately three-quarters of the members maintain affiliation with their parish in addition to the small community. Members are generally better educated and of higher average income than the general public, and they are strongly committed to a social justice agenda.

Typically, the four basic activities are prayer, faith sharing, Scripture, and spirituality (faith in action). Members have social justice concerns, but as a rule they have not actually implemented actions that reflect their values. A necessary ingredient of the base community concept is outreach to others. Christian community doesn't exist for its own members; it must move beyond itself and have an outside mission. This is one of the problems Hebblethwaite sees as the First World adapts the model. Lee confirms this concern. However, the communities he ob-served are still quite early in their development. He feels the outreach mission will grow.

Members are taking that important step in faith development described in Chapter 10, moving from Fowler's stages three and four, entering stage five. This represents a significant change—one that is sure to be reflected in the larger Church as these communities continue to expand. Much of the tension that chafes at the clergy-laity relationship is the need for different theological emphasis among the people. This can be addressed through base community models of Church. Many predict that they will become a regular part of parish life, giving more people the opportunity to engage religion in a meaningful way.

What Lies Ahead?

Although the integrity of its teaching is always a preoccupation of leadership, the recent obsession over orthodoxy is a theological dead end. The culture is moving away from doctrinal preoccupation and toward a more spiritual approach to religion. People are less interested in splitting dogmatic hairs and more interested in exploring the sacred in a variety of ways and places. It's a hard and perplexing world out there, and folks need to find meaning that will add depth to their lives and offset impersonal technology, superhighways, and bigger-is-better consumerism.

If religion is to remain relevant and viable in the new millennium, it will have to keep step with the culture. In *The Complete Idiot's Guide to Understanding Catholicism*, we talked about quantum spirituality—the mystical counterpart of quantum physics—as food for the faithful who are hungry for connection in a fragmented and isolated world.

Physics has taken us past the world of atoms into quarks and finally to cosmic soup. Basically, science is saying that everything is interrelated. As science translates into spirituality, the "big field," or soup, in which all this takes place can be understood as a new manifestation of God. This new view of creation sees a spirited universe, a living cosmos constantly in process, unfolding, always *becoming*. This isn't a new idea—mystics have talked about it for centuries. However, the main thrust of official religion has not embraced or incorporated the concept, until now. It seems that's about to change.

A New and Ancient Path

A growing community of people believes that we are on the brink of a new consciousness: a holistic understanding of the universe as both material and spiritual. This new consciousness suggests that we are at long last moving past duality, seeing how spirit is present in the creation. Holism is about having a significant relationship with the living system in which the flapping of a butterfly's wing sends a ripple felt by the farthest star. Holism contrasts sharply with scientific reductionism that believes analysis, dissection, and categorizing actually bring insight into reality. Holism stands in awe of the great mystery and realizes we probably will never really understand it all—it speaks paradoxically and sometimes in outright contradiction of itself.

Rather than a philosophy, it is more often expressed in spiritual terms by those who identify themselves as seekers. The movement includes a great variety of people—many different faith traditions and academic disciplines. For these, there is no attempt to control creation, but rather to find ways of coexisting with any and all aspects of it. Holism isn't a science or a religion, but is moving us past the rift between science and spirit to a new territory in which physics and religion are talking the same language—a language of diversity, variety, compassion, passion, peace, and uniqueness.

Holism is both new and ancient. We stand at the intersection of two paths—one at which we arrived intuitively long ago and the other recently by scientific discovery.

Western progress has often "discovered" ideas (and places) long known by others, and claimed them as its own. An uncommon characteristic of this new consciousness is that both scientists and philosophers acknowledge that indigenous people already know what they are just now discovering. In looking for their European roots in holism, many seekers go to the Irish mythology of the Celtic people. Despite Greek and Roman influence, the Celts maintained their nonhierarchical relationship with nature, honoring animal spirits, trees, and holy wells of healing water up through the Middle Ages. This consciousness continues to exist just below the surface in stories and songs. It was a society in which men and women shared many of the same roles: as healers, chiefs, priests, peacemakers, and warriors. The Celts kept their pagan character through hundreds of years of Christianity because of their spiritual and creative adaptation.

Structures of the Universe: Holy Holon!

About a quarter of a century ago, Hungarian philosopher and author Arthur Koestler coined the word *holon* to describe a basic organizational pattern by which all biological and social systems interact. The term combines the Greek word *holos*, meaning "whole," and the suffix *on*, meaning "part" or "particle."

Koestler's observations pointed out that there are no self-supporting, isolated, single-unit entities in nature. Every unit of creation, from amoeba to archbishop, exists in relationship. Holon describes the system of subordinate parts and their interrelationship in an identifiable system.

The hierarchal character of holons is determined by complexity, not superior position. Holons are whole/parts, being both whole in themselves and belonging to a more complex organizational structure—as an atom is part of a molecule, part of a cell, and part of a whole organism.

The larger organism holds the system together and can communicate with the other levels of holons. The stability of a holon system depends on the self-supporting smaller unit's ability to handle crucial levels of disturbance without engaging the larger system—or the feedback loop. A key function of a holarchy is the ability to self-organize.

The holon theory applies to the composition of all organizations:

- Physical systems: atoms, molecules, cells, and so on
- Biological systems: genes, nuclei, cells, and so on
- Physiological systems: organs, organisms, and so on
- Psychological systems: children, women, men, family, and so on
- Social systems: cities, states, nations, religions, and so on

When Koestler first used the word holon, he pointed out that hierarchy should actually be holarchy—as the hierarchy is interdependent with all the parts Koestler that compose it.

From Hierarchy to Holarchy

In *The Holy Web: Church and the New Universe Story,* Dominican friar and theologian Cletus Wessels writes that there is nothing intrinsically wrong with hierarchal structures, but they often fail to recognize interplay and interdependence, and seldom operate from the acute awareness of divine presence everywhere as holarchy does. He explores how holon theory might inform Church structure as hierarchy transforms into holarchy. He feels the Church's mission is to become consciously aware of the "web," seeing itself in sacred relationship with the universe. Wessels and others such as mathematical cosmologist Brian Swimme and Fr. Thomas Berry study the evolutionary dynamics of the universe and the earth community in relationship to the bigger story. Native Americans similarly talk about the sacred hoop of creation. These "geologians" are bringing science and religion back into a sacred circle.

The base communities discussed earlier in this chapter reflect holon system theory in relationship with the Catholic Church. The entirety of the Church would be seen as a web of small communities within each parish, and parishes as members of a diocese, which in turn is connected to an archdiocese. This worldwide web of interrelationships forms the Catholic Church, which belongs to an Earth community, and so on, wherever further exploration takes us.

The Natural-Born Christian

Thomas Berry blazed the trail for the new breed writing in the emerging field of science/religion. Berry calls himself a cosmologist and geologian. Cosmology unlocks secrets that tell us how our world works, where we fit into the big scheme—the universe—and into the small scheme—our immediate environment. His work, as well as that of others exploring the same territory, assumes that we are not separate beings. We exist as a corporate body *of* nature, not *in* nature.

Humans are credited by some with being the consciousness of the planet. Others are not so ready to grant us that status because we are the only holon members of the universe who seem bent on self-destruction.

The studies of Berry and others envisage the universe as both a psycho-spiritual and physical reality. Communication with this living universe comes through our imagination, our dream brain—the right brain. As Western culture's preference for "logic" and analytical reasoning overtook faith, we lost our connection to the natural world. We lost sight of the holiness of nature and the presence of God in God's creation. Berry works toward recapturing this sense of the omnipresence of the sacred.

Three principles are key to understanding the universe, according to Berry:

- **Diversity:** "The greater the diversity, the greater the perfection."
- **Subjectivity:** "The universe is a community of subjects, not a collection of objects."
- **Communion:** "Diversity and subjectivity allow us to be in com-

munion with everything and everyone."

Holism theory involves the imagination more than traditional disciplines allowed—recognizing it as the brain's *primary* function. Imagination combined with the senses creates the conditions for intuition—those little twinges that give us all sorts of information. Our experiences—our sensate knowledge of the world—along with the promptings of imagination are processed in the right hemisphere of the brain.

According to this model, thought is a left hemisphere business. It's *secondary*. We think or reflect back on something that has already happened, which means that thinking is always a step behind experience—it is always in the past.

Living spiritually—or by spiritual instinct—is a right brain process. Success in allowing spirit to guide us depends on how well the thinking brain can be quieted. Analytical thinking is a necessary next step in discernment, according to this theory. It tells whether a twinge is from something we ate for lunch or an incoming message! Holism means the *whole brain* is involved—intuition and reason. The new spiritual/ scientific understanding needs and values both.

A Quantum Leap

Holon systems are self-organizing, continuously in progress. The quantum leap in logic here is that we are reorganizing along spiritual, instinctual lines, away from the overdependence on rational thought that has characterized our culture. This is not a flip-flop procedure, from logic to intuition and back to logic, but rather a way of balancing our grip on reality.

The right hemisphere of the brain is our relational center. It connects us to our body, or more accurately it allows us to realize this connection. It likewise allows us to experience connection with nature and with one another. It's where compassion resides.

It is not difficult to see how the overdeveloped left brain, a task-oriented part of the mind, might lead to insensitivity toward others and toward nature—a definite pattern in our culture. Cut off from the senses, the thinking mind is abstract, specializing in intellectual theories. It lacks the ability to connect to the human experience. Thoughts need to be road tested.

The work of Berry and his colleagues is simultaneously taking us into the future and back to our origins. French philosopher Paul Ricoeur, who writes like a theologian, describes the process as second naïvete. Second naïvete lies beyond abstractions and theories that serve to tell us *about* God, and past our preoccupation with biblical and theological treatises, to a fresh encounter *with* the divine reality to which the texts can only bear witness.

Ricoeur describes revisiting a time of simplicity. The perception of oneness we once knew instinctively is now revisited—this time with critical awareness. In terms of Fowler's stages of faith (in the last chapter), this is the sixth or highest level, which he calls universalizing. Here we have a vivid sense of the transcendent, an enlarged vision of universal community. In Catholic terms, it is radical communion.

In Conclusion

We began our story by revisiting our prehistoric indigenous ancestors; then stopped to check on the Greeks and Romans, before entering the common era. History shows us how empires rise and fall. We have witnessed the demise of ancient Greece, seen Rome sacked, observed the crumbling of the Holy Roman Empire, beheld the end of the Aztec and Mayan worlds, yet we still dream of a time when the lion will lie down with the lamb.

The Catholic Church identifies itself by four marks: It is one, holy, catholic, and apostolic. The term *catholic* is often interpreted as universal. Universe, however, connotes a territory separated by a boundary. This is how the Church has often understood itself: a universe distinct from the world. The Greek word *katholokos*, by contrast, means throughout the whole. As the new consciousness begins to invade our dreams, including the dreams of the hierarchal institution, the Church moves toward holarchy, toward a relationship that allows the dream to become a reality.

Like a huge glacier, the Church has inched its way through the last

2,000 years. Like a glacier, it has both shaped and been shaped by the world—sometimes remarkably impervious to whatever lay in its path. Now it seems this maddening slowness has positioned it on the front edge of a new age.

Catholics have never strayed too far past their roots in the earth. We already discussed elemental presence—earth, air, fire, water— integral to our sacramental life. The Liturgy of the Hours is prayed each day and night all over the world by members of religious orders honoring the earth's journey around the sun. At midnight, first light, noon, and sundown, as well as points between, hymns are sung, and Scripture and prayers are recited according to ancient rhythms. In farming communities, the rogation days are still honored, or are being reintroduced, blessing the fields, acknowledging the source of our food. In city neighborhoods and country villages, the Angelus rings out— morning, noon, and night—reminding us of the young Jewish girl who was willing to take a risk for the world.

For the first time in geological history, the evolutionary tables have turned. Today, humans are less at the mercy of their environment than ever before; indeed, quite the opposite is the case: The environment is at the mercy of humans. Those who dream the common dream believe that our unchecked lust for power has brought us to this perilous position. As we teeter on the brink of tomorrow, the Church is ripe for transformation.

All over the world, indigenous people gather in tribal circles, pilgrims journey to temples, churches, mosques, and monasteries—as well as thousands of other places the faithful congregate. They come together offering prayers around the clock, paving the way for our imminent transformation. Those who hold the sacred vision of creation pray in many different tongues. Behind the words the thoughts are the same— thy kingdom come.

Faith is often described as believing that all is well even in the face of overwhelming evidence to the contrary. This is a time of great faith. Earlier in this book, the Catholic Church was described as one of the oldest and possibly the most influential institutions in the Western world, being one billion strong. We have seen how this idealistic, yet flawed entity has influenced the world over time—sometimes annoyingly and sometimes gloriously.

This book examines Catholic power. The Catholic Church is in transition, always. Seeds planted at Vatican II are sprouting. As Catholics move from the hierarchical, authoritarian model of church they have grown used to—and in many cases, grown weary of—they are moving into a new way of being church that is community based and allows faith to find action.

One of the first steps in this transition is to claim one's moral authority—to begin to follow the inner guidance of the Holy Spirit that speaks to each of us. It is helpful to know this follows Catholic tradition.

A big proportion of today's disenchanted Catholics are staying in the Church and working to make changes that are transforming them as well as transforming the larger structure. Others have moved out into new territory—broadening what it means to be a Catholic, exploring new faith models.

As we explore our common story, we realize that the pervasive power we've read about is not locked in a Vatican vault. It's not confined to the hierarchy. It lies in the potential Catholic swing vote that can move us toward a new common consciousness. As holon theory tells us, we're all in it together.

Things are looking good!

Epilogue

There is a momentum of participation in today's U.S. Catholic Church. Two hundred years of democracy and education have trained American Catholics to take responsibility and think for themselves. Confronted by this fierce legacy of independence, Rome seems hell-bent on maintaining control at all costs. Still, when opposing views are sincere and authentic and both sides hunger for resolution, change sometimes happens. The defining need is dialog.

Catholics believe in the ongoing presence of the Holy Spirit. The Spirit moves horizontally (not just from the top down) among the people of God. Wherever the Spirit is, communication, change, growth, and movement seem inevitable. And where is the Spirit not?

Vatican II set the agenda, and the seeds of a new Church were impregnated into the earth—into the hearts of the people. Gestating for the last 40 years, the seedlings seem to be pushing their way above ground. The new Church is one of shared power, maintaining its essential connection to history—its deep sense of itself.

We've seen how science and religion have begun to mend their age-old argument, and we've explored what their union might produce.

Catholics often use the phrase *Holy Mother Church*. Every mother knows that when labor begins, the child will come—there is no way to avoid the inevitable pushing forth of life. Birthing babies involves a good bit of blood, sweat, and tears before the squirming new life is laid across the mother's belly and put to the breast. To be mother is to welcome new life, feed and nurture it, and set it free—transfer the power. I see the Church engaged in this process. The wise Church will mine the image of *Holy Mother Church* and reap the fullness it holds.

A wise friend of mine who raised four spirited offspring used to tell them, "Little birds in their nest must agree." It's wishful thinking, no doubt, but it's a good reminder. This globe we share once seemed so large, but now it feels more like a fragile little nest. Although we might never find ourselves in complete agreement, we can acknowledge our relationship to one another and to "it." We're all in "it" together. We have a mutual agenda—a need to find peaceful solutions. Thankfully, that creative conversation has begun.

The cosmologists tell us we need a new story—one that puts us in relationship with the big creation—not just our walk out of Eden. Some believe that we found the new image for this some years ago in the pictures sent back from space showing the earth as a delicate little orb suspended in a vast cosmos. It was the first time we were able to stand outside ourselves and see us from this unique perspective.

Suddenly, bravado shifted to wonderment. Who are we in this endless sea of space? Who dares to disturb this delicate balance and risk cutting the invisible wires that secure our place among all the other stars, moons, planets, galaxies, and whatever else lies beyond our imagination?

Rather than squandering precious brainpower on petty argumentation, Sophia beckons, whispers, shouts—wise up! We made the mistake once of turning our back on paradise; let's not do it again.

Autumn 2002, offering thanks, getting ready for winter, thinking about spring ...

Appendix A

Resources

Books and Articles

Allen, John L., Jr. *Conclave: The Politics, Personalities, and Process of the Next Papal Election.* New York: Doubleday, 2002.

———. *Cardinal Ratzinger: The Vatican's Enforcer of the Faith.* New York: Continuum, 2000.

Baranowski, Arthur R. *Creating Small Church Communities.* Cincinnati: St. Anthony Messenger, 1996.

Baranowski, Arthur, ed. *Called to Be Church: Faith Sharing for Small Church Communities.* Cincinnati: St. Anthony Messenger, 1993.

Bernstein, CSJ, and Martin F. Connell, eds. *Traditions and Transitions.* Chicago: Liturgy Training Publications, 1998.

Berry, Jason. *Lead Us Not into Temptation: Catholic Priests and the Sexual Abuse of Children.* Urbana: University of Illinois Press, 2000.

Berry, Thomas. *The Dream of the Earth.* San Francisco: Sierra Club Books, 1988.

Bokenkotter, Thomas. *A Concise History of the Catholic Church.* New York: Doubleday, 1990.

Bradley, Ian. *God Is Green: Ecology for Christians.* New York: Doubleday, 1990.

Brown, Joanne Carlson, and Carole R. Bohn, eds. *Christianity, Patriarchy, and Abuse. A Feminist Critique.* Cleveland: The Pilgrim Press, 1989.

Christiansen, S. J., and Walter Grazer. *And God Saw That It Was Good: Catholic Theology and the Environment,* Washington, D.C.: United States Catholic Conference, 1996.

Clark, Susan J. *Celebrating Earth Holy Days: A Resource Guide for Faith Communities.* New York: Crossroad, 1992.

Cooke, Bernard, ed. *The Papacy and the Church in the United States.* New York: Paulist Press, 1989.

Cozzens, Donald B. *The Changing Priesthood.* Collegeville, Minn.: The Liturgical Press, 2000.

Faulkner, Mary. *The Complete Idiot's Guide to Women's Spirituality.* Indianapolis: Alpha Books, 2002.

Fox, Matthew. *One River, Many Wells: Wisdom Springing from Global Faiths.* New York: Jeremy P. Tarcher/Putnam Inc., 2000.

Fox, Thomas C. *Sexuality and Catholicism.* New York: George Braziller, 1995.

Gilles, Anthony E. *People of God: The History of Catholic Christianity.* Cincinnati: St. Anthony Messenger Press, 2000.

Greeley, Andrew M. *The Catholic Myth: The Behavior and Beliefs of American Catholics.* New York: Touchstone, 1997.

———. *Sex, The Catholic Experience.* Allen, Tex.: Tabor Publishing, 1994.

Gutierrez, Gustavo. *A Theology of Liberation.* Maryknoll, N.Y.: Orbis, 1971. (15th ed. 1998)

Hail, Raven. The *Cherokee Sacred Calendar.* Rochester, N.Y.: Destiny Books, 2000.

Hebblethwaite, Margaret. *Base Communities: An Introduction*. London: Paulist Press, 1994.

Investigative Staff of the *Boston Globe*. *Betrayal: Crises in the Catholic Church*. New York: Little Brown and Company, 2002.

Jenkins, Philip. *Pedophiles and Priests: Anatomy of a Contemporary Crisis*. New York: Oxford University Press, Inc., 1996.

Kennedy, Eugene. *The Unhealed Wound: The Church and Human Sexuality*. New York: St. Martin's Press, 2001.

Kung, Hans. *The Catholic Church: A Short History*. New York: Random House, 2001.

Lee, Bernard J. *The Catholic Experience of Small Christian Communities*. New York: Paulist Press, 2000.

Malone, Mary T. *Women and Christianity*. Maryknoll, N.Y.: Orbis Books, 2001.

Marty, Martin. *A Short History of American Catholicism*. Allen, Tex.: Thomas More Publishing, 1995.

McBrian, Richard P., ed. *The Harper Collins Encyclopedia of Catholicism*. New York: HarperCollins publishers, Inc., 1995.

McCarthy, Timothy G. *The Catholic Tradition: The Church in the Twentieth Century*. Chicago: Loyola Press, 1998.

O'Gorman, Bob, and Mary Faulkner. *The Complete Idiot's Guide to Understanding Catholicism*. Indianapolis: Alpha Books, 2000.

O'Murchu, Diarmuid. *Quantum Theology*. New York: The Crossroad Publishing Company, 1997.

Orlandis, Jose. *A Short History of the Catholic Church*. Dublin: Four Courts Press Limited, 1993.

Our Sunday Visitor, Inc. *Our Sunday Visitor's Catholic Almanac.*
Huntington, Ind.: Our Sunday Visitor Publishing Division, 1999.

Pelikan, Jaroslav. *The Christian Tradition: A History of the
Development of Doctrine.* Chicago: University of Chicago Press,
1991.

Pelton, Robert S., CSC, ed. *Small Christian Communities: Imagining
Future Church.* Notre Dame: University of Notre Dame Press,
1997.

Ranke-Heinemann, Uta. *Eunuchs for the Kingdom of Heaven.* New
York: Penguin Books, 1990.

Rich, Adrienne. *The Dream of a Common Language: Poems 1974–1977.*
New York: W. W. Norton Company, 1978.

Rossetti, Stephen J. *A Tragic Grace.* Collegeville, Minn.: The Liturgical
Press, 1996.

Ruether, Rosemary Radford. *New Woman/New Earth: Sexist Ideologies
and Human Liberation.* New York: The Seabury Press, 1975.

———. *Women Church: Theology and Practice.* San Francisco: Harper
and Row, 1986.

Sipe, A. W. Richard. *A Secret World: Sexuality and the Search for
Celibacy.* New York: Brunner-Routledge, 1990.

———. *Sex, Priests, and Power: Anatomy of a Crisis.* New York:
Brunner/Mazel Publishers, 1995.

Swimme, Brian. *The Hidden Heart of the Cosmos: Humanity and the
New Story.* Maryknoll, N.Y.: Orbis Books, 1996.

Swimme, Brian, and Thomas Berry. *The Universe Story.* New York:
HarperCollins Publishers, 1992.

Tilley, Terrence, W. *Inventing Catholic Tradition.* Maryknoll, N.Y.:
Orbis Books, 2000.

Walker, Alice. *In Search of Our Mothers' Gardens: Womanist Prose.* New York: Harcourt, Brace, Jovanovich, 1983.

Wessels, Cletus. *The Holy Web: Church and the New Universe Story.* Maryknoll, N.Y.: Orbis Books, 2000.

Wilkins, Ronald J., and Veronica Grover, SHCJ. *Achieving Social Justice: A Catholic Perspective.* Dubuque: Wm. C. Brown Company, Publishers, 1991.

Wills, Garry. *Why I Am a Catholic.* New York: Houghton Mifflin Company, 2002.

———. *Structures of Deceit: Papal Sin.* New York: Doubleday, 2000.

Magazines

National Catholic Reporter. The National Catholic Reporter Publishing Company, 115 East Armour Blvd., Kansas City, Missouri, 64111.

St. Anthony Messenger. St. Anthony Messenger Press and Franciscan Communications, 1615 Republic Street, Cincinnati, Ohio, 45210.

U.S. Catholic. Claretian Publications, 205 W. Monroe Street, Chicago, Illinois, 60606.

Websites

www.calib.com/nccanch. National Clearinghouse on Child Abuse and Neglect Information.

www.christusrex.org/www1/CDHN/ccc.html. Website for the Catechism of the Catholic Church.

www.halcyon.com/arborhts/chiefsea.html. "Chief Seattle's 1854 Oration" from a column by Dr. Henry A. Smith appearing in the *Seattle Sunday Star*, October 29, 1887.

www.life.ca/family/feminism. A description of eco-feminism which describes the common thread in the oppression of women, of nature, and of all those somehow defined by the dominant culture as "other."

www.library.csi.cuny.edu/dept/history/lavender/walker.html. Alice Walker's biography, information links, study guide for women writers, other African American writers, resources for womanist study, and more.

www.matthewfoxfcs.org/sys-tmpl/door. Matthew Fox's biography, recent articles, books, tapes, events, travel schedule, and contact information for his institute.

www.nccbuscc.org/comm/restoretrust.htm. "Restoring Trust: A Response to Sexual Abuse Essential Norms for Diocesan/Eparchial Policies Dealing with Allegations of Sexual Abuse of Minors by Priests, Deacons, or Other Church Personnel." Final: Charter for the Protection of Children and Young People.

www.religion-online.org. Features more than 4,000 articles and chapters on topics such as the Old and New Testament, theology, ethics, and more.

www.wow2001.org. Women's Ordination Worldwide.

Appendix B

Timeline of the Catholic Church

Before Common Era (B.C.E.)

8000–3000	Catholic tribal roots in the earth-based indigenous cultures of Europe.
1200	Judaism creates its Jewish identity and settles in Israel.
469–322	Socrates, Plato, Aristotle.
400–100	Organization of the Old Testament.

The Common Era (C.E.)

c. 0	Jesus is born.
c. 30–33	The public life of Jesus.
c. 33	Jesus' death, burial, and resurrection.
c. 30–35	Paul persecuting Christians.
	Peter, James, Prisca and Aquila, and others begin missionary work.
	Paul's conversion.
	Decision to preach to Gentiles.
49	Persecutions of Christians begin in Rome.
60	Paul's execution in Rome.
64	Peter is crucified (upside down).
66–70	Destruction of the Jewish Temple—Christianity and Judaism separate.
70	Mark's gospel is recorded, followed by Matthew and Luke.

The Common Era (C.E.) (continued)

80	Acts of the Apostles is written.
90	John's gospel is written.
202	Perpetua and Felicitas are martyred.
270	Anthony goes to the desert beginning the movement known as the mothers and fathers of the desert.
313	Constantine grants religious freedom in Roman Empire.
325	Council of Nicea—the Church structure begins to solidify at this Council. Creed is written; imposed celibacy advocated; order of deaconess is removed from clergy status and becomes lay ministry; hierarchal offices are shaped, laying the ground for authoritative papal office.
330	Monasticism begins in the Egyptian desert.
340	Women's monasticism begins in Rome.
354	Birth of Augustine.
382	Jerome begins his translation of the Bible.
410	Sack of Rome.
430	Death of Augustine.
431	Council of Ephesus—Mary declared Theotokos (God-bearer, or Mother of God).
432	Bishop Patrick is sent to Ireland.
440	Pope Leo I—Papal office becomes authoritative.
476	Death of the last Roman Emperor.
481	Birth of Benedict who establishes rules for monastic life. Monasticism begins in Celtic Britain.
517	End of Western Orders of Deaconess and Widows.
632	Death of the prophet Muhammad.
664	Roman Christianity dominates over Celtic Christianity.
770	Beginning of Boniface's missionary work in Germany. Islam's army occupies Spain
800	Charlemagne crowned emperor by Leo III—birth of the Holy Roman Empire.

829	Council of Paris removes women from performing any liturgical acts.
1012	Pope Benedict enacted legislation to protect Church property from inheritance claims.
1054	Orthodox Church separates from the Catholic Church.
1073	Pope Gregory VII established more consistency in the practice of celibacy.
1095–1291	The Crusades.
1231	First Inquisition begins under Pope Gregory IX.
1274	St. Thomas Aquinas, theologian and Doctor of the Church dies.
1380	St. Catherine of Siena, theologian, Doctor of the Church, and mystic dies.
1431	St. Joan of Arc is burned at the stake.
1479	Spanish Inquisition.
1517	Martin Luther openly challenges Church authority.
1531	Our Lady of Guadalupe appears in Mexico.
1534	Henry the VIII declares the Church of England.
1542	Pope Paul establishes the Roman Inquisition.
1545–1563	Council of Trent—Catholic Reformation. Keeps celibacy, but states that it is a human law and not divine, affirms marriage, maintaining procreation for reproduction only, refocuses Church in the sacraments.
1565	St. Augustine, Florida founded—first Catholic settlement in North America
1582	St. Teresa of Avila, theologian, Doctor of the Church, and mystic dies.
1790	John Carroll elected the first bishop in United States— appointed to the Baltimore see.
1806	The Holy Roman Empire is dissolved.
1854	The doctrine of Mary's Immaculate Conception is declared.

The Common Era (C.E.) (continued)

1869-1870   Vatican I Council. Pope Pius IX presents his *Syllabus of Errors* and declares doctrine of infallibility.

1907–1967   Priests required to take oath against modernism. John

1960   Fitzgerald Kennedy becomes first Catholic president elected in the United States.

1962–1965   Vatican II Council. Image: People of God. Church moves toward collegiality. Doctrine of Religious Freedom declared. Mission: to improve relations with world; to learn from the culture.

1962   John XXIII dies.

1968   Pope Paul VI encyclical *Humanae Vitae* (*Of Human Life*) is published affirming the continued ban on birth control.

1978   Pope John Paul II, first non-Italian Pope since 1523, is elected.

1995   Cardinal Bernardin appoints the first woman pastoral coordinator to head up a Chicago parish.

2002   U.S. Bishops convene to determine actions regarding sex abuse among clergy.

Pedro de San Jose Betancur, seventeenth-century Spanish missionary, becomes the first Central American saint.

Juan Diego canonized—first Indian saint of the Americas. It was to him that the Lady of Guadalupe appeared in the sixteenth century.

Index

Index